# COMPENSATION and REWARD MANAGEMENT

Dr. Biswanath Ghosh

**STERLING PUBLISHERS PRIVATE LIMITED**
A-59, Okhla Industrial Area, Phase-II, New Delhi-110020.
Tel: 26387070, 26386209 Fax: 91-11-26383788
e-mail: mail@sterlingpublishers.com
www.sterlingpublishers.com

*Compensation and Reward Management*
© 2012, Dr. Biswanath Ghosh
ISBN 978 81 207 7742 2

All rights are reserved. No part of this publication may be reproduced, stored in a retrieval system or transmitted, in any form or by any means, mechanical, photocopying, recording or otherwise, without prior written permission of the original publisher.

PRINTED IN INDIA

Printed and Published by Sterling Publishers Pvt. Ltd., New Delhi-110 020.

# Preface

This is a comprehensive textbook on compensation management. This new area has emerged as a separate discipline. Earlier, salary administration was a part of Human Resource Management.

There are good books on the subject by foreign authors but those books do not serve the purpose of our students because the context is different, approaches are different and practices are different. Country-specific discussions are more useful to the students.

Our book deals with concepts, tools, techniques, and designs of salary administration.

The text is written in accordance with the UGC syllabus for MBA students of our universities. The text is divided into 24 chapters, each chapter discusses a specific problem in the light of modern developments.

In a competitive environment, the most important task is to attract and retain the right man. It is therefore necessary to design an attractive compensation package; otherwise the growth of the organization will be adversely affected.

I am personally indebted to Mr. S.K. Ghai, the MD of Sterling Publishers Private Limited for the interest he has shown. Without his active cooperation the book would not have been published so quickly.

There are university questions for the benefit of students.

I extend my thanks to my friends, colleagues and students. Aristotle said guests are the best judge of a feast. Similarly, I think students are the best judge of a book.

**Biswanath Ghosh**

# Contents

1. **Introduction**   1
   • State Employment Policy, 2005 • Objectives of The Mission • Policy Initiatives • Strengthening of Co-operative Movement • Compensation Management at a Glance • Test Questions

2. **Motivation and Reward**   13
   • Role of Rewards and Incentives in motivation • *Instrumentality Theory* • *Needs (Content) Theory* • *Herzberg's Model* • *Expectancy Theory* • *Goal Theory* • *Equity Theory* • *Motivation, Incentives and Rewards* • Factors affecting Satisfaction with Pay • Job Satisfaction, Motivation and Performance • Key message of Motivation Theory • Significance of Needs • Importance of Expectations • Influence of goals • Rewarding Sales Staff – 1. Salary Only, 2. Basic Salary plus Commission, 3. Basic Salary plus Bonus 4. *Commission Only*, 5. *Additional Non-Cash Rewards* • Test Questions

3. **Individual Contingent Pay**   21
   • Arguments for Contingent Pay • *Arguments Against* • *Alternatives to Contingent Pay* • *Criteria for Success* – 1. *Performance-Related Pay* • 2. *Competence-related pay* • 3. *Contribution-related Pay* • 4. *Skill-based Pay* • *Main features* • *Choice of Approach* • Test Questions

4. **Concept of Internal and External Equity**   29
   • Job Evaluation • Methods of Job Evaluation • 1. *Ranking Method* • 2. *Classification Method* 3. *Point Rating Method* 4. *Factors Comparison Method, Job Analysis and Job Description* • External Equity and Pay Surveys • *Pay Surveys* • *Prerequisites before Pay Survey* • *Types of Pay Surveys* • *Survey Method* • Test Questions

5. **Wage Concepts**    39

*1. The Statutory Minimum Wage • 2. The Bare Subsistence or Minimum Wage • 3. The Concept of the Living Wage 4. The Concept of Fair Wage • 5. Minimum Wage • 6. Need-based Minimum Wage • Test Questions*

6. **Factors Affecting Levels of Pay**    43

• *1. Ability to pay • 2. Supply and Demand of Labour • 3. Prevailing Market Rate • 4. Cost of Living • 5. The Living Wage • 6. Productivity • 7. Union Bargaining Power • 8. Job Requirements 9. Psychological and Social Factors 10. Planning of Wages & Salary Administration 11. Steps Involved in Fixing Specific Job Rates 12. Control of Compensation • Test Questions*

7. **Economic Theories Affecting Compensation**    49

• *Macro Theories • Micro-Macro Theories • Test Questions*

8. **Team Pay**    57

• *1. Organizational teams • 2. Work teams • 3. Project teams • 4. Ad hoc teams • Objectives of Team Pay • How Team Pay Works • 1. The team pay formula • 2. Method of distributing bonuses • 3. Team pay and individual pay • 4. Dealing with high and low individual performance in a team • 5. Project team bonuses • 6. Ad hoc bonuses • Advantages and Disadvantage of Team Pay • Test Questions*

9. **Wage Fixing Machinery**    62
**Wage Boards, Pay Commissions, Collective Bargaining and Adjudication**

• *1. Wage Boards • Terms of Reference • Procedure and Methodology • An assessment of Wage Board Method • Recommendations of National Labour Commission • Central Pay Commission • Sixth Pay Commission (2008) • Spotlights of the Sixth Pay Commission, Pay Overhaul • Annual Increment • Group A officers • Pension • Allowances • Health • Defence • Regulators • Work Hours • Performance Sops • Collective Bargaining • Test Questions*

10. **Fringe Benefits**    79

• *Objectives of Fringe Benefits • Evolution of Fringe Benefits • Fringe Benefits in Different Countries • Objectives and Types of Fringe benefits • Fringe Benefits offered in India can be classified into the following five categories • Welfare and Recreational Facilities • Old Age and Retirement Benefits*

• Methods of Computing DA: • *Statutory Provisions* • *Advantages and Disadvantages of having DA as a separate component of Wages* • Abolition of DA • Benefits: British Model • *Pension* • *Company Car and Fuel Benefit* • *Sick Pay* • *Family-friendly Benefits* • *Child care Provision* • *Benefits and Taxation* • *Paid Holidays* • *Growth of Benefits* • *New Pay* • Test Questions

### 11. Retirement Benefits including VRS     93

• 1. Pension • Employer and Employee Contributions • *Pension Fund* • *Dependants* • *Lump sum* • **Defined Contribution (Money Purchase) Schemes** • *Pension Entitlement* • *Contributions* • *Pension Fund* • *Employee's Pension Scheme, 1995* 2. Employees' Provident Funds and Miscellaneous Provisions Act 1952 • Effect on number of employees falling below 20 • Non-applicability of the Act to certain establishments. • Power to apply the Act on Establishment having common Provident Fund. • Employees' Provident Fund Scheme. • Employees' Deposit-linked Insurance Scheme • 3. Gratuity • *Introduction* • *Scope and Coverage* • Employees covered under the Act • *Determination of the Amount of Gratuity* • *Application for claiming Gratuity* • *Rate of Gratuity* • *Piece Rate Employee* • *Seasonal Employee* • *Ceiling of Gratuity* • *Forfeiture of Gratuity* • *Compulsory Insurance* • *Nomination* • *Recovery of Gratuity* • *Penalties* • Voluntary Retirement Scheme (VRS) • Test Questions

### 12. Reservation in Services     105

• List of Scheduled Castes • List of Scheduled Tribes • List of Other Backward Classes • Test Questions

### 13. Bonus     111

• Introduction• Beginnings of Bonus in India. • *Bonus During and Immediately After the Second World War* • Bonus as a Matter of Right • Payment of Bonus • *The Payment of Bonus Act 1965* • Calculation of Amount Payable as Bonus. • Payment of Maximum Bonus • Test Questions

### 14. Contract Labour In India     121

• Introduction • The Contract Labour (Regulation and Abolition) Act, 1970 • Objects and Purposes of The Act • Application • Appropriate Government • The Central and State Advisory Boards • Registration of Establishment and Licensing of Contractors • Welfare and Health of Contract

Labour • *Payment of Wages* • *Penal Provisions* • *Other Provisions* • *Prohibition* • *Exemption* • *Enforcement* • Important Judgments of The Supreme Court • *Streamlining Contract Labour Law* • *Views of Employers' Associations* • Views of the trade Unions • Test Questions

### 15. Tax Planning     128
• Tax Planning of Employee Compensation • Tax implications of employee compensation package to the employer • Tax implications of compensation to the employees • Test Questions

### 16. Oustees from Dam: Resettlement of Project Affected People     135
• Rural Rehabilitation Package • Test Questions

### 17. Equal Pay For Equal Work     142
• **I. Causes of Inequality** • Economic Factors • Social Factors • **II. Wage-Differentials in India** • Cotton Textiles • Jute Mill Industry • Other Factory Industries • Coal Mines • Plantations • **III. Movement for Equalisation** • **IV. Socio-Economic Consequences** • Psychological Effects • Effects on Health and Efficiency • Effects on Marriage and Birth Rate • Economic Consequences • Test Questions

### 18. Methods of Wage Payment     153
• Time-rates and Piece-rates • Bonus Based on Standard Time • Differential Piece-rates and Progressive Bonus Systems • Test Questions

### 19. Job Evaluation     162
• Job Evaluation—Methods • Preliminary Steps—Job Analysis and Job Description • Job Evaluation in India • Methods of Job Evaluation • Use of Job Evaluation • Some conditions for the successful conduct of job evaluation • Test Question

### 20. Incentives     172
• Incentives • Compensation Programme • Executive Compensation Practices • Personalized Compensation Plan for Executives • The Cafeteria Approach in Salary Fixation • Do Fringe Benefits Motivate Employees? • Non-Financial Incentives • Promotion Policies as Motivators • **The Chief Incentive Plans Are** • *1. Halsey Premium Plan* • *2. Rown Premium Plan* • *3. The Bedeaux Point Plan* • *4. Taylor's Differential*

Piece-Rate Plan • 5. Merric's Multiple Piece Rate System • 6. The Gnatt Task and Bonus Plan • 7. Emerson Efficiency Plan • 8. Profit Sharing • Test Question

21. **Wages and Productivity**     180
    • Wages And Productivity • Test Questions

22. **Executive And International Compensation and a Reference to Executive Compensation in India**     187
    • International Compensation • **Executive Remuneration: Indian Perspective** • Test Questions

23. **National Wage Policy**     201
    • What is a Wage Policy? • Objectives of Wage Policy • Why a Wage Policy at all? • International Symposium on Wages in 1967 • The National Commission on Labour (1969) on Wage Policy • The Chakraborty Committee on Wage Policy (1973) • Wage Policy in India under Planning • Wage Policy in the Five Year Plans • Test Questions

24. **Wage Legislation: I. The Payment of Wages Act, 1936**     215
    • **II. The Minimum Wages Act 1948** • **III. Payment of Gratuity Act 1972** • **IV. Equal Remuneration Act 1976** • Test Questions

*University Questions Years 2010*     230

*Employment & Compensation Administration 2011*     234

*Employment & Compensation Administration 2010*     238

# 1

# Introduction

In earlier decades, pay issues had been strongly influenced by tradition and government policy and many writers were critical of the large number of organizations with no salary policy or plan, usually associated with high turnover, poor productivity and low morale.

Pay has undergone a revolution. Increasing competition, globalization, skill shortages and the new technologies have come together to move pay from a peripheral role to central stage in influencing and achieving corporate objectives. Pay is an agent of change.

Public policy provides the basis for pay determination. Within the framework of public policy, wages are determined through one or more of the following methods:

(i) Unilaterally by the employees, (ii) Through collective bargaining between employer and union, (iii) Pay commission for civil service, (iv) Wage boards for select industries and (v) Adjudication by a third party where disputes remain unresolved through negotiation and conciliation.

The term 'compensation' or 'reward' is used to mean employees' gross earnings in the form of financial rewards for their contribution to the organization. Compensation may also be viewed as a (i) system of rewards that motivate employees to perform, (ii) a tool used by organizations to foster the values, culture and the behaviour they require and (iii) an instrument that enables organizations to achieve their business objectives.

Compensation is typically divided into direct and indirect components. The term direct compensation is used to describe financial remuneration, usually cash and includes such elements as basic pay, dearness allowance, overtime pay, incentive bonus, profit sharing bonus, commissions etc. Indirect compensation or wage

---

* with reference to State Employment Policy 2005.

supplements or fringe benefits refer to such benefits as provident fund, pension scheme, medical insurance, sick leave and other benefits.

**Aims of Compensation Management:** Compensation or reward management is concerned with the formulation and implementation of strategies and policies which are to reward people fairly, equitably and consistently in accordance with their value to the organizations and to help the organization to achieve its strategic goals. It deals with the design, implementation and maintenance of reward systems which aim to meet the needs of both the organization and its shareholders.

The aims of rewards or compensation management are to

1. Reward people according to what the organization values and wants to pay for;
2. Reward people for the value they create;
3. Reward the right things to convey the right message about what is important in terms of outcomes and behaviours;
4. Develop a performance culture;
5. Motivate people and obtain their commitment and engagement;
6. Help to attract and retain the high quality people the organization needs;
7. Create total reward processes which recognize the importance of both financial and non financial rewards;
8. Align reward practices with both business goals and employee values and
9. Operate in ways which are fair, equitable, consistent and transparent as stated below.

A. *Fair:* A fair reward system is one in which people are treated justifiably in accordance with what is due to them and their value to the organization. Fairness means that the reward system operates according to the principles of distributive and procedural justice. Distributive justice is provided to people what they believe that rewards have been distributed in accordance with the value of their contribution, that they receive what was promised to them and that they get what they need. Procedural justice conforms to the ways in which managerial decisions are made. The following five factors affect procedural justice:
   (i) The viewpoint of employees is given proper consideration.
   (ii) Personal bias towards employees is suppressed.
   (iii) The criteria for decisions are applied consistently to all the employees.

(iv) Employees are provided with early feedback about the outcome of decision.

(v) Employees are provided with adequate explanations of why decisions have been made.

B. *Equity:* Equity is achieved when people are rewarded appropriately in relation to others within the organization. Equitable reward processes ensure that relativities between jobs are measured as objectively as possible and that equal pay is provided for work of equal value.

C. *Consistent:* Consistency means that decisions on pay should not vary arbitrarily among different people or at different times.

D. *Transparent:* Transparency means that people understand how reward processes operate and how they are affected by them. The reasons for pay decisions are explained to them at the time they are made.

**The Philosophy:** Reward management is based on a sound philosophy, a set of beliefs and guiding principles that are consistent with the values of the organization and help to enact them. These include beliefs in the need to achieve, fairness, equity, consistency and transparency in operating the reward system.

The philosophy of reward management recognizes that it must be strategic in the sense that it addresses longer-term issues relating to how people should be valued for what they do and what they achieve. Reward strategies have to follow the business strategy.

Reward management adopts a 'total reward' approach which requires the integration of reward strategies with other human resource management strategies. Reward or compensation management is an integral part of an HRM approach to managing people.

**Role of Compensation:** Compensation has an important role to play in an organization. It has the following characteristics:

(i) it enables an organization to attract and retain the manpower it requires;

(ii) it motivates employees and provides directions to their efforts;

(iii) it encourages employees to develop skills and competencies which the organization requires and

(iv) it is used to foster values and culture of the organization.

Usually, the focus of compensation management has been primarily on enabling an organization to recruit and retain employees while complying with legal and statutory requirements. Pay was mainly related to status and hierarchical position. It is now looked upon as the key to acquire a competitive advantage. Innovations in compensation are necessary to do more with less by reducing labour cost per unit of output, motivating employees to higher performance, providing an impetus to skill development and higher quality.

Payroll costs have to be seen in the context of overall corporate strategy and performance and its ability to attract and retain adequate manpower. Payroll cost considerations have forced many multinationals to increasingly hire host-country managers, in preference to assigning its employees for overseas duties. Unions can also influence compensation level and practices; collective bargaining agreement induces rigidity in wage rates with the emergence of the new employee with a higher level of education. The influence of the union on compensation management is decreasing. Compensation policy and practices are being considered as an important factor in an organization's survival, profitability, competitiveness and long-term growth.

## State Employment Policy, 2005

*Introduction*

1.1 Organised sector, be it of public or private, cannot absorb the huge pool of the unemployed youth. To mitigate the growing problem of unemployment in the State, Government have initiated a number of steps as part of the overall plan strategy. Development Departments have been advised to explore the scope for innovative self-employment projects under various sectors and to play more proactive role for creation of large scale self-employment and wage employment opportunities ensuring more productive and efficient use of the available human resources.

1.2 Keeping in view the burning problem of unemployment, the State Governments have decided to take up a major initiative for creation of self-and wage-employment opportunities during the years 2003-04 and rest of the 10th Plan period up to 2006-07.

1.3 In the latest Election Manifesto of B.J.P and B.J.D, great emphasis has been laid on expansion of self-employment opportunity. It has been indicated to maximize self-employment opportunities which in turn will generate associated wage employment. In order to achieve this, a High Power Employment Mission (HPEM) has been proposed to be constituted to take over the responsibility of coordination with different departments and related institutions.

1.4 As a part of the State Employment Policy, 2005 an Employment Mission has been proposed. This will be headed by the Chief

Minister and shall include all the members of Council of ministers, 5 M.L.As, 5 M.Ps and 10 members from among Bankers, Professionals, Civil Society Organizations etc.

1.5 While this Apex Body will be determining policies and general directions, there will be an Executive Body of the Mission headed by the Chief Secretary. The Mission may constitute if deemed necessary, an Empowered Committee and Task Forces on different operational aspects.

1.6 The main objectives of this Mission shall be as follows: *Objectives of The Mission*
   i. To facilitate generation of adequate employment opportunities through a policy framework.
   ii. To recommend and initiate bold steps for infrastructure development which will open up avenues for self employment and create a conducive atmosphere for sustainable wage employment.
   iii. To act as a catalyst in opening of marketing opportunities for commodities and goods produced in the State.
   iv. To mount special drive for creation of self-employment opportunities particularly in agriculture and allied sectors and small-scale industries, handicraft and cottage industries and in the I.T. sector.
   v. To encourage and facilitate training of young entrepreneurs on development of small and cottage industries.
   vi. To monitor generation of employment in different sectors and programmes.
   vii. To facilitate launching of training programmes for both uneducated and educated unemployed persons for upgradation of their skill.
   viii. To formulate area-and trade-specific strategies for maximizing employment opportunities on a sustainable basis in the State-supported and private sectors.
   ix. To facilitate proactively substantial wage employment for various development activities with special emphasis on creation of community and individual assets. Sectors like forestry, watershed development, rural communication, horticulture and land development among others will receive priority.
   x. To facilitate a coordinated approach in achieving the above objectives through convergence of various ongoing schemes for maximizing the benefits over time and space and in reaching out the most needy sections of the population.

| Policy Initiatives | 2.1 | Government of Orissa, through the State Employment Policy, 2005, intends to bring synergy in different development sectors in terms of creation of self-employment opportunities. In this regard, following policy interventions are proposed: |

(a) Model Law on Contract Farming

2.2 A model law on contract farming would be introduced so that a legal framework is created linking agriculture with industries.

*Strengthening of Cooperative Movement*

2.3 Cooperatives shall be revitalized through Long-Term Operation Funds to promote agricultural and agribusiness activities. Agricultural Term Loan would be doubled in 3 years which would enhance both self-employment and wage employment opportunities.

(b) New and Innovative Self-Employment Programmes (SEPs)

2.4 Development Departments would formulate more proactive and innovative self-employment programmes so as to provide self-employment and wage-employment opportunities to the youth. Such schemes shall contain training component for up-gradation of skill and entrepreneurial ability.

2.5 Assistance will be provided to educated unemployed persons for their self-employment in urban and rural growth centres in the services and small business sectors.

2.6 Development of infrastructure for marketing shall be given utmost priority.

2.7 Export promotion in Handloom, Coir and Cottage Industries will be given priority.

2.8 Handicraft artisans and Handloom Weavers would be assisted with a particular emphasis on market orientation and linkage with the Small and Medium Enterprise (SME) sector.

2.9 Special measures will be initiated for improving the skills of young persons in order to improve their employability.

2.10 Ancillarisation of large industries and promotion of downstream industries will receive priority of attention.

(c) Reorganization of Directorate of Employment

2.11 The Director of Employment will monitor all sorts of employment programmes particularly the Self Employment Programmes (SEPs). The Director of Employment will be redesignated as Director Employment-cum-Joint Commissioner of Employment Mission. The Employment Exchanges will also be reorganized and District Employment Officers (DEOs) will be given responsibilities for counselling on Self-Employment Programmes and will be redesignated as Project Directors of Employment Mission-cum-District Employment Officers.

## Compensation Management at a Glance

Compensation Management provides an approach for designing a remuneration system that recognizes the contribution of employees.

People gain satisfaction from their work but it is difficult to define and measure satisfaction. Generally we measure employees' satisfaction in the form of reward for the services provided. The focus remains on monetary rewards paid either directly or indirectly by an employer.

1. *The Reward System:* An organization is formed to achieve a specific mission. To do this it must attract and hire men who have some knowledge, skills, aptitudes and attitudes. To attract and retain men, the organization has to pay rewards.

   How rewards affect motivation or modify behaviour has been observed by the behavioural scientists.

   The reward system of an organization includes anything that an employee may value and desire and that the employee is able to offer in exchange for employee contributions. All rewards that can be classified as monetary payments and in-kind payments constitute the compensation system of an organization. Monetary payments have value in use and they simplify exchange transactions. All other rewards constitute the non-compensation system.

2. *Compensation System:* The compensation system results from the allocation and transfer of a portion of the income of an organization to its employees for their monetary claims on goods and services.

   Monetary claims on goods and services are wages or salaries paid to an employee in the form of money. As a medium of exchange, money enables an employee to purchase goods and services available in the marketplace. Wages and salaries in the form of money may be subdivided further into payments earned and acquired at the present time and payments earned but not acquired until some future time-deferred payments.

The following eight dimensions of a compensation system will give an idea of the complexity of a compensation system in a modern organization.

(a) *Pay for Work and Performance:* Pay for work and performance includes money that is provided in the short term and that permits employees to pay for and contract for the payments of desired goods and services. Typical components within this dimension are base pay, premiums and differentials, short-term bonuses, merit pay and certain allowances.

(b) *Pay for Time not Worked:* Over the years, the number of hours worked per week and the number of days worked per year have decreased. During the past 40 years, workers have enjoyed more days off with pay for holidays, longer paid vacations and paid time off for a wide variety of personal reasons. These components of pay for time not worked significantly increase labour costs.

(c) *Loss-of-job Income Continuation:* Job security has always been the main consideration for most workers. They want assurance that their jobs and the income derived from working will continue until they retire. Workers also know that few jobs are guaranteed to continue till retirement. Not only could accident and sickness problems occur but personal performance might cause a temporary layoff or termination of employment. Changes in economic conditions and technology might eliminate the demand for the product of the employer resulting in the demise of the firm. A variety of components such as unemployment insurance and severance pay help unemployed workers subsist until new employment opportunities arise.

(d) *Disability Income Continuation:* The possibility always exists that a worker will incur health or accident disability. Because of these disabilities, employees are unable to perform their normal assignments. Even so, individual and family living expenses continue and medical, hospital and surgical expenses create additional burdens. Social security, worker's compensation, sick leave, and short-term and long term disability plans are examples of components that provide funds for employees who are unable to work for health reasons.

(e) *Deferred Income:* Most employees depend on some kind of employer-provided programmes for income continuation after retirement. These programmes are provided because most employees do not have sufficient savings at retirement to continue the lifestyles they enjoyed while working.

(f) *Spouse (Family) Income Continuation:* Most employees with family obligations are concerned with what might happen if they are no longer able to provide money that will enable their families to maintain a particular standard of living. Certain plans are designed to provide dependents with income when an employee dies or is unable to work due to permanent disability. In India, if an employee of government service dies in harness; his wife is provided with a job.

(g) *Health, Accident and Liability Protection:* When a health problem occurs, employees must be concerned not only with income continuation but also with the payment for the goods and services required to overcome the illness or disability. Organizations provide a wide variety of insurance plans to assist in paying for these goods and services.

(h) *Income Equivalent Payments:* A final set of compensation components may be grouped under the title of income equivalent payments. Many of these components are frequently called perquisites or 'perks'. Employees usually find them highly desirable and both employers and employees enjoy certain tax benefits in them.

3. *Non Compensation System:* The other major part of the reward system consists of non compensation reward. These rewards are more complex than compensation rewards. Non compensation rewards are all the situation-related rewards not included in the compensation package. Any activity that has an impact on the intellectual, emotional and physical well being of the employee and is not specifically covered by the compensations system is part of the non compensation reward system. These rewards satisfy emotional and intellectual demands. The components of non-compensation systems are as follows:

   a. *Enhance Dignity and Satisfaction from Work Performed:* One of the most powerful rewards an organization can offer to an employee is to recognize the person as a useful and valuable contributor. This kind of recognition leads to employee feelings of self worth and pride in making a contribution. Few people want simply to be given something. They would much prefer to know that through their own efforts, they have earned and deserved rewards.

   b. *Enhance Physiological Health, Intellectual Growth and Emotional Maturity:* Considering the number of hours a person spends on the job, on travel to and from the work site and off the job in attempting to resolve job-related problems has a great effect on the health of employees. Modern health practices recognize the direct relationship between the physiological health and intellectual and emotional well being of each individual.

More and more attention is being focused on the emotional strains that result from the extreme specialization of work assignments caused by this specialization. Additional stress is caused by technological advancements that need rapid changes in the knowledge and skills of workers.

Management recognizes the existence of these problems and takes action to limit their negative influence on the performance of each employee. Training employees to perform current jobs in an acceptable manner and offering development opportunities that will help employees attain their potential are non-compensation components that can influence this health-related dimension.

c. *Promote Constructive Social Relationship with Coworkers:* An old proverb says, 'one man is no man'. One human alone is weak, but with joint action, people can accomplish almost anything. In this world of extreme specialization, people rely on others more than ever. One of the most valued rewards gained from working is the opportunity to interact in a socially constructive manner with other people. The chance to communicate and interact with others is an inexpensive but valuable reward. A workplace environment where trust, fellowship, loyalty and love emanate from the top level of management to the lowest levels of the organization promotes the kinds of social interaction most people need in order to thrive.

d. *Design Jobs that require Adequate Attention and Effort:* Organization scientists have discussed the problems arising from boredom related to work. Acting on scientific management jobs are designed so that workers could be taught quickly how to perform a few repetitive tasks. Workers are then required to perform these few tasks as long as they remained on the job. What first appeared to be an efficient way of doing jobs, became a source of boredom. Work-related anxieties and frustration produced behaviour that led to declining performance. Employee turnovers, absenteeism, tardiness and waste of physical resources were behaviours attributed to unacceptable job design. Recognizing these problems managers are implementing new approaches to improve the quality of work life. Employees are being given more opportunity to have a voice in how their jobs should be performed. Workers are given more opportunity to schedule workdays. Managers instruct workers to do their jobs and then leave them alone to perform their assignments in their own ways.

e. *Allocate Sufficient Resources to Perform Work Assignments:* When employees have to perform assignments for which they have neither skill nor knowledge opens the door for problems. Because of the inevitability of failure employee satisfaction and interest are apt to break down. Most employees seek a sense of accomplishment from their work. They want some degree of challenge but they also want to feel sure that they can succeed.

   When employees are told they must produce certain kinds and quantities of output within a specified time, they want to know the resources that are available to help them meet these demands. The most critical resource is sufficient time to accomplish an assignment. Does the employee have the time to perform the assignment? Has the organization assisted the employee to gain the knowledge and skills necessary to perform the assignment? Are the necessary human and physical resources available to support the employee in accomplishing the assignment? These questions must be answered by supervisors as they review performance.

f. *Grant Sufficient Control over the Job to meet Personal demands:* Behavioural scientists have discussed the need to grant employees greater opportunity to participate in organizational decision making process. Organizations are composed of all kinds of people with all kinds of decision making desires. Some people simply want to be told what to do and few others in the organization want to tell the top management how to run the organization. Between these two extremes there are others who want to know how to perform assignments.

   One of the most important decisions made by more and more workers is that of scheduling work activities and, in some case, of choosing the location of assignments. Over the past two decades, flexible work schedules have been implemented. With the advent of personal computer and networking, more employees are allowed to work from home or at a worksite of their choice.

   Another advancement in this area enables two part-time employees to share one full time job. Each of the two may work only 15 to 25 hours per week but together they share and perform all jobs responsibilities.

   Another change to make life easier is the casual dress day. With this option, employees are granted the opportunity to 'dress down' or wear clothing of a more relaxed or casual style. In most cases, the organization provides guide lines regarding clothing to be worn.

g. *Offer Supportive Leadership and Management:* This is a unique dimension of the non-compensation rewards. All people look to certain individuals for guidance and support. They respect those who can help them achieve goals. They look to managers who can bring about desired changes. Followers must have faith in the actions taken by their leaders and the leaders must heed the requests of their followers.

Supportive leadership is demonstrated in many ways: skill and interest in coaching and counselling, praise for a job well done and feedback leading to improvement of job performance. Leaders must be sufficiently flexible with rules and regulations so that an employee can meet job responsibilities satisfactorily. The selection, training and promotion of individuals who will later become effective leaders and managers are the cost components of this dimension.

## Test Questions

1. In earlier decades pay issues were influenced by tradition and government policy.

   What was the result of such policy?

2. Why pay has undergone a revolution? Do you think that pay is an agent of change?

3. In the framework of public policy how pay is determined?

   What do you mean by direct and indirect compensation? Explain them with examples.

4. What are the aims of compensation management? What are its characteristics?

5. State the State Employment Policy, 2005.

# Motivation and Reward

One fundamental question of reward management is how it can help to motivate people so that they can achieve high levels of performance. It is necessary to understand the factors that motivate people, and how reward practices will enhance motivation and positive behaviour can be developed. Motivation theories provide guidance on the practical steps to be developed for effective reward systems.

Motivation theory examines the process of motivation. It explains why people at work behave in the way they do.

A motive is a reason for doing something. People are motivated when they expect that a course of action will lead to the achievement of a goal.

The process of motivation is initiated by the recognition of unsatisfied needs. These needs create wants which lead to achieve something. Goals are then established which will satisfy the needs and a behaviour path is selected which will achieve the goal. If the goal is achieved and the needs are satisfied, the behaviour will be repeated when a similar need emerges. When a need is satisfied, a new need will emerge and the process will continue. According to Maslow, it is unsatisfied needs that motivate behaviour.

As mentioned by Frederick Herzberg there are two types of motivation—Intrinsic motivation and Extrinsic motivation. Intrinsic motivation is the motivation through the work itself. It takes place when people feel that the work they do is intrinsically interesting and challenging and important, and there are opportunities for advancement and growth. Extrinsic motivation is what is done to people to motivate them. This includes rewards such as increased pay, promotion and punishment such as withholding pay or disciplinary action.

Extrinsic motivators have an immediate and powerful effect but it may not last long. The intrinsic motivators are likely to have deeper and long-term effect because they are inherent in individuals and not imposed from outside. Intrinsic motivation is provided when jobs are well designed.

## Role of Rewards and Incentives in motivation:

Rewards provide recognition to people for their achievements and contribution. If rewards are worth having and people know how they can attain them they can act as motivators. Rewards can be either financial or non-financial. Incentives are designed to encourage people to achieve objectives. Incentives are generally financial but can be also non-financial.

The process of motivation is based on a number of motivation theories. The main theories are as follows:

1. Instrumentality, behaviourist reinforcement theories
2. Needs or Content theories
3. Herzberg's Two Factor theories
4. Process theories (Expectancy, goal and equity)

## *Instrumentality Theory:*

Instrumentality is the belief that if we do one thing, it will lead to another. This theory states that people work only for money. It assumes that people will be motivated to work if rewards and penalties are tied directly to their performance. Instrumentality Theory has its roots in Frederick Winslow Taylor's scientific management. This theory is based on the principle of reinforcement which states that people perceive that certain actions help to achieve their goal while others are less successful. Success in achieving goals and rewards therefore acts as a positive incentive and reinforces the behaviour which is repeated the next time a similar need emerges. Conversely, failure or punishment provides negative reinforcement. This process has been called the law of effect.

Motivation using this approach has been widely adopted, but it is based exclusively on a system of external controls and fails to recognize a number of other human needs.

## *Needs (Content) Theory:*

The basis of this theory is the belief that an unsatisfied need creates tension and disequilibrium. To restore the balance a goal is identified which will satisfy the need and a behaviour pathway is selected which will lead to achievement of the goal. Hence, all behaviour is motivated by unsatisfied needs. The best known contributor to need theory is Abraham Maslow. He said, "Man is a wanting animal; only an unsatisfied need can motivate behaviour and the dominant need is the prime motivator of behaviour."

## Herzberg's Model:

Herzberg's Two Factor model states that factors giving rise to job satisfaction (and motivation) are distinct from the factors that lead to job dissatisfaction. It is also known as motivation-hygiene theory.

There are two groups of factors: the first consists of the satisfiers or motivators which are intrinsic to the job. These include achievement, recognition, the work itself, responsibility and growth. The second group comprises what Herzberg calls the "dissatisfaction avoidance" or hygienic factors which are extrinsic to the job and include pay, personal relations and security. These cannot create satisfaction but can cause dissatisfaction. He also noted that any feeling of satisfaction resulting from pay increases was likely to be short lived. Hence, we can conclude that pay is not a motivator although unfair payment system can lead to de-motivation. The more relevant approaches are the process theories. They are known as process theories because they describe the psychological processes or forces which affect motivation as well as basic needs. Process theories can be more useful to managers than needs theory because it provides more realistic guidance on motivation techniques.

Process theories are covered by
 i) Expectations (Expectancy theory)
 ii) Goal Achievement (Goal theory)
 iii) Feelings about Equity (Equity theory)

*Expectancy Theory:*

The core process theory is Expectancy theory. Most other approaches adapt on it. The concept of expectancy was originally contained in the valence-instrumentality-expectancy theory formulated by Victor Vroom. Valence stands for value, instrumentality is the belief that if we do one thing it will lead to another and expectancy is the probability that action will lead to an outcome.

The strength of expectations may be based on past experience, but individuals are presented with new situations–a change of job, payment system or working conditions imposed by management where past experience is an inadequate guide to the implications of the change. In these circumstances, motivation may be reduced.

Motivation is likely when a perceived and usable relationship exists between performance and outcome, and outcome is seen as a means of satisfying needs. This explains why extrinsic financial motivation, for examples, and incentive or bonus scheme works only if the link between effort and reward is understood and the value of reward is worth the effort. It also explains why intrinsic motivation arising from the work itself can be more powerful than extrinsic motivation.

This theory was developed by Lyman W. Porter and Edward E. Lawler into a model which follows Vroom's ideas by suggesting that there are two factors determining the effort people put into their jobs: i) the value of the reward to individuals in so far as they satisfy their need for security, social esteem, and self actualization; ii) the probability that reward depends on effort as perceived by individuals. Thus, the greater the value of a set of rewards and the higher the probability that receiving each of these rewards depends on effort, the greater the effort will be made in a given situation.

*Goal Theory:*

Goal Theory, as developed by Latham Locke, states that motivation and performance are higher when individuals set specific goals, when the goals are difficult but accepted and when there is feedback on performance. Participation in goal-setting is important as a means of securing agreement to the setting of higher goals. Difficult goals must be agreed and achieving them must be helped by guidance and advice.

*Equity Theory:*

Equity Theory as described by John Stacey Adams states that people will be better motivated if they are treated equitably and demotivated if they are treated inequitably. It is concerned with people's perceptions of how they are being treated in relation to others. To be dealt with equitably is to be treated fairly in comparison with another group of people.

*Motivation, Incentives and Rewards:*

Financial incentives and rewards can motivate. People need money and therefore want money. It can motivate but it is not the only motivator. Money can serve the following reward functions:

i) It can act as a goal that people generally strive for.
ii) It can act as an instrument which provides valued outcomes.
iii) It can be a symbol which indicates the recipient's value to the organization.
iv) It can act as a general reinforcer.

Money motivates because it is linked with satisfaction of many needs. It satisfies the basic need for survival and security, and can also satisfy the need for self esteem and status. Money may by itself have no intrinsic meaning but it acquires significant motivating power because it comes to symbolize so many intangible goals. Pay is often a dominant factor in the choice of employer and pay is an important consideration when people are deciding whether or not to stay with an organization.

But doubts have been cast on the effectiveness of money as a motivator by Herzberg. He claimed that while the lack of it may cause dissatisfaction, money does not result in lasting satisfaction. Do financial incentives motivate people? The answer is absolutely not. Mr Kohn challenges what he calls the 'behaviourist dogma about money and motivation'. He claims that no controlled scientific study has ever found a long-term enhancement of the quality of work as a result of any reward system.

Jeffrey Pfeffer contends that people do work for money, but they work even more for meaning in their lives. In fact, they work to have fun. In contrast, N. Gupta and J. D. Shaw emphasize the instrumental and symbolic meanings of money. The instrumental meanings of money concerns what we get for ourselves and others. When certain behaviours are followed by money, then they are more likely to be repeated. In other words, employees will do the things for which they are not rewarded; it also means that they ignore the things for which they are rewarded.

The views expressed by Kohn are convincing except he seems to think that the only types of rewards to be considered are financial. He does not seem to recognize that non-financial rewards can motivate, if handled properly.

To assume that financial incentives will always motivate to perform better is as simplistic as to assume that they never motivate people to perform better. Some people will be motivated by money than others and an incentive scheme can encourage them to perform more effectively as long as they can link their effort to the reward and reward is worth having. Sometimes cash bonuses can be more effective rewards because they can be immediately converted into things that people want.

As Lawler points out, people's feelings about the adequacy of their pay are based upon comparisons they make between their own and others. External market comparisons are the most critical because they are the ones that strongly influence whether individuals want to stay with the organization.

**Factors affecting Satisfaction with Pay:**

No research evidence has been found that there is always a positive relationship between job satisfaction and performance. A satisfied worker is not necessarily a high performer and a high performer is not necessarily a satisfied worker. Satisfaction may lead to good performance but good performance may just as well be the cause of satisfaction. The relationship can be reciprocal.

**Job Satisfaction, Motivation and Performance:**

The practical messages delivered by Motivation Theory are as follows:

Extrinsic reward provided by employers in the form of pay will help to attract and retain employees and may increase effort and minimize dissatisfaction. Intrinsic non-financial rewards may have a long-term and deeper impact on motivation. Reward systems should therefore include a mix of extrinsic and intrinsic rewards.

**Key message of Motivation Theory:**

**Significance of needs:** People will be better motivated if their work satisfies their social and psychological needs as well as economic needs. Needs theory highlights the concept of total reward which recognizes the importance of the non-financial rewards as motivators.

**Importance of Expectations:** The degree to which people are motivated will depend not only upon the perceived value of the outcome of their actions-the goal or reward-but also on their perceptions of the likelihood of obtaining a worthwhile reward, i.e., their expectations. They will be highly motivated if they can control the means of attaining their goals. This indicates that where pay is related to performance, contribution or skill are effective as motivators only if (i) people know what they are going to get in return for certain efforts, (ii) they feel that what they may get is worth having and (iii) they expect to get it.

**Influence of goals:** Individuals are motivated by having specific goals to work for; and they perform better when they are aiming at difficult goals which they have accepted and when they receive feedback on performance.

**Rewarding Sales Staff**

Rewards for sales staff are often different from other employees. Sales representatives are more likely to be eligible for commission payments or bonuses because it is expected that their sales performance will be improved by financial incentives. It is believed that owing to the special nature of selling and the type of person required for sales job demand some form of additional bonus or commission. In the case of sales representatives, target is fixed and performance is measured against it, that is, a clear link is maintained between effort and performance. There are five different approaches to rewarding sales staff. These are as follows:

1. Salary Only
2. Basic salary plus commission
3. Basic salary plus bonus
4. Commission only
5. Sales incentives

**1. Salary only:** Companies may adopt a salary only approach (no commission or bonus) when sales staff has practically no influence over sales volume. Basic salary may also be paid to sales staff who work in highly seasonal industries where sales fluctuate considerably and in businesses where there is little opportunity for creative selling. If no commission or bonus is offered, it is necessary for companies to ensure that the salaries paid to their sales staff are competitive.

**2. Basic Salary plus Commission:** Salary plus commission plans provide for a proportion of total earnings to be paid in commission, the rest is being paid in the form of a fixed salary. The commission is a percentage of the value of sales. The proportion of commission varies widely. Generally, it is higher when results depend on the ability and enterprise of a salesman. Most sales managers believe that the commission will not motivate their staff unless they can earn at least 20 per cent.

The commission may be fixed percentage of all sales or the commission rate can increase at higher levels of sales on a rising scale to encourage sales representatives to make even greater efforts.

**3. Basic Salary plus Bonus:** Cash bonuses may be paid on basic salary. They are given on the achievement of targets for sales volume or profit. They differ from commission payments in that the latter are based simply on a percentage of whatever sales have been attained. In a bonus scheme targets or objectives may be set just for sales volume but they can also focus on particular aspects of the results that can be achieved by sales staff which has to be stimulated. These may include the sales of more profitable products or services in order to encourage staff to concentrate on them rather than simply aiming to achieve sales volume with low-margin products that are easier to sell.

There are many methods by which bonuses can be determined. The method used will take into account the following considerations:

I. The formula for relating bonuses to sales–a bonus may be offered when a sales threshold is reached.
II. The size of bonus payments available at different levels of performance.
III. The maximum bonus that will be paid.
IV. The bonus criteria-sales revenue is often used.

**4. Commission only:** In this case sales staff who are at the 'hard' end of selling may receive only a straight commission on the basis of a percentage of the value of their sales. No basic salary is paid.

**5. Additional Non-Cash Rewards:** The prime motivator for a typical sales representative is cash but there are a number of other non-cash methods of providing motivation, as described below:

1. **Incentives:** Gifts and vouchers provide a tangible means of recognizing achievements. They may be linked to the achievement of specific targets.
2. **Competitions:** Prizes can be given to individuals or teams for significant sales achievements.

3. **Cars as perks:** Sales representatives can be motivated by the opportunity to get a better car if they are particularly successful.
4. **Non-financial motivators:** Sales people have a high level of achievement motivation when they have the opportunity to make use of their talents in more challenging work. Public applause is also very important.

## Test Questions

1. What factors motivate employees? Discuss the roles of rewards and incentives in motivation.
2. Discuss different approaches to rewarding sales staff.
3. Discuss the non-cash methods of providing motivation to sales representatives.

# 3

# Individual Contingent Pay

Contingent pay is used to describe schemes for providing financial rewards which are related to individual performance, competence, contribution or skill. However, pay related to service is also in a sense contingent pay.

Individual contingent pay relates financial rewards to the performance, competence, contribution or skill of individual employees. It provides an answer to the two fundamental reward management questions: a) What do we value? and b) What are we prepared to pay for? Contingent pay may be consolidated in base pay or provided in the form of cash lump-sum bonuses. The latter arrangement is called 'variable pay', sometimes referred to as 'pay at risk'.

Contingent pay schemes are based on processes for measuring performance, competence, contribution or skill. These may be expressed as ratings which are converted by means of a formula to a payment. Alternatively, there may be no formal ratings and pay decisions are based on broad assessments.

A distinction is made between performance (what a person achieves) and contribution (the impact made by the person on the performance of the team and the organization). The level of contribution will depend on the competence, knowledge, skill and motivation of individuals, the opportunities on which they have to apply their knowledge and skill and the use they make of the leadership, support and guidance they receive.

Many people see contingent pay as the best way to motivate people. But it is not correct to assume that it is only the extrinsic motivators in the form of pay that creates long-term motivation about financial rewards. The total reward concept highlights the importance of non-financial rewards as an integral part of a complete package. The intrinsic motivators which can arise from the work itself and the working environment might have a long-lasting effect. When

## Compensation and Reward Management

considering contingent pay as a motivator a distinction is made between financial incentives and rewards.

Financial incentives are designed to provide direct motivation while financial rewards act as indirect motivators because they provide a tangible means of recognizing achievement as long as people expect that what they do in the future will produce something worth while rewards can be retrospective.

### Arguments for Contingent Pay:

The most powerful argument for contingent pay is that those who contribute more should be paid more. It is proper that achievement is recognized with a financial reward.

The following were the main reasons for using Contingent Pay:
* To recognize and reward better performance.
* To attract and retain high quality people.
* To improve organizational performance.
* To focus attention on key results and values.
* To deliver a message about the importance of performance.
* To motivate people.
* To influence behaviour.
* To support cultural change.

### Arguments Against:

1. The main arguments against contingent pay schemes question the level of motivation. The amounts available for distribution are so small that they cannot act as an incentives.
2. The requirements for success are difficult to achieve, money by itself will not result in sustained motivation.
3. People react in widely different ways to any form of motivation. The contingent pay schemes are based on the premise that money will motivate all people equally which is not correct.
4. Financial rewards may possibly motivate those who receive them but they can demotivate those who do not receive rewards, and the numbers who are demotivated could be much higher than those who are motivated.
5. Contingent pay schemes can create more dissatisfaction than satisfaction if they think it to be unfair or badly managed.
6. Contingent pay schemes depend on the existence of accurate methods of measuring performance, competence, contribution, or skill which might not exist.

7. Contingent pay decisions depend on the judgment of managers which might be partial, prejudiced or inconsistent.
8. The concept of contingent pay is based on the assumption that performance is completely under the control of individuals when, in actuality, it is affected by the system in which they work.
9. Contingent pay may militate against quality and teamwork.

Another powerful argument against contingent pay is that it has proved difficult to manage. It has been aptly remarked that 'performance pay is beautiful in theory but difficult in practice'.

**Alternatives to Contingent Pay:**

The arguments against contingent pay convince many people that it is unsatisfactory but the question, what is the alternative? One answer is to rely more on non-financial motivators. But it is still necessary to consider what should be done about the pay. The reaction to the adverse criticisms of performance-related pay was to develop the concept of competence related pay. This approach in theory overcame some of the cruder features of performance-related pay but still created a number of practical difficulties. In the late 1990s the idea of contribution-related pay emerged as advocated by Michael Armstrong. This combines the output-driven approach of performance-related pay with the input (competence-oriented) approach of competence-related pay and is better than either performance-or competence-related pay. The traditional alternative is service-related pay. This treats everyone equally (and therefore appeals to trade unions) but pays people simply for being there and this could be regarded as inequitable because rewards take no account of relative levels of contribution. The other alternative is a spot rate system where there is a single rate for job and no scope for pay progression. Spot rates are often used for senior management and at the other end, for manual workers and sales representatives. They are sometimes adopted by newly started organizations and in smaller companies where pay is market driven and a matter for individual contracts rather than being determined by a company-wide system.

The criteria for effective contingent pay are as follows:

**Criteria for Success:**

1. Individuals should have a clear vision on what they do and what they will get for doing it. This expressed the essence of expectancy theory: that motivation will take place when people expect that their effort and contribution will be rewarded.
2. Rewards are worth having.

3. Fair and consistent means are available for measuring performance, competence, contribution or skill.
4. People must be able to change their performance by changing their behaviour.

**1. Performance-related pay:**

The main features of performance-related pay (PRP) are described below:

Targets or outcomes — Performance measures — Performance — Rating — Formula — Performance pay.

Pay increases are related to the achievement of agreed result defined as targets or outcomes. Scope is provided for consolidated pay progression within pay brackets attached to grades in a graded family structure or in a broad-banded structure. Such increases are permanent.

Alternatively, high levels of performance may be rewarded by cash bonuses which are not consolidated. Persons may be eligible for such bonuses when they have reached the top of the pay bracket for their grade or when they are assessed as being fully competent.

The rate and limits of progression through the pay brackets are determined by performance ratings which are often done at the time of the performance management review.

Pay progression in a graded structure is planned to decelerate through the grade for two reasons: First, in line with learning curve theory that pay increases should be higher during the earlier period in a job when learning is at its highest rate. Second, it may be assumed that the central point in a grade represents the market value of fully competent people.

PRP has all the advantages and disadvantages for contingent pay. It has attracted a lot of adverse comments, mainly because of the difficulties organizations have met in managing it. Contribution-related pay schemes are becoming more popular.

**2. Competence-related pay:**

The main features of competence-related pay schemes are illustrated below:

Agreed Competence Requirement — Competence level definitions — Evidence of Competence level achieved — Rating or assessment — Methodology — Competency pay.

Individuals receive financial rewards in the shape of increases to their base pay by reference to the level of competence they demonstrate in carrying out their roles. It is a method of paying people for paying their ability to perform.

As in the case of PRP, there is scope for consolidated pay progression within pay brackets attached to grades.

Competence-related pay is attractive in theory because it can be part of an integrated competency-based approach to HRM. Organizations are finding that success depends on a competent workforce. Paying for competence means that an organization is looking forward not back. It is attractive because it rewards people for what they are capable of doing, not for results over which they might have little control.

The notion of contribution-related pay or linking the reward to outcomes (performance) as well as inputs (competence) is a better approach.

**3. Contribution-related pay:**

Contribution-related pay is a process for making pay decisions which are based on assessments of both the outcomes of the work carried out by individuals and the inputs in terms of levels of competence and competency which have influenced these outcomes. It focuses on what the people contribute by their skills and efforts to the achievement of the purpose of their organization.

Contribution-related pay is a holistic process taking into account all aspects of a person's performance. Performance means both behaviours and results.

The case of contribution-related pay has been made by Duncun Brown and Michael Armstrong in this way: Contribution captures the full scope of what people do, the level of skill and competence they apply and the results they achieve, which all contribute to the organization achieving its long-term goals: Contribution-related pay works by applying the mixed model of performance management, assessing inputs and outputs and coming to a conclusion on the level of pay for people in their roles and their work; both to the organization and in the market; considering both past performance and their future potential.

The main features of contribution-related pay are shown in the following figure:

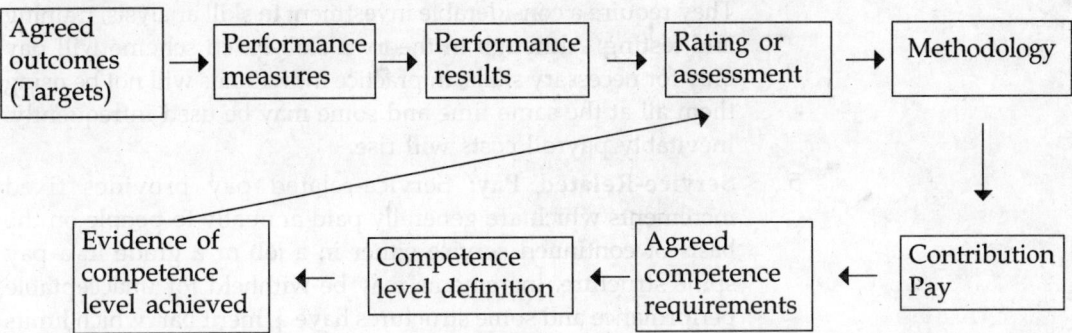

Contribution-related pay rewards people for both their performance (outcomes) and their competence (inputs).

Pay awards can be made as consolidated pay increases but in some schemes there is also scope for cash bonuses.

4. **Skill-based pay:**

Skill-based pay provides employees with a direct link between their pay progression and the skills they have acquired and can use effectively. It focuses on what skills the business wants to pay for and what employees must do to demonstrate them. Therefore, it is a people-based rather than a job-based approach to pay. Rewards are related to the employee's ability to apply a wider range or a higher level of skills to different jobs.

A skill may be defined broadly as a learnt ability which improves with practice over time. For skill-based pay purposes the skill must be relevant to the work. Skill-based pay is also known as knowledge-based pay.

Skill based pay was originally applied mainly to operations in manufacturing firms. But it has been extended to technicians and workers in retailing, distribution, catering and other service industries.

*Main features:*

1. Skill blocks or modules are defined. These incorporate individual skills or clusters of skill which workers need to use and which will be rewarded by extra pay when they have been acquired.
2. The skill blocks are arranged in a hierarchy with natural break points between different levels of skills.
3. The successful completion of a skill module will result in an increment in pay. This indicates how the pay of individuals can progress as they gain extra skills.
4. Methods of verifying that employees have acquired and can use the skills at defined levels are established.

Skill-based pay systems are expensive to introduce and maintain. They require a considerable investment in skill analysis, training and testing. Although in theory a skill-based scheme will pay only for necessary skills, in practice individuals will not be using them all at the same time and some may be used infrequently. Inevitably payroll costs will rise.

5. **Service-Related Pay:** Service-related pay provides fixed increments which are generally paid annually to people on the basis of continued service either in a job or a grade in a pay spine structure. Increments may be withheld for unacceptable performance and some structures have a 'merit bar' which limits increments unless a defined level of merit has been achieved. This is the traditional form of contingent pay and is widely used.

Service-related pay is supported by unions because they perceive it as being fair in which everyone is treated equally. Some people believe that the principle of rewarding people for loyalty by continued service is a good practice.

The arguments against service-related pay are that:
i) It is inequitable in the sense that an equal allocation of pay increase according to service does not recognize the fact that some people will be contributing more than others and should be rewarded accordingly.
ii) It does not encourage good performance.
iii) It is based on the assumption that performance improves with experience but it is not automatically the case.
iv) It can be expensive, everyone may drift to the top of the scale but the cost of their pay is not justified by the added value they provide.

*Choice of Approach:*

The choice is whether or not to have contingent pay related to performance, competence, contribution or skill. Public sector organizations with fixed incremental systems where progression is solely based on service may want to retain the system because they do not depend on biased judgments by managers and they are perceived as being fair-everyone gets the same and easily managed. However, fairness of such system can be called in question. It is not fair for a poor performer to be paid more than a good performer simply for being there.

The alternatives to fixed increments are either spot rates or some form of contingent pay. If it is decided that a more formal type of contingent pay for individuals should be adopted, the choice is between the various types of performance pay, competence-related or contribution-related pay and skill-based pay.

## Main features of Contingent pay schemes

| Types of scheme | Main Features |
| --- | --- |
| Performance-related pay | Increase in basic pay or bonuses are related to assessment of performance |
| Competence-related pay | Pay increases are related to level of competence. |
| Contribution-related pay | Increases in pay or bonuses are related both to competence and performance. |
| Skill-based pay | Increments related to the acquisition of skills. |
| Service-related pay | Increments related to service in grade. |

## Test Questions

1. What is individual contingent pay? The most powerful argument for contingent pay is that those who contribute more should be paid more.

   Explain the reason for using contingent pay

2. Describe the main features of contingent pay schemes as under
   a) Performance-related pay
   b) Competence-related pay
   c) Contribution-related pay
   d) Skill- related pay
   e) Service-related pay

# 4

# Concept of Internal and External Equity

The basic binding factor for an employee with the organization is the compensation he gets for the service he renders to achieve the desired goal of the organization. We know that the salary is the main compensation to an employee for working in the organization. The employee compares his salary with others working in the same organization and expects an equitable compensation in relation to similar task performed within his organization. The approach is also to compare the compensation levels of similar jobs in the industry or the region.

The is how the concept of Internal Equity and External Equity has emerged. The basic tenets of Frederick Winslow Taylor's scientific management with respect to human resource management involve.

1. Right man for right job
2. Right pay for the right job

If the right pay is offered to the right man, the man is motivated to associate himself with the work. This is where the issue of determining the relative worth of a job within his organization to establish internal equity assumes relevance. The method of determining the internal worth of the jobs is known as Job Evaluation, which establishes the rational differentials that are required between jobs, ultimately leading to a wage structure across the jobs in the organization. Accordingly, wage surveys in the industry or region attempt to compare the internal wage structure of an organization with those prevailing in the market. Such an External Equity enables the management to evolve a suitable wage structure to attract required skills and retain them with the organization.

Therefore, Job Evaluation is a means to establish the internal worth of a job relative to others, whereas wage surveys are the means to evolve suitable wage structure to attract and retain employees by establishing External Equity. These two techniques of scientific management would enable the management to locate the right man and retain him motivated by wages.

**Job Evaluation:**

With the advent of Scientific Management, job evaluation is widely used. Job Evaluation is a generic term covering methods of determining the relative worth (Equity) of jobs. It is a systematic (Quantitative and Qualitative) method for determining the relative worth of a job in comparison within and outside the organization. It helps to eliminate wage inequities and to establish a basis for sound salary and wage structure. Job Evaluation consists of the following steps:

i) Job Analysis examining the content of a job, breaking it down into its tasks, functions, processes and operations.
ii) Job description
iii) Job Specification–statement of the content of a job.
iv) Job Grading–ranking of a job, as a result of a job analysis.
v) Job Classification–grouping of jobs according to their worth.
vi) Job Assessment–assignment of a money value to a job.

Job Evaluation is concerned with the evaluation of the job and not with evaluation of the man performing the job.

**Methods of Job Evaluation:**

The methods of Job Evaluation are divided in the following categories:

A) Conventional
    I) Non-quantitative
        a) Ranking Method
        b) Classification Method
    II) Quantitative
        a) Points Rating Method
        b) Factor Comparison Method
B) Non-Conventional
    a) Time Span of Discretion Method
    b) Decision Band Method
    c) Direct Consensus Method
    d) Guide Chart Profile Method
    e) Urwick Orr Profile Method

**1. Ranking Method:**

In this method simple and easy job description are made and sorted in the sequential order of their worth as a whole. The jobs common in various organizations are checked and ranked by interpolation.

All jobs in an organization are ranked in the order of complexity, responsibility and demands they make on the respective employees. Ranking of all the jobs is made easier by first identifying those that come at two extreme ends of the scale and locating the rest in the middle region.

*Advantages:*
  i) It is a very simple procedure;
  ii) It is not time consuming;
  iii) It leaves more room to bargain.

*Disadvantages:*
  i) Evaluation committee members are not likely to be familiar with all jobs.

**2. Classification Method:**

In this method a limited number of job grades are established on the basis of knowledge about the existing jobs in the organization. Each of these grades is defined in terms of general functions and qualifications. This is followed by development of job descriptions which briefly state the nature of duties of each job. These global job descriptions are matched with the grades and jobs are classified into different grades.

*Advantages:*
  1. It is comparatively easier method and
  2. It is less time consuming.

*Disadvantages:*
  1. It is difficult to determine the prerequisites of classes and
  2. Nearly similar jobs are put in different classes.

**3. Point Rating Method:**

In this method the whole job is analyzed through factors and sub-factors on the basis of requirements. These factors are given points which totals out as the overall position of the jobs. It is a systematic and the most popular method in use. The steps involved in this system are as follows:

1. Job analysis through interview and actual observation and
2. Writing up of job description from the data collected through job analysis.

The next important step in the selection of an appropriate plan is evaluation of the job. A plan should contain such job factors into a number of degrees which would provide suitable scales for measuring the extent of a particular characteristic present in the job being evaluated. Further, a plan should be developed in such a way as to cover the types of jobs, which are to be evaluated. For example, a plan for clerical employees is not suitable for factory operatives. In such a plan, the inclusion of the factor of physical effort may not be necessary because of the sedentary natures of the job, but physical effort is an important factor in almost all factory jobs. After factors have been decided upon, they should be defined to make their meanings clear. Due weightage should be given to them. Factors are then divided into a suitable number of degrees between their extremes and each degree is defined clearly. Point values are then assigned to each degree. This step would involve development of an appropriate plan which involves:

a) Selection and definition of factors and giving due weightage to them;

b) Deciding on the number of degrees and defining them and

c) Assigning point values to degrees.

### 4. Factors Comparison Method:

Here important factors of jobs are evaluated in terms of monetary value, and relative jobs are positioned in terms of those factors and values. The factors usually considered in this system are five in number-mental requirement, skill, physical requirements, responsibility and working conditions.

The system involves detailed job analysis, ranking jobs in respect of predetermined factors, apportioning the total money paid to the different factors of the job, fitting key jobs into the system and locating all other jobs in relation to the key jobs. The main features of the system consist of evaluating important elements of the job in terms of money value and establishing the relative positions of the job in terms of specific factors.

*Advantages:*

i) Internal comparison and External comparison of the job within and out of industry are considered.

ii) Monetary units are used for comparison.

*Disadvantage:*

i) It is difficult to apportion the total wage in various factors.

ii) Conflict may arise on the valuation of each factor.

**Factors Comparison vis-a-vis Point Rating System:** Both systems are basically analytical and quantitative in their approach. Unlike the ranking and grading systems, these systems are based on detailed analysis of the jobs and assessment of the different factors of the jobs.

Second, factor comparison system ranks jobs in relation to each other, while the point system relates each job to a descriptive scale and arrives at a numerical value. There is no clearly stated scale used in factor comparison, whereas the point system defines the factors, their degrees and point values in specific terms.

Third, these stages are more clear in the case of the point system than in factor comparison.

Fourth, money units are used in the factor comparison system while the point system makes no reference to money units.

Fifth, the ranking of jobs is easier on the point system while such ranking is difficult in the factor comparison.

Sixth, both the systems recognize the need for giving weightage to factors. But the point system uses point values for giving weightage to different factors. Use of numerical values provides for greater flexibility.

Lastly, the point system is usually restricted to evaluation of jobs at the operative level while the factor comparison system can be applied to a wider range of jobs including executive positions.

## Job Analysis and Job Description:

Job analysis is the process which results in establishing the components of a job and ascertaining the human qualifications necessary for its successful performance.

Job analysis, which is the first step in the job evaluation process consists of analyzing the jobs in detail. The idea of such analysis is to find out all relevant facts in respect of the job. Job analysis is carried out by gathering information in respect of the job either through interviews or questionnaires. Where workers are illiterate, job information is collected through interviews. Where workers can fill up the particulars about the job, information is collected through questionnaires. The nature of information gathered through job analysis comprises the requirements of skill in performing the job, responsibilities involved and the surroundings in which it is performed. The job is studied when it is actually performed.

**Job Description:** It is essential that the jobs are described accurately so that job description can give a clear picture of the work involved. Job descriptions are used for various purposes such as selection of employees, training and job evaluation. Job description is a description of jobs on the basis of job analysis sheets and contains the following information:

i) Identification of data,
ii) Summary of job,

iii) Work performed,
iv) Responsibilities of Tools and Materials etc.,
v) Work Environment and
vi) Required qualities.

Data is collected on the job through Observation, Interviewing of employees, Questionnaire Method and Consulting Supervisors.

**Linking with Wage Fixation:** After all the jobs have been evaluated and reviewed, the next step is to link the wages to point and derive a final wage structure. The major steps involved in this are

i) Deriving the company wage curve;
ii) Job classification and
iii) Pricing of the jobs.

The wage curve is a graphic relationship between the job points and the corresponding wages paid for the job. The points evaluated for each job is plotted on the X-axis and the corresponding wages on the Y-axis. When all the jobs have been plotted, a scatter diagram would be obtained. A line of best fit is obtained for the plotted points by drawing a freehand line.

The ultimate objective of the job evaluation is to determine equitable wage rates for each job. Therefore, these points have to be connected into monetary values.

Establishing pay rates for each job is extremely difficult to operate. Hence the normal practice is to classify the jobs into a definite number of categories and establish a wage for each category which will be applicable to all the jobs falling in that category.

The jobs are arranged as per their evaluated points in an ascending or descending manner. This will facilitate in determining the point range for each classification.

When all the jobs in the company have been classified into a definite number of categories, each category needs to be fixed with proper wage scales. For this it is necessary to make sure whether the existing wage structure of the company is sound and comparable with practices obtaining in other industries. This is done through a wage survey.

The idea of carrying out job evaluation work mostly comes from the top management and there are three alternatives open for getting the job done. The work of Job Evaluation is carried out by i) the company employees; ii) consultants or iii) jointly by the company employees and consultants.

## External Equity and Pay Surveys:

One of the major problems in wage and salary administration is that proper wage differentials are established and maintained within an organization on the basis of relative worth of job. This is known as Internal Equity. Another important consideration is that a wage structure should be built in such a way that would be attractive enough to retain good employees. In other words, the structure should be built up by composing the prevailing wages in the area of the industry. Such comparison of internal wage structure with external wage structure is known as establishing External Equity.

Pay or wage is the basic means to compensate for the work performed by an employee. Pay has three components. They are

i) Basic ii) Allowances such as DA and Perks and iii) Incentives or Bonus payments including overtime.

The basic pay is the most important consideration of the employer for the intrinsic worth of the jobs in the organization. Monetary allowances are supposed to ameliorate the needs of the employee to meet the extra demands that arise as a result of inflation or increased house rent etc. The third component under the incentive scheme is to reward the productive effort.

One of the basic principles of Taylor's Scientific Management is 'Fair pay for Fair work'. The fair day's work is determined by scientific approach of work study when the output expected from an employee is estimated and norms of output are determined. Accordingly fair pay which is expected to compensate adequately to attract and retain as well as motivate the employee is determined by the following factors:

i) Paying capacity of the organization;
ii) The prevailing compensation in the market;
iii) The differentials between a particular job with respect to others in the same industry and
iv) Needs of an employee as stipulated by the statutory agencies.

The paying capacity of the enterprise emerges from the performance and competitiveness as well as the policy of the management vis-a-vis the bargaining capacity of the employees. The prevailing rate or going rate is usually determined by Pay surveys. Job evaluation provides the rational basis to explain and establish the differentials required to be maintained between jobs. The ideas of fair day's pay for a job is normally arrived from the minimum wages concept and are generally available from the wage boards, labour departments and other statutory agencies.

**Pay Surveys:** To build up a competitive wage structure, it is necessary to know what are the rates prevailing for similar jobs in the same industry in the area. Unless the wage structure is competitive it will be difficult to get and retain efficient workers. The purpose of a pay or wage survey is to obtain the desired information.

**Prerequisites before pay survey:** It has to be decided on

i) What is the information to be sought?
ii) Selection of jobs about which information should be sought. and
iii) The units which should be approached to furnish the desired information.

Furthermore, one has to ensure that information sought through survey should be for jobs having identical job content.

i) Information is usually sought about basic wage rate or scale, different allowances incentives, mode of increment etc.
ii) The important considerations which should govern the selection of jobs are that, the jobs selected must cover the range of jobs evaluated and jobs which are to be found in other units in the area.
iii) Units selected should be on the basis of similar size and be in the same locality as the firm conducting the survey.

When the required information is gathered from different units, a summary should be prepared from the data so collected and comparison made with the company's existing wage structure so that future rates are constructed accordingly.

**Types of pay surveys:** External Equity is the comparison of both intra-and inter-industry pay rates. There are three main types of pay survey–informal, external and commissioned. Informal surveys are conducted in an informal way and can vary from personal contacts to specific arrangements for exchanging information with a number of local companies or with companies in a particular industry.

External surveys are almost entirely confined to salary earnings groups. Few comparable surveys of wage earners are produced. They fall into three main categories: first those produced by professional bodies about their own members' pay; second, those prepared by consultants and third, published surveys of employment agencies.

Commissioned method is the most reliable among all the three existing methods. This is what is done either by commissioned consultant or by the company itself. Whether the pay survey is commissioned through a consultant or by the enterprise itself, the approach is the same.

## Survey Method:

There are three methods of wage survey: i) by job title; ii) by job description and iii) by job evaluation.

In the job title method, the company collecting information gets the pay details for similar job titles in other companies. The information obtained from various companies for each job title is tabled and compared with the wages paid to each of these jobs in the company in question. This method is easy but not accurate. Many companies may have the same job titles but the job content may be different. There may be variations in skill, working conditions and other factors. Hence, a wage survey on the basis of job titles does not provide correct information.

Job description method is the most common method used in the pay survey. The comparison is made on the basis of the job description. The wage data of other industries are collected for these jobs which have the same job descriptions in the company doing the pay survey. This is a more realistic basis for comparison.

Job evaluation method is no new method – it is simply an improvement over the job description method. The descriptions are collected for the jobs selected for wage survey in other industries. These jobs are evaluated and if the points obtained by similar jobs in other industries are the same as the ones for the company then the jobs are supposed to be identical and a comparison of wages for these jobs would be made. This method being time-consuming is not normally used in wage surveys.

While making a pay survey, it may not be possible to collect information for all the jobs that have been evaluated. If the information is collected for representative jobs from which it would be possible to derive the wage curve, it would serve the purpose. These jobs are known as key jobs or benchmark jobs. One has to ensure that these jobs should be distributed over the whole range of jobs and the jobs should exist in competing companies and these jobs should remain relatively stable in recent years.

In practice, similar units are selected for wage survey. Units situated in the same locality should be selected since location has an important bearing on the wages paid. But this is not always practicable since there may be only one such organization in a locality. Competing organizations are included, for example, a jute industry may include all the jute factories throughout West Bengal in a wage survey.

Collection of information is a vital aspect in a wage survey and requires careful planning. Information may be collected by the job

analyst or through questionnaire filled up by participating companies. The following types of information are to be collected in pay survey:
  i) General Information;
  ii) Number of weekly and daily working hours;
  iii) Holidays;
  iv) Basic wages, scales of pay;
  v) Allowances;
  vi) Incentives and Bonuses and
  vii) Facilities such as convenience, accommodation etc.

**Test Questions**

1. What do you mean by internal and external equity of compensation? How internal and external equity is done? Explain them.
2. What do you mean by job evaluation? Describe the different methods of job evaluation.
3. Explain the following terms;
   a) Job Analysis
   b) Job Description
   c) Pay Surveys
   d) Survey Methods

# 5

# Wage Concepts

Wages have been classified into six broad categories:
1. Statutory minimum wage
2. Basic subsistence or minimum wage
3. Living wage
4. Fair wage
5. Minimum wage
6. Need-based minimum wage.

The statutory minimum wage is determined according to the provisions of the Minimum Wages Act, 1948. The statutory minimum wage is higher than the bare subsistence or minimum wage, providing for some measure of education, medical requirements and amenities.

**1. The Statutory Minimum Wage**

The bare minimum wage is a wage that would be sufficient to cover the bare physical needs of the worker and his family i.e., a rate which has got to be paid to the worker, irrespective of the capacity of the industry to pay.

**2. The Bare Subsistence or Minimum Wage**

Justice Higgins of the Australian Commonwealth Court of the Conciliation defined the living wage as one appropriate for the normal needs of the average employee, regarded as a human being living in a civilized community. According to him, living wage must provide not merely for absolute essentials such as food and clothing but for a condition of frugal comfort estimated by current human standards. He explained it further by saying that it was a wage sufficient to insure the workmen, food, shelter, clothing, frugal comfort, provision for evil days etc. as well as regard for the special skill of an artisan if he is one.

**3. The Concept of the Living Wage**

Our political aim is living wage though, in actual practice living wage has been an ideal which has included our efforts like a ever receding horizon and will so remain for some time to come. Our general wage structure has at best reached the lower levels of fair wage though some employers are paying much higher wages than the general average.

In a classic judgment, the Supreme Court held that the management, specially of public undertakings, are bound by the Directive Principles of State policy enshrined under Part IV of the Constitution. The workers must, therefore be ensured a living wage, just and human conditions of work and a decent standard of life. The management accordingly must endeavour to secure for the workmen apart from wages, other amenities like supply of essential commodities at concessional rates, medical aid, housing facility, education for children, old age benefits and opportunities for social, cultural and sport activities.

### 4. The Concept of Fair Wage

The Committee on Fair Wages said that the fair wages lies between a minimum wage and a living wage. The Committee envisaged that while the lower limit of the fair wage must obviously be the minimum wage, the upper limit is equally set by what may broadly be called the capacity of the industry to pay. This will depend not only on the present economic position of the industry but on its future prospects. Between these two limits the actual wages will depend on (i) the productivity of labour; (ii) the prevailing rates of wages in the same or similar occupations in the same or neighbouring localities; (iii) the level of the national income and its distribution and (iv) the place of the industry in the economy of the country.

The Supreme Court defined fair wages as something above the minimum wage which may roughly be said to approximate to the need-based minimum wage, in the sense of a wage which is adequate to cover the normal needs of the average employee, regarded as a human being in a civilized society.

In another judgment the Supreme Court observed that the fair wage will grow with the growth and development of the national economy and the progress made by the industry must approximate to the capacity of the industry to pay.

Thus the concept of fair wage implies a wage sufficiently high to enable a worker with a standard family to provide with for food, shelter, clothing, medical care and education of children appropriate to his status in life.

### 5. Minimum Wage

The Committee on Fair Wages stated that the minimum wage must provide not merely for the subsistence of life but for the preservation of the worker. It must provide for some measure of education, medical requirements and amenities. The Committee also stated that an industry which was incapable of paying this minimum wage had no right to exist, and for fixing the minimum wage, no regard should be paid to the capacity of the industry to pay and it should be based on the requirements of the worker and his family.

The Supreme Court explained the concept of minimum wage and observed: At the bottom of the ladder, there is the minimum basic wage which the employer of any industrial labour must pay in order to be allowed to continue as industry. Above this, it is the fair wage which may roughly be said to approximate to the need-based minimum in the sense of a wage which is adequate to cover the normal needs of the average employee regarded as a human being in a civilized society. Above the fair wage is the living wage which will maintain the workmen in the highest state of industrial efficiency which will enable him to provide his family with all the material things which are needed for their health and physical wellbeing, enough to enable him to qualify to discharge his duties as a citizen.

**6. Need-based Minimum Wage**

The 15th Indian Labour Conference held in 1957 at New Delhi for the first time delineated the concept of minimum wage for all workers industry reproduced below, which is with regard to the minimum wage was 'need based' and should ensure the minimum human needs of the industrial workers, irrespective of any other considerations. To calculate the minimum wage, The committee accepted the following four norms and recommended that they should guide all wage-fixing authorities including minimum wage committees, wage boards, adjudicators etc.

i) In calculating the minimum wage, the standard working class family should be taken to consist of three consumption units, for one earner; the earnings of women, children and adolescents should be disregarded.

ii) Minimum food requirements should be calculated on the basis of a net intake of 2,700 calories, as recommended by Dr. Wallace Aykroyd for an average Indian adult of moderate activity.

iii) Clothing requirements should be the minimum, rent charged by Government in any area for houses provided under the subsidized industrial housing scheme for low income groups and

iv) Fuel, light and other miscellaneous items of expenditure should constitute 20 per cent of the total minimum wage.

The Second Pay Commission examined the norms set by the 15th Session of ILC. The National Commission on Labour which examined this aspect came to be observed that most of the wageboards have taken into consideration, the capacity to pay in fixing the minimum for the respective industries and the wages fixed by them fall in the realm of fair wages, though at its lower level. The need-based minimum wage is also a level of fair wage and represents a wage higher than the minimum obtaining at present in many industries, though it is only on the lower reaches of the fair wage. It therefore held that in fixing the need-based minimum, the capacity to pay will have to be taken into account.

The Third Pay Commission also examined the feasibility of a need-based minimum for Central Government employees in the light of norms laid down by the Indian Labour Conference.

## Test Questions

1. Explain the following concepts:
   a) Statutory minimum wage
   b) Basic minimum wage
   c) Living wage
   d) Fair Wage
   e) Minimum wage
   f) Need-based minimum wage

# 6

# Factors Affecting Levels of Pay

The compensation policies of different organizations vary somewhat. Marginal units pay the minimum necessary to attract the required number and kind of labour. Often, these units pay only the minimum wage rates required by the labour legislation and recruit marginal labour. At the other extreme, some units pay well above the ongoing rates in the labour market. Some managers believe in the economy of higher wages. They feel that by paying higher wages, they would attract better workers who will produce more than the average worker in the industry. This greater production per employee means greater output per manhour. Hence, labour costs may turn out to be lower than those existing in firms using marginal labour. Some units pay high wages because of a combination of favourable product market demand, higher ability to pay and the bargaining power of a trade union. But a large number of them seek to be competitive in their wage programme, i.e., they aim at paying somewhere near the ongoing rate in the labour market for the various classes of labour they employ. Most units give greater weight to two wage criteria, viz. job requirements and the prevailing rates of wages in the labour market. Other factors such as changes in the cost of living, the supply and demand of labour and the ability to pay are accorded a secondary importance.

A sound wage policy is to adopt a job evaluation programme in order to establish fair differentials in wages based upon differences in job contents. Besides the basic factors provided by a job description and job evaluation those that are usually taken into consideration for, compensation administration are

1. The ability to pay;
2. Supply and demand of labour;
3. The prevailing market rate;
4. The cost of living and
5. Living wage.

6. Productivity
7. Trade Union's bargaining power
8. Job requirements
9. Psychological and sociological factors.

*1. Ability to pay*  Wage increases should be given by those organizations which can afford them. Companies that have good sales and therefore high profits tend to pay higher wages than those which are running at a loss or earning low profits because of the high cost of production or low sales. In the short run, the economic influence of the ability to pay is practically nil. All employers, irrespective of their profits or losses, must pay no less than their competitors and need pay no more if they wish to attract and keep workers. In the long run, the ability to pay is very important. During times of prosperity, employers pay high wages to carry on profitable operations because of their increased ability to pay. But during a period of depression, wages are cut because of the shortage of funds. Marginal firms and non-profit organizations (like hospitals and educational institutions) pay relatively low wages because of low or no profit.

*2. Supply and Demand of Labour*  Wages and salaries are affected by the market conditions of supply and demand. If the supply of particular labour skills is scarce, employers may offer higher wages. If the supply is excessive, lower wages are usually given. Similarly, if there is a great demand for labour expertise, wages rise, but if the demand for a manpower skill is minimal, wages will be relatively low. The supply and demand compensation criterion is very closely related to the prevailing pay, comparable wage and ongoing wage concepts are determined by immediate market forces and factors.

*3. Prevailing Market Rate*  This is also known as the comparable wage or going wage rate and is the most widely used criterion. An organization's compensation policies generally tend to conform to the wage rate payable by the industry and the community. This is done for several reasons. First, competition demands that competitors adhere to the same relative wage level. Second, various government laws and judicial decision make the adoption of uniform wage rates an attractive proposition. Third, trade unions encourage this practice so that their members can have equal pay for equal work and geographical differences may be eliminated. Fourth, functionally related firms in the same industry require essentially the same quality of employees with the same skills and experience. This results in a considerable uniformity in wage and salary rates. Finally, if the same or about the same general rates of wages are not paid to the employees as are paid by the organization's competitors, it will not be able to attract and maintain sufficient quantity and quality of manpower. Belcher and Aitchison observe: "some companies pay on the high side of the market in order to obtain goodwill or to ensure an adequate supply of labour while other organizations pay lower wages because economically they have to or by lowering hiring requirements they can keep jobs adequately manned."

**4. Cost of Living**

The cost of living pay criterion is usually regarded as an automatic minimum equity pay correction. This criterion calls for pay adjustments based on increases or decreases in an acceptable cost of living index. In recognition of the influence of the cost of living, "escalator clauses" are written into labour contracts. When the cost of living increases, workers and trade unions demand adjusted wages to offset the erosion of real wages. However, when living costs are stable or decline, the management does not resort to this argument as a reason for wage reductions.

**5. The Living Wage**

The living wage criterion means that wages paid should be adequate to enable an employee to maintain himself and his family at a reasonable level of existence. However, employers do not generally favour using the concept of living wages as a guide to wage determination because they prefer to base the wages of an employee on his contribution rather than on his need. Also they feel that the level of living prescribed in a worker's budget is open to argument since it is based on subjective opinion.

**6. Productivity**

Productivity is another criterion and is measured in terms of output per manhour. It is not due to labour efforts alone. Technological improvements, better organization and management, the development of better methods of production by labour and management, greater ingenuity and skill by labour are all responsible for the increase in productivity. Actually productivity measures, the contribution of all the resource factors-men, machines, methods, materials and management. No productivity index can be devised which will measure only the productivity of a specific factor of production. Another problem is that productivity can be measured at several levels–job, plant, industry on national economic level. Thus, although theoretically it is a sound compensation criterion, operationally many problems and complications arise because of measurement and conceptual issues.

### 7. Union Bargaining Power

Trade unions do affect the rate of wages. Generally, the stronger and more powerful the trade union, the higher wages. A trade union's bargaining power is often measured in terms of its membership, its financial strength and the nature of its leadership. A strike or threat of a strike is the most powerful weapon used by it. Sometimes, trade unions force wages up faster than increases in productivity would allow and become responsible for unemployment or higher prices and inflation. However, for those remaining on the pay roll, a real gain is often achieved as consequence of a trade union's stronger bargaining power.

### 8. Job Requirements

Generally, the more difficult a job, the higher are the wages. Measures of a job difficulty are frequently used when the relative value of one job to another in an organization is to be ascertained. Jobs are graded according to the relative skill, effort, responsibility and job conditions required.

### 9. Psychological and Social Factors

These factors determine in a significant measure, how hard a person will work for the compensation received or what pressures he will exert to get his compensation increased. Psychologically, persons perceive the level of wages as a measure of success in life; people may feel secure, have an inferiority complex, seem inadequate or feel the reverse of all these. They may or may not take pride in their work or in the wages they get. Therefore, these things should not be overlooked by the management in establishing wage rates. Sociologically and ethically, people feel that equal work should carry 'equal wages', that wages should be commensurate with their efforts, that they are not exploited and that no distinction is made on the basis of caste, colour, sex or religion. To satisfy the conditions of equity, fairness and justice, a management should take these factors into considerations.

### 10. Planning of Wages & Salary Administration

The generally accepted principles covering the fixation of wages and salary are

i) There should be a definite plan to ensure that differences in pay for jobs are based upon variations in job requirements, such as skill, efforts, responsibility of job or working conditions and mental and physical requirements.

ii) The general level of wages and salaries should be reasonably in line with that prevailing in the labour market. The labour market criterion is most commonly used.

iii) The plan should carefully distinguish between jobs and employees. A job carries a certain wage rate, and a person is assigned to fill it at that rate. Exceptions sometimes occur in very high level jobs in which the job-holder may make the job large or small, depending upon his ability and contributions.

iv) Equal pay for equal work, i.e., if two jobs have equal difficulty requirements, the pay should be the same, regardless of who fills them.

v) An equitable practice should be adopted for the recognition of individual differences in ability and contribution. For some units, this may take the form of rate ranges, with in-grade increase; in others, it may be a wage incentive plans and in still others, it may take the form of closely integrated sequences of job promotion.

vi) There should be a clearly established procedure for hearing and adjusting wage complaints. This may be integrated with the regular grievance procedure, if it exists.

vii) The employees and the trade union, if there is one, should be informed about the procedure used to establish wage rates. Every employee should be informed of his own position, wages and salary structure. Secrecy in wage matters should not be used as a cover-up for haphazard and unreasonable wage programme.

viii) The wage should be sufficient to ensure for the worker and his family a reasonable standard of living. Workers should receive a guaranteed minimum wage to protect them against conditions beyond their control.

ix) The wage and salary structure should be flexible so that changing conditions can be easily met.

## 11. Steps Involved in Fixing Specific Job Rates

Usually, four steps are involved in arriving at specific, job rates, viz. performing a job analysis, grading a job, assigning a price to each job, and administering the resulting programme.

The process of job analysis results in job descriptions which lead to job specifications. A job analysis describes the duties, responsibilities, working conditions and inter-relationships between the job as it is and the other jobs with which it is associated. It attempts to record and analyze details concerning the training, skills, required efforts, qualifications, abilities, experience and responsibilities expected from an employee.

After determining the job specifications, the process of grading, rating or evaluating the job occurs. A job is rated in order to determine its value relative to all the other jobs in the organization, which are subject to evaluation.

The next step is that of providing the job with a price. This involves converting the relative job values into specific monetary values or translating the job classes into rate changes.

Finally, after the wage range for each job is established, the specific wage rate within the range for each employee must be determined. This leads to the process of employee appraisal.

## 12. Control of Compensation

Wage and salary administration should be controlled by some appropriate agency. This responsibility may be entrusted to the personnel department or the general company organization or to some job executive. Since the problem of wages and salary is very delicate and complicated, it is usually entrusted to a committee composed of high ranking executives representing major line organizations. The major functions of such committee are

i) Approval and/or recommendation to management on job evaluation methods and findings;

ii) Review and recommendation of basic wage and salary structure;

iii) Help in the formulation of wage policies;

iv) Co-ordination and review of relative departmental rates to ensure conformity and

v) Review of budget estimates for wage and salary adjustments and increases.

This committee should be supported by the advice of the technical staff. Such staff committees may be for job evaluation, job description, merit rating, wage and salary surveys in an industry and for a review of present wage rates, procedure and policies.

## Test Questions

1. Discuss the factors usually taken into consideration for compensation administration.
2. What do you mean by the economy of higher wages?
3. Discuss steps involved in fixing specific job rates.

# Economic Theories Affecting Compensation

Economic theories affecting compensation that have developed over the centuries are

1. **Social Wage Theories:** The social wage theories, often classified as the classical wage theories, attempt to explain what society ought to pay to one of its members, based either on the need or right of that member. In no case these theories mention talents of the individual or the quality or quantity of work produced by that individual.

    a) *Subsistence Theory of Wages:* Although the fundamental concept of the Subsistence Theory of Wages existed long before the Christian era, David Ricardo is given the credit for its development. In 1817, he proposed this theory which deals with population rather than labour. This theory suggests that each member of society be provided enough food, clothing and shelter to continue to exist. It further implies that when the income of the workers exceeds their subsistence level, they respond by further procreation, thereby increasing the labour force and consequently lowering wages as a result of supply and demand. The works of Thomas Mun and Thomas Malthus influenced Ricardo in the development of this theory. This theory also is known as the Iron Law of Wages.

    b) In the pre-Christian eras of Greece and Rome, early philosophers began developing theories to explain and describe the economic relationships among social groups. *The Just Price Theory,* originally proposed by Plato and

**Macro Theories:**

Aristotle some 300 years before Christ, suggested that each person born into the world is foreordained to occupy exactly the same status and to enjoy the same creature comforts as did his parents. Therefore, society owes these individuals sufficient compensation to maintain exactly the same position of life into which they were born.

c) The Just Price Theory of the pre-Christian era evolved into a *Just Wage Theory* and was firmly established during the feudal Middle Ages in Europe. The construction of churches and government buildings and continued expansion of commercial activities, provided more and more job opportunities for artists, artisans and traders. The artists and artisans felt that they should receive better wages than the unskilled lower class who provided physical work that required minimal intellectual effort.

 The Just Wage Theory received strong church support because of the philosophy proposed by St. Thomas Aquinas. He suggested that the price of any article should be adequate but no more than adequate to cover the cost of production, which in turn is based upon the accustomed standards of living of the producers of the item. Aquinas continued to promote the view that society owes each individual sufficient compensation to maintain exactly the same position of life in which he was born.

d) *The Wages Fund Theory* was advanced by John Stuart Mill in 1830s. It suggests that the wages of an employee are paid from a fund, which presumably has been accumulated by entrepreneur from operations of previous years. The fund is to be divided evenly among all employees. An obvious shortcoming of the theory is that wages are paid from current business operations rather than from past operations. However, the theory seems to possess some validity when applied to not-for-profit organizations such as government and public service whereby the wage fund is actually forecasted and drawn from tax monies.

e) In the late nineteenth century Francis Walker proposed the *Residual Claimant Theory,* a version of the Wage Fund Theory, in which he stated that the wage fund was derived not from previous years' operations, but simply from the residue of total revenues after deducting all other legitimate expenses of business operations such as rent, taxes, interests and profits. If the other expenses consumed all of the revenue, labour being the "residual claimant" would receive no wages and would not be entitled to them.

f) *The Marxian Theory or Surplus Value Theory* of Karl Marx is essentially the inversion of Residual Claimant Theory in as much as he suggests that labour is the sole source of economic value and therefore labour should exercise the prime claim on revenue. This means that the price of an article consists solely of labour value and any other value collected by the entrepreneur represents unacceptable exploitation of labour. According to Marx, the surplus between labour cost and product price should be paid to labour. Marx further suggests that the displacement of labour through technological progress is dysfunctional to the system and eventually will destroy capitalism. This appears to be the ideological basis for the opposition to automation by some segments of the labour union movement.

II. **The Wage Control Theories** suggest that somewhere between a pure dictatorship and a pure democracy, room can be found for a mode of governing that openly permits some degree of indirect control of wage levels.

In the 30s Lord Maynard Keynes recognized that a thriving middle class economy required full employment. Keynes developed his National Income Theory, also called Full Employment Wage Theory or General Theory. This theory states that full employment is a function of national income. National income, in turn, is equal to the total consumption plus private and public investment. If the national income falls below a level that commands full employment, it is the responsibility of the government to manipulate any or all of the three variables to increase national income and return to full employment.

This suggests that government is the one agent powerful enough to control monetary and fiscal policies as well as to enforce direct edicts upon private enterprise, thereby maintaining full employment and indirectly the desired wage level.

g) The *National Income Theory* treats the labour supply fixed. In reality, the national labour force continually varies within wide limits. This short-term variation is a result of the fact that a substantial segment of the population can, in the short run, exercise a personal choice as to whether they are actually a part of or not a part of the labour force. This personal choice can be exercised by a second wage earner in the family, by teenagers who have not previously been in the labour force, by older people who may be able to choose whether to be employed, by recipients of unemployment compensation, who for the short term might not be available for alternative employment or simply by those who are unwilling to work under any conditions. Thus the critics of the National Income Theory suggest that a fault of the theory is the fact that it does not recognize this fluctuating labour force.

h) *The Neo-Keynesian Distribution Theory:* The Neo-Keynesian Distribution Theory is an extension of the National Income Theory which attempts to explain how full employment conditions can be achieved without conflicting with general living standards or with stable prices. This is a theory of the general wage level in the long and short terms. It also recognizes the fact that entrepreneurial decisions can determine the general level of wages in the short run. Money wage rates, within limits, is determined by bargaining between the capitalist and the employee. This is a departure from the theories previously mentioned in which economic forces alone determined the wage level. Thus the ever-changing labours supply is given some consideration in this theory.

i) By the 20th century, wage theories became closely linked to employment practices. Henry Ford, the great industrialist of USA developed the *Consumption Theory*, sometimes referred to as the Purchasing Power Theory. In 1913, Ford introduced the $5 a day wage for workers in his automobile plant. This wage was about double than that being paid by competitors at that time.

The pay-related actions of Ford took much of steam away from Marx's *Manifesto*. Ford's simple philosophy was that higher-paid workers could buy more products, which would, in turn, improve their lifestyles. This, in turn, would generate more business and higher profits for entrepreneurs, employers and stockholders. Ford, better than Marx, recognized the strength of an upward mobile middle class that in a capitalistic–democratic society would increase in numbers. Ford operated in a democratic society whereas Marx lived within absolute and constitutional monarchies.

Those who support Ford's action as a New Wage Theory suggest that high wages encourage consumption, increase demand for products and thereby lower commodity prices.

III. **The Justification Theories:** The Justification Theories so labelled because their authors attempt to explain or justify an individual worker's compensation level. This first three theories approach the wage level from an overall macroeconomic viewpoint, whereas the remaining theories use a microeconomic approach.

   j) *The Investment Theory* developed by H.M. Gitelman, recognizes that labour markets vary in the scope of "worker investment" required for their particular industry. Generally, the wider the labour market is, the higher the wages are. The individual worker's 'investment' consists of the education, training and experience that the worker has invested in a lifetime of work. Individual workers vary in their desire to maximize income, just as employing organizations vary in their worker investment requirements. Thus Gitelman says that an individual worker's compensation is determined by the rate of return on that worker's investment. This theory has combined broad economic influences on compensation with the specific means whereby workers can control the level of their own compensation.

   k) *The Institutional Wage* Theory makes an attempt to place the 'level of compensation' on a system or establish an empirical and quantitative basis. It is an interdisciplinary approach to compensation that includes such considerations as wage experience, variability of wage relationships, latitude of decision makers, the influence of collective bargaining etc. It suggests that a wage level depends on a variety of choices of decision makers and that weights can be assigned to these choices. It considers all types of wage structures such as interpersonal and inter-industry and suggests that one must analyze compensation from a dynamic changing basis rather than assuming that we can hold all factors affecting compensation constant.

   i) A review of wage theories would be incomplete without reference to the classic *Supply and Demand Theory*.

Probably the most acceptable theory of compensation is the assumption that if jobs are few and the supply of workers is higher, then wages will fall. Conversely, if jobs are plentiful and there is a shortage of workers, wages will rise. However, in the long run wages will seek a level at a point at which the demand curve intersects the supply curve.

*Micro Theories:* The theories outlined previously are basically macro in nature because each attempts to describe the broad economic influences of society that affect the level of compensation of all workers. The following theories have been termed micro because they consider the wage structure within a given industry or even a given company involving the bargain and the exchange between employer and employee.

m) *Marginal Productivity Theory:* In 1876, Von Thunev, a German economist proposed the basis for the Marginal Productivity Theory which was further developed by Philip Henry Wicksteed and J.B. Clark. According to this theory, the wage that is paid to an employee should be equal to the extra value of productivity that the employee adds to the total production. The value of the worker's production is determined by the revenue the employer can realize from the worker's productivity. As the employer hires additional workers, a point will reach at which the last worker hired just produces enough products to pay his own wages. The hiring of an additional worker would result in revenue that did not equal that worker's wages. The last worker hired is called the marginal employee and the increased production attributed to the worker is called marginal productivity. The wage paid to the latest marginal employee determines the wages of all workers who are doing similar work. Despite criticism, this theory at least represents the first formal theory embracing the principle that a worker should be paid according to the quantity and quality of work contributed.

n) *The Productivity Efficiency* is a refinement of Marginal Productivity Theory in that each worker is provided the opportunity to increase his wages by increasing his productivity efficiency. This theory provides the basis for various monetary motivational tools such as incentive systems, bonuses and profit sharing plans.

o) The beginning of the *Bargaining Theory of Wages* is found in the writings of Adam Smith. This is the first clear presentation of the simple principle that compensation is dependent upon a bargain between an employer and an employee. The Bargaining Theory is based on the assumption that there is no single fixed wage rate for a particular kind of work; rather there is a range of possible wage rates. The upper limit of this range is determined by the highest wage the employer is willing to pay and the lower limit is determined by the lowest wage for which the employee is willing to work.

The Bargaining Theory remains probably the most practical and valid explanation for the level of a given employee's compensation. When an employee chooses to designate the union as a bargaining agent with the employer, then this theory becomes the Collective Bargaining Theory.

IV. **Behavioural Economic:** Theories were developed in the last half of the 20th century. Earlier economic models lacked behavioural models. Economic Theories viewed the organization as a 'black box' that transformed inputs into outputs. The developers of micro-macro economic theories recognized that management practices could influence the productivity of the organization and that internal managerial and compensation management practices must be recognized.

**Micro-Macro Theories:**

p) Harvey Leibenstein developed the **X-Efficiency Theory** model which recognized the influence of internal management practices on organizational productivity. Firms operating under competitive market conditions could produce additional levels of output by changing internal work process without changing the scale of operations. He assumed that the actual output levels of a firm seldom matched its competitive optimal level. The difference, X-Inefficiency was established to recognize the difference between the firm's production attributable to its internal operations rather than the allocative efficiency of the market. Libenstein felt that the optimizing behaviour assumed under neoclassical theories was the exception rather than the rule. He stated that productivity was significantly influenced by the internal structure of rewards and incentives, work effort and the management system of the organization.

V. A. set of theories and models related to behavioural economics that centres on the nature of the firm can be called **Organizational Economic Theories**. Organizational economics consist of transaction cost economics and agency theory.

q) **Transaction Cost Economic Theory** has been largely associated with the writings of Oliver Williamson. The theory centres on the nature of exchange of goods and services among parties; it assumes complexity and uncertainty in the process of the exchanges. Transaction costs consist of negotiating, monitoring and enforcement costs that must be borne to allow an exchange between the two parties to take place. When these costs of exchange in the market become too great, an incentive arises to remove them from the market and produce them internally. It is clear how a compensation system plays a major role in the operation of the firm. A compensation system will take into account these transaction costs and attempts to reduce them.

r) One contribution to organizational economics is the **Agency Theory**. It provides the most relevant implications for the design of a compensation system for the organization. Under conditions of imperfect information, divergent interests among stock holders (principals), management (agent) and employees may prevail. The fundamental compensation problem is how to develop an incentive reward contract that aligns the interests of management with those of the stockholders.

### Test Questions

1. Discuss briefly two important macro theories affecting compensation.
2. Explain how you can explain an individual worker's compensation level.
3. Explain a) Marginal Productivity theory of wages b) Bargaining theory of wages and c) Efficiency Theory of wages.

# 8

# Team Pay

There are two factors which have combined to create interest in rewarding teams rather than individuals. The first is the belief that team pay would enhance good team work and the second is dissatisfaction with the individual nature of performance-related pay. Team pay is an attractive idea but it is difficult to put it into practice.

Team pay links payments to members of a formally established team to the performance of that team. The rewards are shared among the members of the team in accordance with a formula or on an ad hoc basis in the case of exceptional achievements. Rewards for individuals may also be influenced by assessment of their contribution to team results.

Now it is necessary to understand the nature of a team and the different types of teams to which team pay applies.

A team may be defined as a small number of people with complementary skills who are committed to a common purpose, set of performance goals and approach for which they are mutually accountable.

A team has the following seven characteristics:

1. Shared leadership roles.
2. Individual and mutual accountability.
3. Specific team purpose that the team itself delivers.
4. Collective work products.
5. Open-ended discussion and active problem-solving meetings.
6. Performance measured directly by assessing collective work products.
7. Real work discussed, decided on and completed together.

There are four different types of teams. These are

## 1. Organizational teams

These comprise individuals who are linked together organizationally as members of the top management team: departmental heads in an operational division, section heads in a department or even people carrying out separate functions as long as they are all contributing to the achievement of the objectives of their department.

Members of organizational teams can be related to one another by the need to achieve an overall objective. Organizations are entirely constructed of such teams but team reward processes may be inappropriate unless their members are strongly united by a common goal and are interdependent. If such is not the case, some form of bonus related to organizational performance might be better.

### 2. Work teams

These are self-contained and permanent teams whose members work together to achieve results in the form of output or development of products or the delivery of services to customers. The members are united by a common purpose and interdependent. For this type of team, continuing team pay schemes rewards may be appropriate if team targets can be established and team performance be measured accurately.

### 3. Project teams

These consist of people brought together from different areas to complete a task lasting several months. When the project is completed the team is dissolved. A team formed to a new plan is an example. Project teams may be rewarded with cash bonuses paid on satisfactory completion of the project on time and within the budget cost.

### 4. Ad hoc teams

These are functional teams set up to deal with an urgent problem. They are usually short lived and operate as a taskforce. Usually no bonus is paid to such teams.

### Objectives of Team Pay

The aim and objective of team pay is to encourage the type of behaviour that leads to and sustain effective team performance by-

  i) giving incentives and other means of recognising team achievements;
  ii) clarifying what teams are expected to achieve by relating rewards to the achievement of predetermined targets and standards of performance and
  iii) conveying the message that one of the firm's core values is effective team work.

Research conducted in the field indicates that the main reason organizations give for developing team reward processes was the perceived need to encourage group effort and co-operation rather than to concentrate only on individual performance.

### How Team Pay Works

The most common method of providing team pay is to distribute cash sum related to team performance among team members. There are different formulas and ways of distributing team pay as follows:

| | |
|---|---|
| This establishes the relationship between team performance and the reward. It also fixes the size of the bonus pool or fund earned by the team to be distributed among the members. Bonuses may be related to performance in such areas as sales, achievement of targets in the form of delivery of results for a project levels of service or an index of customer satisfaction. Targets are fixed and performance is measured against the targets. | 1. **The team pay formula** |
| Bonuses can be distributed to team members in the form of either a percentage of base salary or the same sum for each member. Payment of bonus as a percentage of base salary is the most popular method. It is assumed that the base salary reflects the value of the individual's contribution to the team. | 2. **Method of distributing bonuses** |
| There are firms which pay team bonuses only. There are few firms which pay individual bonuses as well that are often related to an assessment of the competence of the person thereby providing impetus to develop skills and rewarding them for their contribution. | 3. **Team pay and individual pay** |
| It is assumed by the supporters of team pay that all members of a team contribute equally and should therefore be rewarded equally. But in practice the contribution of members of the team will be different and if this is the case, team pressure will force every member to work at the same rate so as to avoid 'rate busting'. When designing a team pay scheme, it may be assumed that some people will perform better or worse than others. If this happens it will be detrimental to single out anyone for different treatment. However, it could be considered that 'special achievement' or high performance bonuses should be given to high performers while poor performers should receive no bonus at all. | 4. **Dealing with high and low individual performance in a team** |
| The scheme described above apply to permanent work teams. Different types of arrangements are necessary for project teams set up to do a particular task and disbanded after the task has been completed. Project team bonuses should be self-financing—they should be related to increases in income or productivity or cost savings arising from the project. Project teams may have set targets and their bonus can be linked to achieving targeted results. | 5. **Project team bonuses** |

**6. Ad hoc bonuses**

Where there is no pre-determined scheme for paying bonuses to teams, a retrospective bonus can be given to the ad hoc team for exceptional achievement.

## Advantages and Disadvantages of Team Pay

*Advantages: Team pay can*

1. encourage team working and co-operative behaviour;
2. enhance flexible working within teams and encourage multiskillings, clarify team goals and provide for the integration of organizational and team objectives;
3. encourage less effective performers to improve with a view to meet team standards and
4. serve as a means of developing self-managed teams.

*Disadvantages:*

1. The effectiveness of team pay depends on the existence of well-defined and mature teams and they may be difficult to identify and if they can be identified, they are not motivated by a purely financial reward.
2. Team pay appears to be unfair to personnel who feel that their own efforts are not rewarded.
3. It is difficult to develop methods of rating team performance that appears to be fair. Team pay formula may be based on arbitrary assumptions about the correct relationship between effort and reward.
4. There may be a tendency of the employees to migrate from poorly performing teams to high performing teams which would cause disruption and stigmatise the teams from which individuals transfer.

Despite the problems that may involve team pay, if it is decided to introduce it, the following steps should be taken:

1. Initial Analysis: It is necessary to identify the team which satisfy the necessary requirement, e.g., it is stable, it is mature, composed of people whose work is interdependent, have a considerable degree of autonomy and performing units for which there are clear targets.
2. Scheme design: Decisions have to be made on which teams will be eligible for team pay and the team bonus formula.
3. Team pay is likely to be unfamiliar and therefore it should be introduced very carefully. Introduction will be easier if employees are involved in developing the scheme.

It is easier to introduce team pay into mature teams whose members are accustomed to working together, trust one another and can recognize the team pay will work to their mutual advantage.

**Test Questions**

1. What do you mean by Team pay? What are the different types of teams? What are their characteristics?
2. Discuss the different methods how team pay works.
3. Describe the advantages and disadvantages of Team pay.

# 9

# Wage Fixing Machinery:
## Wage Boards, Pay Commission, Collective Bargaining and Adjudication

**Wage Boards**

For industrial workers not covered by the Minimum Wages Act, India has several well-established procedures or practices for wage-fixation and wage revision: Wage Board, Pay Commission, Collective Bargaining at the plant level, Settlements in conciliation of wage disputes, Adjudication and Arbitration.

The First Five Year Plan talked of fair wage for workers in an industry to be adjudged by an impartial authority, with a view to evolving a scientific wage structure. But earlier, in 1948, by an amendment to the Bombay Industrial Relations Act (1946), the then provincial government had provided for the setting up of statutory Wage Boards. The Second Plan also considered the Wage Board a more acceptable machinery for settling wage disputes, a platform which gives the parties a more responsible role in reaching decision. The 15th Labour Conference (1957) accepted the principle of appointing industry-wise Wage Boards. The first Wage Board was set up on 30 March, 1957, for the cotton textile industry, with a Chairman, 2 independent members, 2 members representing employers and 2 labour. This has been the normal composition since then except that, at times, workers' and employers' representatives have been 3 instead of 2 each. One independent member is generally an economist and the other one generally an MP who is supposed to represent the consumers' interest. The employers' and workers' representatives are nominated by the organizations of the two interests which are prominent in the concerned industry, others are nominated by the government.

So far 24 Wage Boards covering most of the major industries have been set up by the Centre. Cotton textiles, cement, sugar, jute, tea, coffee, rubber plantation, iron and steel, iron ore, coal mining, ports and docks, engineering, heavy chemicals and fertilizers, electricity undertakings, road transportation, newspapers etc. are among the industries covered. Barring the Working Journalists (Conditions of Service) and Miscellaneous Provisions Act, 1955, no Central Act contains any provision for setting up wage boards. These are set up by a resolution of the government only, as we have seen. Under the Bombay Industrial Relations Act, the Maharashtra and Gujarat Government can set up statutory Wage Boards. The former has set up Wage Boards for cotton textile, silk and sugar industries and the latter on cotton textile and silk industries. These are standing or permanent Boards with power to review and modify their own orders. The decision of these Boards are judicial and appealable but no appeal can be made to the Industrial Court against the unanimous decision of such a Wage Board. The non-statutory Wage Board's awards are not enforceable in any court of Law-except in the UP where under section 3 of the UP Industrial Disputes Act, 1947, the recommendations made by some Wage Boards can be legally enforced. Such ad hoc non-statutory Wage Boards have also been set up by the Kerala Government (on plantation), by the Bihar Government (on the engineering industry) and by Delhi administration (on the hotel industry). The Jammu and Kashmir Government set up a tripartite Wage Committee in 1972.

On the government's acceptance of a Central Wage Board's recommendations, these are notified for general acceptance and persuasion and relied on for their implementation. On non-implementation by an industry, an industrial dispute can be raised and eventually a reference can be made to a tribunal. The governments have always accepted the unanimous recommendations, at times majority recommendations and only rarely modified any recommendations. Discussions with the parties precede government decisions. Those industries which have or had a regulated price structure (cement, iron and steel, coal etc.) generally ask for price increases being allowed by the government before they can implement Wage Board recommendations.

These are generally in conformity with the terms of the reference of the first Wage Board viz. (a) to determine which categories of employees are to be covered (manual, clerical, supervisory etc.), but generally the definition of workman in the Industrial Disputes Act is followed; (b) to work out a wage structure on the basis of principles of fair wages as formulated by the Committee on Fair Wages; (c) the needs of the industry in a developing economy; (d) the system of payment by results; (e) the special characteristics of the industry in different regions and are as including the working hours in an

**Terms of Reference**

## Procedure and Methodology

industry. The Wage Boards being set up by the government naturally work within the broad framework of the government's economic and social policy.

Generally, the questionnaire method is used and protracted public hearings are held. No workstudy or job evaluation or any of the scientific methods accepted in Western countries are resorted to. The Wage Boards determine the minimum wage for the unskilled worker and then build upon it a structure of differentials. The average capacity of the industry to pay as a whole is taken into account and not that of individual units or of the weakest units. The capacity to pay would generally be related to the profitability of an industry and its future prospects. The prevailing rates of wages, the place of the industry in the economy, the development needs of the industry, the growth of national income and the level of productivity are also taken into account in varying degrees.

## An assessment of Wage Board Method

The system is almost peculiar to India-the only analogies are with the Wage Councils of the UK and with the Australian Conciliation Committees, Wage Boards and Industrial Boards on an industry-wise basis which are set by the different States of Australia. These are standing boards-their decisions can be appealed against to courts.

The Main Criticism (1) Delays caused by extremely dilatory procedure (public hearings etc.) e.g., the Rubber Wage Board took 5 years one month; the Tea Wage Board 5 years 6 months and the Coal Mining Wage Board 4 years 7 months. So a series of interim awards become inevitable and cause distortions or pre-empt decisions; (2) no definite linkage between higher wages and productivity has been established; (3) these have not introduced by any scientific elements into the wage structure. Horse-trading has been at times, the deciding factor; (4) the operations of the Wage Boards have certainly narrowed down the area of collective bargaining in the country while the anomalies created by many 'unscientific' awards have been a prolific source of industrial disputes.

Merits. (1) Standardisation of wages over a wide area has taken place; (2) involvement of workers' and employers' representatives in the process was a step in the right direction.

## Recommendations of National Labour Commission

(i) Independent members are not needed but they can be particularly economists, appointed as assessors; (ii) the Wage Board procedure should be a kind of collective bargaining; (iii) the Chairman's appointment should be agreed to by both the parties preferably, so that he can arbitrate if necessary; (iv) unanimous recommendations should be made statutorily binding; (v) Wage Boards should finish their work within a year; (vi) a permanent Secretariat in the Labour Ministry producing standard questionnaires, collecting data etc. should be set up; (vii) awards should be operative for 5 years generally.

## Central Pay Commission

The pay structure of the Central Government employees is based on the recommendations of the Pay Commissions set up by the Central Government. While some State Governments also broadly follow the recommendations of the Central Pay Commissions for their employees, a few other state governments set up their own pay commissions. During the past 50 years, the Government of India set up six pay commissions. The recommendations of the Sixth Pay Commission, which submitted its report in 2007, as accepted by the Government are currently in force. Pay Commissions also cover a wide range of employees in the public sector.

There are significant differences between the methods of settlement of wage disputes available to workers in the private sector and those concerned government employees. The latter are at a disadvantageous position as none of the wage settlement methods such as collective bargaining, adjudication or arbitration is available to these employees to settle wage claims and disputes.

A Joint Consultative Machinery was set up by the Central Government to discuss matters relating to the welfare of the employees and improvement of efficiency and standards of work. The scheme provides for a limited extent of compulsory arbitration on the following subjects: (i) pay and allowances; (ii) weekly hours of work and (iii) leave of a class or grade of employees. The Government however, becomes the final authority in deciding whether an issue can or cannot go for arbitration.

Despite these arrangements, the effective method available to government employees is that of enquiry by the Pay Commission. The Central Government has so far set up Six Pay Commissions which reported in 1947, 1959, 1973, 1984, 1994 and 2006, respectively. Sixth Pay Commission submitted its report at the end of 2007. Most State Governments have also set up Pay Commissions from time to time.

Pay Commissions which were set up at regular intervals function non-statutorily, study the problems establishing their own procedures for the collection of data and information and make recommendations to the Government. Though these recommendations are given much weightage, the ultimate responsibility lies with the Government whether to accept, or modify or reject some of them.

The First Central Pay Commission recognized that the influence of the law of demand and supply cannot be wholly ignored in fixing the salaries of public servants. The fairness and adequacy of the salary proposed must be judged balancing the interests of the employee, employer and the public. The Commission stated that an employee must be paid a 'living wage'. However, with the Fair Wages Committee's clarification of the concept of living wage it becomes clear that the living wage which was recommended by the Commission should actually be the minimum wage.

The Second Pay Commission also referred to the principle that as a matter of social policy, the lowest rate of remuneration should not be lower than a 'living wage and the highest salaries also should be kept down, consistent with the essential requirements of recruitment and efficiency. The Commission reached the conclusion that the minimum wage or salary should not be determined merely on economic considerations, but should also satisfy a social test-both because of its intrinsic validity and because of its bearing on efficiency. Even above the minimum level the Government should remunerate their employees fairly; for those who serve the State, as well as others, are entitled to fair wages (Second Central Pay Commission Report).

The first two Central Pay Commissions stressed that the minimum wage must satisfy a social test and that wages above the minimum should be fair.

The major requirements of a second pay system quoted by the Third Pay Commission included inclusiveness, comprehensibility and adequacy.

(a) **Inclusiveness-**the pay structure and career pattern adopted for the civil service should broadly be adopted by autonomous quasi-governmental organizations also. Secondly, the large-scale appointment of casual, contingency and work-charged employees should be discouraged and kept to the minimum.

(b) **Comprehensibility-**the pay scale should provide a true and comprehensible picture of the total remuneration given to the Government employee.

(c) **Adequacy-**the pay structure should be adequate both internally and externally. Individual attributes such as education, training and skill should be taken into account for internal adequacy. For being externally adequate, the pay structure should provide for some measure of protection of living standards.

None of the above pay commissions viewed that the Government should be assigned the role of 'model employer' by paying higher wages and salaries. However, it was observed that the Government must be guided by the objectives and principles prescribed by the Pay Commission.

Though the feasibility of need-based minimum wage was examined by the two Pay Commissions, they differed in their views on the 15th Session of the Indian Labour Conference specifications on the minimum wage. The Third Pay Commission viewed that the minimum wage fixed should be realistic and should match the conditions prevailing in the economy. The Commission concluded that "the adoption of the minimum remuneration based on the 15th ILC norms at this stage would be tantamount to a misdirection of resources."

An important criteria in wage determination in industry is that of comparison. The First Pay Commission considered that a 'fair relativity' should be maintained between government employees and outside rates. The Second Pay Commission felt that though fair comparison between rates of remuneration for comparable work could be adopted, it involves practical difficulties in the application of the principle. The Third Pay Commission paid considerable attention to fair comparison under the principle of 'equal pay for equal work'. However, there can be no fair comparison between establishment with a profit motive and a public service motive. The Fourth Central Pay Commission dealt with the criteria of comparability on how it is not satisfactory as an absolute factor for fixing the governmental pay structure by comparison with that prevailing pay structure in the private sector. A market price cannot be assigned to the value of work in the public services. The Commission viewed that comparison should be used in determining pay of government employees. As far as possible, the effort should be to provide comparable emoluments for comparable work.

Capacity to pay is another criterion applicable to the remuneration of government employees but the method of assessment of Government's capacity is entirely different from that in the private sector, since, the Government could pay its 'fair wages' to employees. The Fourth Central Pay Commission observed that the capacity of the employer to pay its employee is a factor to reckon and be given due consideration. The Commission said that the fairness of the payments has to satisfy a double test in the sense it has to be fair from the point of employees as well as the people they serve.

The Fourth Central Pay Commission (1984 p. 84) disagreed with the First and Second Pay Commissions which rejected the 'model employer principle'. The Commission expressed that a model employer need not necessarily pay higher wages than other good employers. "A 'model' is above the ordinary or above that which is the minimum, or higher than what others are content with or what is good enough to serve their purpose."

Another important factor in wage determination is the cost of living. The approach of most Pay Commissions has been to devise a salary structure with reference to a certain consumer price index at which the Commission believes that prices may eventually get stabilized or, at any rate, below which prices are unlikely to fall and to provide for neutralisation of any rise in the cost of living thereafter through dearness allowance linked to, and generally varying with, the consumer price index.

The various commissions expressed different views on the subject of dearness allowance payable to government employees. The First Central Pay Commission observed that the dearness allowance is relevant not only to the needs of the most vulnerable section of the employees, but some of the upper grade employees also require a measure of relief. The quantum of dearness allowance will be raised, lowered and discontinued for a rise or fall in the consumer price index. The same principles would apply to all classes of employees except that when the consumer price index fell considerably below the existing level, DA was to be discontinued at different index levels for employees on different pay scales. The Commission recommended DA to all employees drawing a salary up to Rs. 1000.

The Second Central Pay Commission considered DA as a device to protect the real income of wage earners and salaried employees from the effects of rise in prices. The Commission, however, limited payment of DA to those drawing a salary of less than Rs. 300) per month. The Third Pay Commission observed that DA should be treated as compensation to the wage earners and salaried employees against the rise in prices over the index level to which the structure was related.

After examining the consumption pattern of employees in the higher pay range, the Commission recommended extending payment of dearness allowance to all employees getting pay not exceeding Rs. 2250 per month.

The Fourth Central Pay Commission also viewed that the compensation should provide full neutralisation of price rise to employees drawing basic pay up to Rs. 3500, 75 per cent to those getting basic pay above Rs. 6000 subject to marginal adjustments.

This compensation may continue to be shown as a distinct element of remuneration.

Doubts were expressed regarding the suitability of the Consumer Price Index for calculating DA for Central Government employees which is used for industrial workers. It has been argued that this index does not truly represent the consumption pattern of all central Government employees and should be replaced by an index specially prepared for the purpose.

The Fifth Central Pay Commission, which submitted its report in 1996, made some proposals linking pay revision with work organization and manpower planning. It recommended 40 per cent increase in pay and 30 percent reduction in manpower over a three-year period, new modes of recruitment, including contract employment and innovative suggestions on training, performance appraisal, career progression, transfer policies and accountability. The Government accepted the first part of the recommendations and not the second part.

The problem with pay commissions is two fold: firstly, they are not able to relate recommendations with the principles they enunciate. Secondly, governments usually tend to take economic decisions on political considerations.

## Sixth Pay Commission (2008)

The eagerly awaited Sixth Pay Commission on Monday 24 March 2008 recommended pay hikes in the range from 40 to 60 per cent for central government employees at various levels, with effect from January 2006, if all benefits are considered. It has also recommended liberal pension scheme.

The increase is in the range of 40 per cent at the junior most and the senior most levels, but only around 20 per cent in the middle to senior ranges, up to joint secretary. Unions are putting pressure on the Government to modify the recommendations to rectify what they see as a systematic attempt to increase disparities within the service.

Secretaries to the Government will now get a salary of Rs. 80,000 per month from the present Rs. 56,000. At the lowest level the new pay would be Rs. 6600 pm instead of Rs. 2550. However, at the level of joint secretary, the rise would be limited to about 20 per cent.

The exchequer will have to take a hit of Rs. 12,561 crore in 2008-09, if the Government decides to implement the report next fiscal. The additional outgo is lower than the Fifth Pay Commission's Rs. 21,000 crore.

Besides, the Government would have to pay Rs. 18060 crore as one time expenditure on paying arrears from 1 January, 2006. This is inclusive of the Rs. 5418 crore, which would have to be borne by the Indian Railways. However, the Government could segregate the arrears in two parts, in which case it would have to pay Rs. 9030 crore in each installment.

In 2008-09, the total outgo on account of pay and allowances for the Government with an employee strength of over 3 lakh, has been pegged at Rs. 51,782 crore exclusive of defence. The Government total employee strength is around 5.4 million including of defence and railways.

In a major recommendation aimed at removing stagnation, the Commission has introduced the concept of running pay bands for all posts in the government. The total number grades has been reduced from 35 to 20 which run across four pay bands.

Transport allowance which was at a maximum of Rs. 800 per month, has been increased four times to Rs. 3200. Moreover, reimbursement of education allowance has been increased from existing Rs. 50 to Rs. 100 per child per month subject to a maximum of two children. Hostel subsidy has also been hiked from Rs. 300 per month to Rs. 3000 per month. Seeking to bring cheer to the armed forces personnel, the Commission recommended that like their civilian counterparts, the soldiers and officers would get at least a 40 per cent hike in pay packets across the board.

It has also recommended an increase in the salary of chairpersons of regulators including SEBI, Trai and IRDA to up to Rs. 3 lakh per month and delink them from government salaries, a move to attract expertise from outside the government.

Scientists would also get a better deal as their salaries would be delinked from the government.

Women and disabled employees have been given a special treatment in the report through a recommendation for improved leave and working conditions. The commission has also recommended a way for awarding performers through a higher 3.5 per cent rate increment against the normal 2.5 per cent. There has been demand for the performance-related incentive scheme.

A liberal severance package has been put together for employees leaving service between 15 and 20 years of service. It has recommended an overall increase of 40 per cent increase in pensions and higher rates of pensions for retirees and family pensioners on attaining the age of 80, 85, 90, 95 and 100 years.

The pension suggests fixing pensions at 50 per cent of average annual emoluments or last pay drawn (whichever is more) while delinking it with the 35-year service qualifier. A higher rate of pension has been proposed on employee attaining 80, 85, 90, 95 and 100 years of age. Full Family Pension would be provided for 10 years in case the pensioner dies.

The Commission has recommended the continuation of a five-day week but said that the government offices should remain closed only on three national holidays. All gazetted holidays would be abolished and compensated by the increasing number of restricted holidays from 2 to 8 days.

In a significant gesture to the men in the bottle figure the Sixth Pay Commission elevated the 3 defence services chiefs to be the highest paid public service men drawing a salary of Rs. 90,000 per month, equal to the Cabinet Secretary. Though the Army, Navy and Air Force chiefs got a hefty hike of about of Rs. 60,000 per month in emoluments, they would continue to be at par with the Defence Secretary in protocol. So far the three chiefs had been drawing a fixed monthly pay packet of Rs. 30,000 per month.

Seeking to bring cheer to the armed forces personnel, who guard the country's frontiers from the snowy Himalayan heights, monsoon jungles to the Thar desert, the Commissions recommended that like their civilian counterparts, the soldiers and officers would get at least 40 per cent hike in pay packets across the board.

But for the armed forces facing acute shortage of officers and new alarming shortfalls in attracting talent to military schools, the Commission instituted a special military service pay up to the rank of brigadiers.

For all officers up to the brigadiers, the special pay would be Rs. 6000 and for personnel between officers' rank it would be Rs. 1000 per month.

Military nursing service officers would get Rs. 4200 per month. The Commission also elevated the rank of the Director General of armed forces medical services to the secretary, Government of India and would draw a fixed salary of Rs. 80,000 per month.

The Commission in a single stroke has doubled the special Siachen and high altitude allowance payable to soldiers serving in a freezing heights at the world's highest battlefield, Kargil and in the North East.

It has also doubled the flying allowance of fighter and transport pilots and submarine allowance for naval personnel serving in deep seas.

Reaction : "India Inc. has welcomed the Sixth Pay Commission report that suggested an average increase of 40 per cent in salaries of central government employees and said the move will not lead to a rise in inflation and revenue deficit of the Government."

The industry body, FICCI said the pay hike would not lead to inflationary conditions and revenue deficit buoyant revenue collections.

"The revenue collections and the overall economy are growing. If these trends are kept intact, then this additional expenditure should not be too much of a problem", FICCI Secretary General Amit Mitra said.

Echoing similar sentiments Assocham, said increase in salaries would not fuel inflation and increase revenue deficit as the country is witnessing increased direct and indirect tax collections as a result of higher tax compliance.

"The Government is going to witness substantial hike in its revenue collections, benefits of which ought to be given to its employees and there should be no grudge against such pay commissions recommendations", Assocham President Venugopal Dhoot said.

Assocham said the move would make the central government employees more accountable, productive and responsive as the exchequer would shed Rs. 12,561 crore in 2008-09 itself on account of higher package.

Also FICCI said the hike would reduce the problem of governance and attract talented personnel besides making the employees more responsible.

The Sixth Pay Commission headed by Justice B.N. Srikrishna submitted its report to Finance Minister P. Chidambaram recommending implementation of the revised pay from 11 January 2006, which would impose an arrear payout burden of Rs. 18,060 crore on the Government.

The reaction of the Leftist parties is very adverse. The recommendations of the commission have failed to cut ice with the Left and its trade unions even as the BJP adopted a wait and watch approach. Castigating the proposals, the Leftist said these will widen the disparities in pay scales, open doors for outsourcing and encourage 'favouritism'.

Describing the pay commission reports as a 'hoax' and discriminatory, Left trade unions said they would oppose it and compel the Government to negotiate with employees for real wage revision. The AITUC said that the commission's report was totally disappointing and a rude shock for central government employees.

Claiming that the Report was discriminatory they said, "As against the demand of Rs. 10,000 as the minimum wage computed on the basis of 15th Indian Labour Conference Norms, the Commission has recommended a paltry sum of Rs. 5,740 as the minimum wage. On the other hand, the maximum has been fixed as Rs. 90,000."

"The very fact that the amount of final implication is only Rs. 7500 crore proves that the benefit is nothing but hoax", M.K. Pande added.

Alleging that the panel's recommendation took away much more than what it gave, the Left said it will be not be acceptable to employees' organizations as the raise for the lower level workers was 'too small'.

"The revised salary of a cabinet secretary would be Rs. 90,000 a month while the minimum entry level monthly was proposed at Rs. 6600. This will increase the disparity in wages. At the lower level, employees are getting very insignificant benefits", said Gurudas Dasgupta. He also said the monetary benefit to employees was disproportionate.

The Confederation of Central Government Employees has conveyed its disappointment with the recommendations and threatened to launch a movement seeking benefits for workers at the lower levels.

The Left is also dissatisfied with the arrear payout burden of Rs. 18,000 crore on the development saying that considering this amount was Rs. 15,000 crore in the Fifth Pay Commission 12 years ago, it was insignificant. The soaring prices should have been kept in mind.

What has further upset the leftists is that the Pay Commission has recommended a ban of further recruitment of Group D employees. Apprehending that the jobs will not be outsourced, they said the move would be resisted by the trade unions.

The Commission has proposed to eventually scrap Group D services and start the government hierarchy from group C. It has suggested a retraining system for those in Grade D for taking them to their higher scale.

Rejecting the proposal for giving performance-related annual increment of 3.5 per cent to 20 per cent of the workforce, the Leftists are of the view that this would lead to favouritism. The annual increment is 2.5 per cent. Why are they suggesting that 20 per cent of employees be given 3.5 per cent. This would be unfair.

The Left and the trade unions are also opposed to a liberal severance package for Voluntary Retirement Scheme saying it would mean further reduction in manpower.

The proposals confirm that Central Government staff along with their counterparts in defence and paramilitary forces could get hikes up to 52 per cent in salaries an work done currently by babus can be outsourced to private firms. The Government should reduce the number of clerks, secretaries and peons and downsize itself.

While it may be that because their salaries are out of sync with the market, that there is a high propensity for corruption among the babus, hiking their salaries alone will not work. They should be made more accountable. The private sector is less corrupt because it has more accountability. The salary hike should be approved only after taking steps to improve organizational competence. If not, the pay hike will be another affliction on the economy which is already slowing down.

There is indeed a genuine case to increase salaries of government employees but this has to be linked to better performance and their playing genuinely productive roles.

Steps need to be taken so that the enormous funds spent on the government's wage bill are utilised efficiently. It is unfortunate that political parties in power use the Pay Commission as a tool to placate the massive vote bank among the babus. They dole out the pecuniary benefits alone without carrying out the administrative reforms suggested by successive Commissions for increasing efficiency. The pay hike will bring about massive strain on the exchequer.

With the implementation of the Fifth Pay Commission's recommendations, the Central Government wage bill shot up by nearly 99 per cent. The present recommendations, when implemented, are expected to cause an additional annual encumbrance of Rs. 20,000 Crore.

Higher salaries should, as a natural corollary, bring about more efficiency. The Government must learn from the private sector, which is far more efficient because its salaries, perks and promotions are linked to productivity. Market salaries will help to attract talent to the Government in competition with the private sector. The Government's aim must be to become a lean organization. A truly efficient bureaucracy will require less people. Many of the positions in our bureaucracy do not exist in advanced societies. A lot of work done by babus currently can be outsourced to private firms. The

Government should reduce the number of clerks, secretaries and peons and downsize itself.

### Spotlights of the Sixth Pay Commission Pay Overhaul

- Minimum entry level pay is Rs. 6650, Cabinet Secretary, Chiefs of Army, Navy and Air force to get fixed pay of Rs. 90,000.
- Number of grades reduced to 20 from 35. Each of four pay bands to have grade pay, minimum of Rs. 1800 per month, max of Rs. 13,000.
- Group D scrapped, employees to be retrained, assimilated into Group C.

*Annual Increment*
- 2.5 per cent for all employees.
- 3.5 per cent for 20 per cent performing.

### Group A officers

*Pension:*
- Pension to be paid at 50 per cent of average emoluments or last pay drawn, delinked from service length.
- Higher rates of pension at the age of 80, 85, 90 and 100.
- Full family pension for 10 years if employee dies within 10 years of retirement.

*Allowances:*
- Most allowances to be doubled.
- City compensatory allowances to be merged with transport allowance and increased four times.
- HRA raised for A, B1, B2 cities to 20 per cent; C and other cities to 10 per cent.
- Monthly education allowance to be Rs. 1000 per child, up from Rs. 50.

*Health:*
- New Medical scheme for employees and pensioners insurance scheme to meet pensions' OPD needs.

*Defence:*
- Defence forces at a par with civilians in pay and grades. Special military pay of Rs. 6600 up to the rank of brigadier.

*Regulators:*
- Salary of Chiefs of regulatory bodies, including SEBI, Trai and IRDA up to Rs. 3 lakh per month.

*Work Hours:*
- Five-day week to continue.
- Only 3 national holidays–26 January, 15 August and 2 October. No gazetted holidays; restricted holidays up to 8 from 2.
- Maternity leave of 180 days.

**Performance Sops:**
- Market-driven pay for young scientists and specialists.
- Contract for high skill posts.
- Performance-linked incentive plan to replace existing annual bonus honorarium overtime.

### 3. Collective Bargaining

Collective bargaining is a process whereby standards are created to govern labour relations including wages. ILO conventions No. 87 and 98 establish the right of workers to organise and bargain collectively. In India, union density is about 6 per cent of the labour force in the country. Of them nearly two-thirds are in governmental and quasi-governmental organizations including defence and are not covered by collective bargaining. The Trade Union Act does not provide for statutory recognition of collective bargaining and legislation puts a premium on adjudication rather than collective bargaining. Refusal to bargain collectively with recognised trade unions has made an 'unfair labour practice' under the Industrial Disputes Act and subject to punishment.

1. Sectoral Bargaining at National Level: Before the 1970's, wage boards appointed by the Government were given awards on wages and working conditions. Since early 1970s, sectoral bargaining is occurring at national level mainly in industries where the Government is a dominant player. These include banks and coal, steel and ports and docks. Fifty-eight private and public banks are members of the Indian Banks Associations. They negotiate long term settlements with the all-India federations of bank employees. Over 200 coal mines were nationalized in the 1970s. They are spread all over the country and are all owned by the government. There is one national agreement for the entire coal industry. In steel, there is a permanent bipartite committee for the integrated steel mills in the public and private sectors.

   Since 1969, the committee which is called the National Joint Consultative Committee for Steel Industry has signed six long-term settlements. The major parts in the country have formed the Indian Ports' Association. They hold negotiations with the industrial federations of major national trade union centres in the country. A peculiar feature of sectoral bargaining at the national level is the presence of a single employer and the involvement of concerned administrative ministry from the employers' side. In many sectors, 2 to 5 major national centres of trade unions, which have a major presence through respective industry federations of workers' organizations, negotiate. In banks, coal and ports and docks invariably all agreement were preceded by strikes or strike threats. Only in the steel industry this did not happen during the past 30 years. Even though industry wide bargaining is not extended to the oil sector, which was nationalized in the late 1970s, the Oil-Coordination Committees accomplished a great deal of standardization in pay and service conditions even if collective bargaining occurs at the plant level.

2. Industry-Cum-Region wide Agreements: These agreements are common in jute, cotton textiles, engineering and tea which are dominated by the private sector. But such agreements are not binding on enterprise management in the respective industries/regions unless they authorize the respective employer associations to bargain on their behalf.

3. Decentralized Firm/Plan Level Agreements: In the rest of private sector while employers generally press for decentralization at plant level, unions insist on bargaining at least at company level where the employees are formed into federations at company level. In 1998 there was a prolonged strike in Escorts, a private sector automobile and engineering conglomerate with over 14 factories on the issue of decentralized bargaining. It does not mean, however, that employers in multi-unit at sector enterprise do not bargain with trade union federations at company level. Brooke-Bond, till it was merged with Lipton and became a part of Hindustan Lever, in one of the recent mega mergers in the country provides such an example. Plant-level bargaining reduces the bargaining power of unions particularly during crisis. There is a general tendency on the part of unions and the Government to think of the public sector as a whole. Uniformity is sought at the Highest level and the concept of capacity to pay is altogether ignored in public sector wage negotiations. In the private sector the capacity to pay continues to be reckoned for the purpose of wage negotiations.

Till the 1970s the collective agreements were for a period of 2 to 3 years. During the 1970s and the 1980s, the durations of agreements increased to 3 to 4 years. During the 1970s, over four-fifths of the central public sector agreements were signed for a duration of five years each. The Government proposal to extend wage agreements for 10 years is meeting with stiff resistance from the unions. Collective agreements in most private sector organizations continue to be valid for period of 3 or in some rare cases, 4 years.

4. **Adjudication:** Pay Commission and Wage Boards submit the reports and the Government accepts the recommendations

with or without modifications. When collective bargaining and conciliation fail to resolve disputes between labour and management, the case may be decided through voluntary arbitration or compulsory adjudication. When wage disputes persist Government refers them for adjudication. Through the adjudicators, award is normally binding on labour and management, it is not uncommon for parties to move to courts over the award of the adjudicator. In such cases, the Supreme Court is the final arbiter. However, there have been instances where even the Supreme Court Verdicts had problems in implementations because of ground realities. In such instances, either labour or management makes amends and agrees with the latter for something less than what the Supreme Court mandated.

In most industrialised countries, it is realised that interest issue (wages, allowances etc.) can not be adjudicated but right issues (right to bargain, right to consultation, right to join union etc.) can be. In India, however, there is no such distinction and both issues are subject to bargaining and adjudication.

## Test Questions

1. Explain briefly the different wage fixing machineries in India.
2. The Second Plan considers the Wage Board an acceptable machinery for settling wage disputes. Discuss the rationale of setting up industrywise wage boards.
3. "The pay structure of the Central Government employees is based on the recommendations of the pay commission set up by the Central Government." Discuss the Statement.
4. Discuss briefly the recommendations of the Sixth Pay Commission (2008).
5. What do you mean by collective bargaining? Discuss the settlement of wage disputes by collective bargaining.
6. When Adjudication is resorted to for the settlement of industrial disputes? Explain it.

# 10

# Fringe Benefits Including British Model

The 1950s have been marked by a new concept in labour-management relations-that of fringe benefits. The term 'fringe benefits' refers to the extra benefits provided to employees in addition to the normal compensation paid in the form of salary. These benefits were called fringe benefits because they were insignificant components of compensation. The term 'fringe benefits' was first used in 1943, by a regional Chairman of the National War Labour Board in the USA. Since the end of the II World War the payment of fringe benefits has become a regular feature of the industrial wage system. Managements expect that the cost of fringe benefits will be offset by increased efficiency, reduced turnover and other tangible benefits to the company.

To get a true measure of labour costs, the economists must take fringe benefits costs into account, since international survey suggests that such cost can be a considerable proportion of total labour costs. In the wider sense, fringe benefits include all expenditure by the employer on labour other than basic wages and in the narrow sense it includes those benefits which the employee can convert into cash. As there is no generally accepted definition, it is better to describe fringe benefits by its characteristic rather than define it. Fringe benefits have the following characteristics: (i) they all cost the employer money; (ii) they all either add to the employee's pay or are of some service to him; (iii) they are available to all or most of the employees; (iv) their cost rises or falls as the size of the workforce changes; (v) they may be statutory or voluntary-PF is a statutory benefit whereas transport is a voluntary benefit.

Fringe benefits in the guise of supplementary labour costs are an addition to wage costs which an employer incurs in providing labour. In general, fringe benefits which are very broadly 'welfare', represent an investment in labour resources.

Using the term 'fringe benefits' to describe payments other than wages to employees or for their services is becoming more and more misleading and may soon be anachronistic. This follows from the fact that the cost of these benefits has become so substantial that they have ceased to constitute a 'fringe' and have become, instead, an important segment of the compensation of employees.

### Objectives of Fringe Benefits.

The objectives of fringe benefits are as follows:

(i) To motive employees by satisfying their unsatisfied needs.

(ii) To improve sound industrial relations.

(iii) To promote employee welfare.

(iv) To provide security to the employees against social risks like old age and disablement benefits.

(v) To provide safety to the employees against accidents.

(vi) To provide a sense of belonging among the employees and to retain them. Hence fringe benefits are called 'golden handcuffs'.

### Evolution of Fringe Benefits:

It would be a misconception to think fringe benefits as entirely a 20th century development. Various items of non-wage remuneration were introduced before the Industrial Revolution. When firm workers had something like an employee status, the contract of employment was a long-term one including many matters which would now be thought of as fringe benefits. Fringe benefits were certainly available to industrial employees in the 19th century but they were of rather a different type and were provided for a different purpose.

Thus fringe benefits are not new but have changed in character over the last 50 years. They have become especially important in the post-war period because of the development of our attitudes towards social security.

During the 20th century two significant trends have emerged which have had some effect on the development of fringe benefits. First, the increase in the number of salaried workers resulting from the growth and professionalism of management and second white-collar occupations and from the increasing complexity of production technique. It is a fact that salaried workers have always been given somewhat better treatment in the matter of additional benefits from work and the greater the number of salaried workers the more important fringe benefits will be. Secondly, collective bargaining has had some influence on the growth of fringe benefits. But at the same time it should be remembered that collective bargaining has not generally been the medium through which fringe benefits have been introduced. Pension schemes, sickness benefits, company subsidized facilities, even in some cases longer holidays, have until the very recent past been introduced unilaterally by the employer. Trade unions' reactions ranged from mild interest or indifference to hostility if there was a suggestion that the employer was attempting to wean allegiance from the union to the firm.

Fringe benefits are now attracting much attention simply because of some recent events and their developments have led to the realisation that in terms of cost to the employer and advantages for employees, these benefits could be important.

The following two arguments are generally used as economic justification for fringe benefit expenditure. First, fringe benefits help to attract better employees to the firm, so increasing productivity by changing the structure of the labour force and secondly, the quality of existing labour force and its efficiency are improved if certain fringe benefits are offered without the firm attracting any additional employees.

*Fringe Benefits in Different Countries*

In the UK the payment of fringe benefits started in the early years of the Industrial Revolution. Some social-minded employers then sought to ameliorate the conditions of their employees by providing certain amenities and facilities. Initially, the benefits provided by employers consisted of gratuitous payments made to employees to enable the latter to meet such contingencies as sickness, physical disability or insecurity on retirement. However, with the high profits made by employers under technological advances and the pressure exerted by trade unions, the practice of providing voluntary benefits made further progress. The exposition of social ideas by such thinkers as Robert Owen in the UK and Leclaire in France, also had its impact. Owen advocated such benefits as shorter hours, minimum wages, medical and sickness benefits, good housing while Leclaire advocated profit sharing. In most European countries, these ideas extensively influenced the course of social welfare legislation till the end of the 19th century.

By the first decade of the present century, the system of fringe benefits gained currency in almost all countries of the west. Medical benefits, workman's compensation, maternity benefits, and compulsory social insurance were introduced in most of the countries of Europe, Australia and New Zealand.

After the World War I, the system of fringe benefits expanded rapidly due to many influences. First, the end of the War witnessed the emergence of the ILO, which through numerous conventions and the recommendations, promoted joint international action to secure the enforcement of several benefits-such as, the provision of holidays, sickness insurance, compensation for accidents and occupational diseases, old age and invalidity, paid holidays etc. Secondly, modern researches into scientific management and industrial psychology also establish positive correlation between fringe benefits and higher productivity. Thirdly, the emergence of a new, enlightened managerial class contributed much to the extension of the system of fringe benefits. Lastly, tax consideration was another important factor accounted for the rapid growth of fringe benefits in the USA. The federal war-time tax structure was designed to confiscate excessive profits; yet it did recognise contributions to health and welfare and pension plans as legitimate business expenses and therefore non-taxable.

In India, fringe benefits paid in the early phases of industrial development consisted mainly of gratuitous payments made by employers to deserving employees. With the Factories Act of 1881, a new chapter began in labour welfare. This Act as amended in 1891, provided for the first time the benefit of paid-weekly holidays. No statutory addition to fringe benefits took place until after the World War I, although voluntary benefits continued to increase. In 1923, the Workmen's Compensation Act was passed, which provided for compensation in case of accidents resulting in death or disablement or occupational disease of an employee. The Factories Act of 1934 made an attempt to increase the material welfare of industrial workers. Fringe benefits increased considerably during the II World War. In addition to voluntary benefits provided by employers such as, housing, medical care and retirement benefits, the Government also enforced welfare measures by promulgating ordinance. Despite these efforts, the development of benefits remained rather uneven and varied from factory to factory. The Labour Investigation Committee of 1946, underlined the need to extend these activities so as to cover mines, plantations, communications as well as factory industries. In 1948, a new Factories Act was passed, incorporating a separate chapter on welfare. A number of social welfare legislations were passed to provide amenities to workers. Apart from State action, the awards given by Industrial Tribunals and in many cases, the collective agreements concluded between employers and workers also, contributed much to expand the scope and coverage of fringe benefits.

Although fringe benefits have become a regular feature of industrial wages system in the modern times, the proportion of fringe benefits in the total wages of employees has varied widely from country to country. In some countries, fringe benefits constitute only negligible amounts while in other countries they constitute significant proportions namely 14 per cent in the UK; 25 per cent in India and 22.8 per cent in the USA to as high as 52 per cent in Italy.

The main objectives with which fringe benefits are offered with a view to (i) induce happier employer-employee relations; (ii) generate good morale in the employees; (iii) provide a psychologically satisfactory work environment; (iv) cater to the health and safety of the employees; (v) promote employee welfare; (vi) induce loyalty to the company and (vii) meet the legal requirements.

*Objectives and Types of Fringe Benefits*

These employee fringe benefits may be a result of the management's policy decisions made voluntarily or may be those forced upon it by government legislation or as a result of bargaining with trade unions. Benefits such as PF, gratuity, maternity benefits and workmen's compensation are those made compulsory by government legislation. Facilities regarding health, recreation etc. are often introduced voluntarily by management. Benefits such as overtime, paid holidays and housing are often a result of trade union pressures.

Richard Cockman has made a two-fold classification of fringe benefits: (1) Those which are offered on the basis of status – car, entertainment facilities, holiday, foreign travel, telephone; Security-insurance and medical benefits, children's educational facilities and work benefits-office accommodation, secretarial services, management training, company scholarships and (2) Those which are key benefits that is, share schemes, profit-sharing, retirement benefits, counselling services and house purchase facilities.

(1) **Employee Security.** Job security to the employee should be provided to ensure security to the employee. When the employee's services is confirmed, his job becomes secure. The Payment of Wages Act, 1936, The Minimum Wages Act 1948, the Payment of Bonus Act 1965 and the Gratuity Act, 1972, provide income security to the employees.

*Fringe Benefits offered in India can be classified into the following four categories:*

The Industrial Disputes Act 1947, provides for the payment of compensation in case of lay off and retrenchment. Lay off compensation is paid up to 45 days in a year at the rate of 50 per cent of the total basic wage and dearness allowances.

(2) **Payment for time not worked.** These benefits include hours of work, Factories Act specifies that no adult worker shall be required to work in a factory for more than 48 hours in a week. As per Factories Act, an adult worker shall have at least one weekly paid holiday. When a worker is deprived of weekly holiday, he is eligible for compensatory holiday.

Companies pay a premium to the workers who work in the night shift. Usually, companies offer double the normal rate of salary to those workers who work during the holidays.

(3) **Workmen's Compensation.** The Workmen's compensation Act 1923, provides for the contingency of invalidity and death of a worker due to an employment injury or an occupational disease specified under the Act as the sole responsibility of the employer. Amount of compensation varies depending upon the nature of injury.

(4) **Health Benefits.** In a welfare state various medical benefits are provided not only to employees but also to their family members.

Employees' State Insurance Act 1948 provides following medical benefits to the employees whose wages do not exceed Rs. 10,000/- p.m.

(i) **Sickness Benefit.** Insured employees are entitled to get cash benefits for a maximum of 56 days in a year.

(ii) **Maternity Benefit.** Insured women employees are entitled to maternity leave for 12 weeks (six weeks before the delivery and 6 weeks after the delivery) in addition to cash benefit of 75 paise per day or twice of sickness benefit, whichever is higher.

(iii) **Medical Benefit.** This benefit is provided to the insured employee in the following forms: (a) outpatient treatment or attendance to a hospital treatment as an in-patient in the hospital or (c) visit of doctors to the home of the patient.

(iv) **Disablement Benefit.** Insured employees who are disabled temporarily or permanently or suffering from occupational disease are entitled to cash benefit under this head.

(v) **Dependents Benefits.** If an insured person dies as a result of an employment injury, his dependents are entitled to compensation.

## Welfare and Recreational Facilities

Welfare and recreational benefits include (i) canteen, (ii) credit societies; (iii) housing; (iv) legal aid; (v) employee counselling; (vi) transportation; (vii) holiday homes and (viii) educational facilities for employee's children.

Canteens are statutory obligation for factories with employees' of 250 or more and foods are supplied at subsidized prices in these canteens. The objective of setting up credit societies is to provide loan facilities at reasonable terms and conditions. The problem of housing is a serious one and most of the large organizations provide housing accommodation to its employees. It is a statutory obligation to provide housing to the employees in plantation industry. Railways provide housing to all its employees. As a result of staff welfare, many large organizations have set up holiday homes in hill stations and seasides at nominal charges. Good organizations run schools for the children of the employees. Many companies also provide libraries and reading rooms for the benefit of the employees. Many organizations provide transport facilities to the employees from their residence to the place of work. Many big organizations have their own sporting clubs and encourage sports and games among the employees.

## Old Age and Retirement Benefits

After retiring, people have three main sources of income: Social security, personal savings and retirement benefits. Because social security provides only about a small amount of pre-retirement earnings, retirees must rely on retirement benefits and personal saving to maintain their standard of living. Retirement benefits support an employee's long-term financial goal of achieving a planned level of retirement income.

An important service that the HR Department can provide to the employees nearing retirement is the pre-retirement counselling. Such sessions give employees information about their retirement benefit so that they can plan their retirement years accordingly.

## Dearness Allowance or Cost of Living Allowance:

It is an accepted principle of wage-fixation that the erosion of the purchasing power of employees (i.e., real wages) should be prevented, to the fullest extent possible, at least that of those of the lower income groups.

The term 'Dearness Allowance' does not belong to the corpus of economic terminology. Its use is peculiar to India, Pakistan and Sri Lanka. At some centres in India at one time, the term used was to mean 'dear food allowance'. As a separate component of the wage and salary it is almost unknown elsewhere–the exceptions being India, Pakistan, Sri Lanka and Japan. Such compensation may also include house rent allowance, city allowance etc. However, here we are concerned with what is specifically termed as Dearness Allowance.

DA has been defined by National Labour Commission thus: The words Dearness Allowance primarily suggest and refer to an allowance paid to employees in order to enable them to face the increasing dearness of essential commodities.

Historically, the payment by the employer of such compensation to the workmen for rise in the cost of living may be traced back to the conditions prevailing during and after the World War I.

## Methods of Computing DA:

Different methods are adopted by industrial undertakings for computing and paying DA. The methods generally followed are:

(i) Computation of DA on the basis of changes in the Consumer Price Index.

(ii) Computation of DA linked to pay slabs and to Consumer Price Index.

(iii) Payment of DA at a flat rate without linking it to the Consumer Price Index and

(iv) Fixing of DA in relation to graduated pay scales.

## Statutory Provisions:

In India, compensation only to the workers governed by the Minimum Wages Act for rise in the cost of living is statutory requirement, to be paid either in cash, as an allowance or in kind, as supplies of essential commodities at concessional rates or in both.

Section 4 of the Act provides: (i) Any minimum rate of wages fixed or revised by the appropriate Government in respect of scheduled employments under section 3 may consist of (a) a basic rate of wages and a special allowance at a rate to be adjusted, at such intervals and in such manners as the appropriate Government may direct to accord as nearly as practicable with the variation in the cost of living index number applicable to such workers; or (b) A basic rate of wages with or without the cost of living allowance and the cash value of the concessions in respect of supplies of essential commodities at concession rates where so authorized or (c) An all inclusive rate of allowing for the basic rate the cost of living allowance and the cash value of the concessions; if any. The cost of living allowance and the cash value of the concessions, in respect of supplies of essential commodities at concessional rates, shall be computed by the competent authority at intervals and in accordance with such directions as may be specified or given by the appropriate Government.

**Neutralization of Cost of Living Index:** The linking of DA to the consumer price index or the cost of living is in conformity with the principle enunciated by the Supreme Court that neutralization should be provided on the basis of changes in the consumer price index. Even where the dearness allowance is linked to the consumer price index, there is a difference of opinion as to which price index should be taken; for example, a study of index numbers chosen by the Central Wage Board indicates that 17 out of 20 Boards favoured the All India Consumer Price Index, while 3 Boards recommended the use of Local Consumer Price Index numbers.

As against this the collective agreements were more in favour of the Local Consumer Price Index Numbers. In addition, there is a divergence in the adoption of index numbers with the old base year and new base year. Besides, there is a variation in the rates prescribed for payment of dearness allowance being 50 paisa per point, 75 paisa per point, 78 paisa per point etc. Whatever the rates fixed, the objective was to neutralize to some extent the increase in the cost of living. For example; in the case of 7 Central Wage Boards, neutralization was granted in respect of the lowest paid employees to the extent of between 90 to 100 per cent. In most organized industries, collective agreement have provided for full or near full neutralization to the lowest paid employees. Different committees have often recommended that, for obvious economic reasons, neutralization should be less than one hundred percent.

DA as a separate component, may at times be several times the basic wage, a rather undesirable practice. On the average, 30 per cent of the wages have been in the form of DA. There are great disparities in the extent of neutralisation of the rise in the cost of living–the range being from 60 per cent to 100 per cent. In some industries even the highest paid officers draw a DA of several hundred rupees although generally the higher income groups draw DA at a tapering rate and at a certain level, particularly in the government employment till recently, no DA at all. There has, however, been some policy changes of late in this regard. An Ad hoc payment is now made to the excluded categories of Central government employees.

*Advantages and Disadvantages of having DA as a separate component of Wages:*

*Advantages:*
(i) Flexibility: This element can fluctuate with the trends of rising and falling prices; (ii) Provides expeditious relief: Wage revision is slow but this method reduces the time-lag between price increase and wage increase.

*Disadvantages:*
(i) Causes distortion in wage structure as it may become larger than the basic wage causing difficulties. The employees may be deprived of certain benefits because of their linkage with low basic wage there have been adverse repercussions on incentives and productivity as DA is paid irrespective of productivity. Again, it may reduce the skill differentials – a kind of wage freezes for skilled categories takes place, while for the unskilled and semiskilled categories, it very amount to a kind of wage-revision through the backdoor, so to say. (ii) May add to the inflationary tendencies. Even the announcement of the sanction of additional DA causes price-rise of certain essential

commodities in the Delhi area. Thus, some sort of a vicious circle is introduced whereby money costs go up, prices are increased and the latter in turn leads to wage increase.

**Abolition of DA:**

As a result of the anomalies produced by different DA schemes some have even advocated complete abolition of the system. The reasons are as follows:

1. An automatic increase in DA (being linked with the price index) can result in an automatic increase in wages paid to the workers without a corresponding increase in productivity. In the ultimate analysis, this would harm the working of the unit and the industry concerned.
2. Linking DA with the consumer price index is linking it with an extraneous factor, instead of with the profitability of an industrial unit.
3. The system results in inflation of wage costs and therefore has to be matched with corresponding rise in the selling price, which may not be possible in a highly competitive situation.
4. Payment of DA can lead to inflation and instead of neutralizing the price rise, it can result in a further price rise.
5. DA payment increases the disparity in earnings and can result in further labour unrest.

However, there are equally strong arguments in favour of the DA system, which include the following:

(i) The living standards of workers in real terms are protected by the DA scheme.
(ii) Substituting DA with a revision in the wages would result in inflexibility in the wage system as if there is a fall in price or cost of living, it will be difficult to reduce the wages.
(iii) Linking DA with the consumer price index provides for an automatic change in the compensation payable which would otherwise have to be substituted by early wage revisions.

Obviously there is merit in the arguments on both sides. Perhaps the time has now come when an appropriate part of the DA should be merged in the basic wage. The position of supervisors and managers should also be considered and not ignored merely because they are not viewed as workers. After all, supervisors, managers and workers are still employees of the same unit. However, it does not seem possible at this stage to remove the linking of DA with the consumer price index.

## Benefits: British Model

Benefit is a generic word used to describe the components of a substantial element of the total remuneration provided by the employing organizations to their workers. This element is a unique part of the payroll in that, it is normally provided in non-cash form, although there are exceptions to this. Benefits include a wide variety of provisions variously termed 'fringe benefits', 'perquisites, 'assistance or simply 'something extra'. These terms cover an extensive range of benefit categories which can be regarded as extras to wage and salary.

Perquisite refers to something of value which is in addition to payment for work, for example the company car. In recent years 'benefit' has superseded 'fringe benefit' (i.e., elements of remuneration on the fringe of pay) and is used as the word to encompass the wide range of benefits in kind, in addition to cash payments which companies provide for their employees. These may include items such as pensions, cars, training and education, accommodation, loans, child care assistance, sick pay and maternity leave with pay.

Benefits represent a substantial cost for employers and can account for up to 50 per cent of basic salary. They therefore have value to the employee. It can affect recruitment, retention and motivation and can impact on individual performance or contribution to the organization.

At the end of the 19th century, pensions were provided to army and navy officers from an early date and civil servants were included in the 19th century. It was the enlightened business owners who were the first to develop welfare facilities and benefits for employees. Innovations included sick-pay, subsidies for meals, and housing for all workforces. Despite these early visionary initiatives, the development of benefits provision in the UK has been a slow affair. Until recently, employers have taken the view that the provision of basic social welfare benefits for the majority of the workforce was the Government's responsibilities. In some cases, the Government has provided a legal obligation on employers to provide minimum levels of benefits to workers (e.g., sick pay, maternity pay etc.)

*Pension:*

Pensions have their roots in local community provision in the form of relief funds for the elderly, sick and destitute during the reign of Richard II. In the 19th century, friendly societies and some trade unions provided a form of insurance against need and set a framework for fund management. Yet the majority of working class people often only had recourse to the workhouse and the Poor Law when incapacity forced them to retire. The company pension emerged in the second half of the 19th century and provision by the beginning of the century, was greatest in civil service, banking and among railway managers, clerks. The emphasis upon pension provision for white collar employees has continued since that time.

State encouragement for individual pensions was extended during the 20th century. Liberal Governments introduced the first state pension scheme in 1908, which was made more generous and realistic by Winston Churchill in 1925.

Employers responded to these initiatives from the 1920s with many larger companies adopting the elements. Trust Law was a means to introduce and administer occupational funds. The growth of occupational pensions was to some extent, a reaction to external pressures, particularly working class militancy during and after the World War I, the presence of a Labour Party and the experience of the 1926 General Strike which prompted large employers to move away from the hire and fire practices of the 19th century and seek to create a long-run identity of common interest with their employees. Company pensions were intended to encourage employee retention and foster long service.

It was in 1945, with the arrival of the Labour Government there was further development, in the form of 1946 National Insurance Act which introduced the contributory state pension for all.

State pensions have proved to be very expensive and by 1986, Margaret Thatcher's Government drastically reduced State Earnings Related Pension Scheme.

Pensions represent a deferred income for employees and company pensions are usually the most costly supplement to the payroll. Membership of such scheme is estimated to include more than 10 million employees in the UK. Schemes are normally financed by employer and employee contribution to a fund.

*Company Car and Fuel Benefit:* The second most expensive outlay after pensions, namely company cars remains a very popular benefit despite increase in taxation over two decades.

*Sick Pay:* State Sickness Benefit has been provided since the National Insurance Act of 1911. Additional sick pay provided by the company is more likely to ensure security than performance and might be regarded as a 'hygiene' factor, with company provision traditionally underpinned by significant government provision. Over the last decade government policy pushed the financial burden for sick pay increasingly towards the employer with the introduction of Statutory Sick Pay in 1983.

*Family-friendly Benefits:* Maternity and paternity leave, compassionate leave, holidays and childcare provisions are sometimes termed as family-friendly benefits. Currently employers are liable to pay Statutory Maternity Pay to qualifying employees and to allow maternity absence for a period of 18 weeks.

*Childcare Provision:* A key element of the government policy is a National Childcare Strategy which aims to encourage businesses to provide access to good quality childcare for their employees. Childcare is a very recent feature of the benefits scene in the UK as the growth in female employment during the past 20 years begins to impact on human resource management policies. The limited growth of childcare provision has been concentrated on the parents of the "under fives".

*Benefits and Taxation:* As benefits have grown, the Government has come to see them as a useful source of tax revenue. These are two categories under the heading of taxation: tax free and taxable benefits. Taxation on benefits has increased markedly since the late 1970s.

*Paid Holidays:* Holidays with pay were an exception until 1938, when the Holidays with Pay Act was passed. This empowered statutory wage-fixing bodies to establish them and from this point, paid holidays also featured in collective agreements.

*Growth of Benefits:* Growth in benefits provision has been noticeable since the beginning of the 1960s. Between 1964 and 1981, benefits increased from 11 per cent of average pre-tax remuneration to 19 per cent in UK manufacturing.

*New Pay:* The New Pay paradigm surfaced in the USA during the 1990s and has been presented as something radically different to traditional methods. The features of New Pay embrace the strategic performance issues and the placement of benefits with a reward model aimed at the achievement of corporate success. The main elements of the New Pay are as follows:

1. Remuneration practices, including benefits, are to support the business strategy.
2. Remuneration is for the pension, not the job.
3. Remuneration practices are to be appropriate to the organization's requirements.
4. Remuneration should support them based and flexible organizations.

5. Reward should be given for skills acquisition and performance.
6. Rewards help shift the employee's focus to key business objective including quality and customer care.

Variable pay is an important element of the New Pay and it is intended that performance will be driven by performance-related or merit business which be re-earned every year. Variable Pay is designed to provide attractive rewards to staff when company performance is good, but offers less attractive rewards in years when performance fall. Reducing the cost of benefits is a key component within the New Pay. The availability of benefits becomes dependent on the ability to pay.

## Test Questions

1. What do you mean by fringe benefits? What are its objectives?
2. What are the objectives and types of Fringe benefits? Do you think that fringe benefits are not entirely a 20th century development?
3. Give a list of fringe benefits offered to industrial employees in India.
4. What is D A? What are its objectives?
5. What do you mean by DA? Discuss the advantages and disadvantages of having DA as a separate component of wages.

# 11

# Retirement Benefits including VRS

The most important retirement benefits of an employee are discussed below under three heads: Pension, Provident Fund and Gratuity.

Pensions provide an income to employees when they retire and to their surviving dependents, on the death of the employee and deferred benefits to employees who leave schemes offered by organizations (occupational pensions) as distinct from State pensions, are funded by contributions from the organizations and usually the employee. Pensions are the most significant benefit and are a valuable part of the total reward package.

Pensions are provided because they demonstrate that the organization is a good employer concerned about the long-term interests of its employees who want the security provided to be a reasonable pension when they retire. Good pension schemes help to attract and retain high-quality people by maintaining competitive levels of total remuneration.

The range and level of benefits from pension schemes depend on the type of scheme and the level of contributions. In general, schemes provided.

i. **Benefits on retirement** - these are related to the final salary of individuals when they retire or the amount that has been paid into a defined contribution scheme while the individuals were members.

ii. **Benefits on Death** - the pensions of widows or widowers and children are normally related to the member's anticipated pension; the most common fraction is half.

iii. **Benefits on leaving an employer** - individuals leaving an employer can elect to take one of the following options - a deferred pension from the occupational scheme they are leaving, the transfer of the pension entitlement from the present employer to the new employer or refund of their

## 1. Pension

contributions, but only if they have completed less than two years' membership of the pension scheme.

The two main types of pensions schemes are as follows:

1. Deferred Benefit or Final Salary Scheme. The main features of final salary schemes are as follows:
    (i) On retiring, the employee is entitled to a pension which is calculated as a fraction of their final salary multiplied by the length of pensionable service.
    (ii) The maximum proportion of salary allowed is two-thirds of final salary after 40 years' service.
    (iii) The amount of the pension depends on the final salary, the value of the annuity that provides the pension and the accrual rate. The accrual rate refers to the fraction of final salary that can be earned per year of service.

**Employer and Employee Contributions**

Employer contributions can be a fixed percentage of salary. Alternatively, the percentage increases with service or is a multiple of the employee's contribution.

Employee contribution rates vary considerably.

*Pension Fund*

Employee and employer contributions are paid into a combined fund and there is no direct link between fund size and the pensions paid.

The money remaining in the fund after any lump sums have been taken out is invested in an annuity to provide a regular income, the amount of which, may be revised upwards periodically to compensate for inflation.

*Dependants*

Dependants are entitled to a percentage of the employee's pension entitlement if he dies during retirement or in service with the company.

*Lump sum*

Part of the pension may be exchanged for a tax-free lump sum up to a maximum of 1/80th year for up to 40 years' service.

## Defined Contribution (Money Purchase) Schemes

2. The main features of Defined Contribution Schemes are as follows:

*Pension Entitlement*

The employee receives a pension on retirement which is related to the size of the fund accumulated by the combined contributions of the employee and employer. The amount of pension depends on the size of contributions, the rate of return on the investment of the accumulated fund and the rate of return on an annuity purchased by the employer. It is not related to the employee's final salary.

## Contributions

The employer contributes a defined percentage of earnings which may be fixed, age-related or linked to what the employee pays. One survey shows that the level of employer contribution averages 6 per cent. The employee also contributes a fixed percentage of the salary.

## Pension Fund

The contributions are invested and the money used at retirement to purchase a regular income, usually via an annuity contract from an insurance company. The retirement pension is therefore whatever annual payment can be purchased with the money accumulated in the fund for a member. Members have individual shares of the fund, which represent their personal entitlements and which will directly determine the pensions they receive.

One quarter of the pension can be taken as a tax-free lump sum on retirement.

## Employee's Pension Scheme, 1995

Employee's Pension Scheme 1995, was implemented in India for the industrial workers with effect from 16 November, 1995. Under the scheme, pension at the rate of 50 per cent of pay is payable to the employees on retirement/superannuating on completion of 33 years of qualifying service. A minimum 10 years/service is required for entitlement to pension. Depending upon the salary and service of the employees at the time of death, the scheme also provides for grant of family pensions ranging from Rs. 460 per month to Rs. 2,500 per month. In addition, children pension at the rate of 25 per cent of widow pension subject to a minimum of Rs. 150 per child is also payable up to two children. The scheme is financed by diverting the employer's share of provident fund representing 8.33 per cent of the monthly wage to the pension fund. In addition, the Central Government also contributes to the scheme at the rate of 1.16 per cent of the wage. The upper limit has been raised from Rs. 5,000 to Rs. 6,500 with effect from 1 June 2001. The government contribution to the Pension Scheme increased from Rs. 600 crore compared to Rs. 450 crore during the previous years.

## 2. Employees' Provident Funds and Miscellaneous Provisions Act, 1952

Provident Funds and Pension are the retrial benefits but unlike pension where all the financial burden falls on the employer, provident funds are contributory in the sense that, besides putting in service, a worker has also to contribute a part of his wages.

The Employees' Provident Funds and Miscellaneous Provision Act, 1952 is one of the important social security measures to workers on his retirement and for the benefit of dependents in case of his/her death.

The Act seeks to provide for institution of (i) provident funds; (ii) pension fund and (iii) deposit linked insurance funds for employees in factories and other establishments.

The objective of the Act is to provide for social security to the industrial worker on his retirement and for the benefits of the dependent in case of his death. The Act extends to the whole of India except the State of Jammu and Kashmir.

Three conditions must be satisfied before the Act may apply to any establishment.

(i) The establishment must be engaged in any industry specified in Schedule I.

(ii) At least 20 persons must be employed in it.

(iii) In case of an establishment employing 50 or more persons 3 years and in case of an establishment employing 20 or more but less than 50 persons, 5 years must have elapsed from the date of its establishment.

**Effect on number of employees falling below 20**

Once the aforesaid conditions are fulfilled, it applies and continues to be applicable even if the Act ceases to apply to the establishment. The ceasing of the applicability of the Act to the establishment will not automatically bring about the ceasing the applicability of the scheme because the applicability of the scheme depends upon its own contents and not upon the provisions of the Act.

**Non-applicability of the Act to certain establishments**

Section 16 (1) provides that the Act shall not apply to certain establishments mentioned therein. Such establishments include:

(i) establishments registered under the Co-operative Societies Act 1912 or under any other law for the time being in force in any State relating to co-operative societies employing less than 50 persons and working without the aid of power or

(ii) to any other establishment belonging to, or under control of the Central Government or a State Government and whose employees are entitled to the benefit of contributory provident fund or old age pension, in accordance with any scheme or rule framed by the Central Government or the State Government governing such benefits or

(iii) to any other establishment set up under any Central, Provincial or State Act and whose employees are entitled to the benefits or contributory provident fund or old age pension in accordance with any scheme or rule framed under that Act governing such benefits or

(iv) to any establishments newly set up, until the expiry of period of three years from the date on such establishments has been set up.

However, mere change of location does not make the establishments a newly set up one.

Under Section 16 (2) if the Central Government may, having regard to the financial position of any class of establishments or other circumstances of the case, it is necessary to be expedient to do so, it may exempt that class of establishments from the operation of this Act for such period as may be specified in the notification.

*Power to apply the Act of Establishment having common Provident Fund*

The Act empowers the Central Government to extend the provision of the Act to any such other establishment, whose employees have a provident fund common with the employees of any other establishment, to which this Act applies by a Gazetted notification, provided the provident fund is in existence in the establishment immediately before this Act applies to such establishment.

Under Section 4, the Central Government may by a Gazetted notification add any other industry in Schedule. After such addition, the provision of the Act shall apply to any establishment engaged in the industry so added by the Central Government.

*Employees' Provident Fund Scheme*

Section 5 empowers the Central Government to frame Employees' Provident Fund Scheme for the establishment of Provident Fund under this Act. The scheme shall apply to employees or any class of employees of an establishment or class of establishments as specified in it.

*Contribution.*

Under Section 6, the contribution paid to the Fund by employer shall be 10 per cent of the basic wages and dearness allowance and retaining allowance and the contribution payable by the employees shall be equal to the employer's contribution. If an employee so desires he may contribute an amount exceeding 10 per cent of his basic wages, dearness allowance and retaining allowance if any, subject to the condition that the employer shall not be under an obligation to pay any contribution over and above his contribution payable under this section.

Employees' Pension Scheme (Sec. 6-A). The Central Government may frame a scheme to be called the Employee's Pension Scheme for the purpose of providing for:

(i) superannuation pension, retiring pension or permanent total disablement pension to the employees of any establishment or class of establishments to which this Act applies; and

(ii) widow or widower's pension, children pension or orphan pension payable to the beneficiaries of such employees.

2. There shall be established a Pension Fund into which these shall be paid from time of time in respect of every employee who is a member of the Pension Scheme.
   (a) such sums from the employer's contribution not exceeding 8.13 per cent of basic wages, dearness allowance and retaining allowance, if any, of the concerned employees, as may be specified in the Pension Scheme.
   (b) such sums, as are payable by the employer of excepted establishments under subsection (6) of Section 17;
   (c) the net assets of the Employees' Family Pension Fund as on the date of the establishments of the Pension Fund.
   (d) such sums as the Central Government may specify.
3. On the establishment of the Pension Fund, the Family Pension Scheme shall cease to operate and all assets of the ceased scheme shall vest in and shall be transferred to and all liabilities under the ceased scheme shall be enforceable against the Pension Fund and the beneficiaries under the ceased scheme shall be entitled to draw the benefits, not less than the benefits they were entitled to under the ceased scheme from the pension fund.

**Employees' Deposit-linked Insurance Scheme**

The Central Government may frame a scheme to be called the Employees Deposit-linked Insurance Scheme for the purpose of providing Life Insurance benefits to the employees of any establishment or class of establishments to which this Act applies.

2. There shall be established after the framing of the Insurance Scheme, a Deposit-linked Insurance Fund into which shall be paid by the employer from time to time in respect of every such employee in relation to whom he is the employer, such amount, not being more than 1 per cent of the aggregate of the basic wages, DA and retaining allowance, if any, for the time being payable in relation to such employee as the Central Government may specify.
3. The employer shall pay into the Insurance Fund such further sums of money, not exceeding one-fourth of the contribution which he is required to make under subsection (2), as the Central Government may determine to meet all the expenses in connection with administration of the Insurance Scheme other than expenses towards the cost of any benefits provided under the scheme.
4. **Modification of the Scheme.** The Central Government may add to, amend or vary either prospectively or retrospectively, the Pension Scheme or the Insurance Scheme, as the case may be.

## 3. Gratuity

### Introduction

In its earlier concept, gratuity was viewed as a gift made by the employer at his discretion gratuitously to the employee. Thereafter, gratuity began to be looked upon as a legitimate claim of the workman. Whilst the provident fund is aimed at inculcating thrift in the employee with a view to provide for his old age, gratuity is a retiral benefit earned by the employee for rendering service.

Gratuity is a retiral benefit of employees for their long and continuous service. "It is a lump sum payment made to a worker or to his heirs by the employer on termination of his service due to retirement, retrenchment, invalidity or death."

### Scope and Coverage

The Payment of Gratuity Act, 1972 was passed as Act No. 30 of 1972 and received the assent of the President of India on 21 August, 1972. It was enforced with effect from 16 September, 1972.

This Act extends to the whole of India. However, in so far as it relates to plantation or ports, it shall not extend to the State of Jammu and Kashmir.

According to Sub-section (3) of Section 1, this Act shall apply to:

(a) Every factory, mine, oil-field, plantation, port and railway company.

(b) Every shop or establishment within the meaning of any law for the time being in force in relation to shops and establishments in a State in which 10 or more persons are employed or where employed, or any day of preceding 12 months.

(c) Such other establishments or class of establishments, in which 10 or more employees are employed or were employed, of any day of the preceding twelve months, as the Central Government may, by notification specify in this behalf.

(3A) A shop or establishment to which Act has been applicable shall continue to be governed by this Act, notwithstanding that number of persons employed therein any time after it has become so applicable falls below 10.

### Employees covered under the Act

The Act applies to employees drawing wages not exceeding Rs. 10,000 per month, employed in factories, plantation, shops, establishments, mines, oil-fields, port and railway company in the event of superannuation, retirement, resignation and death or disablement due to accident or disease. It extends even Administrative and managerial staff subject to prescribed wage limit.

| | |
|---|---|
| **Determination of the Amount of Gratuity** | It is the duty of the employer to determine the amount of gratuity as soon as it becomes payable and to give notice of the same to the person to whom gratuity is payable and also to the controlling authority. The employer shall arrange to pay the amount of gratuity to the person concerned within 30 days from the date it becomes payable; the employer is to complete the formalities of gratuity, failure to do so would render him liable to pay interest at the rate of 10 per cent. Looking to the matter from the practical point of view the machinery of payment of the gratuity is to be moved by the person entitled to receive the amount. |
| **Application for claiming Gratuity** | Any person to whom gratuity is payable, may apply to the same of the employer. |
| **Rate of Gratuity** | For every completed year of service or part thereof in excess of six months, the employer shall pay gratuity to an employee at the rate of 15 days wages based on the rate of wages last drawn by the employee concerned. |
| **Piece-Rate Employee** | In the case of piece-rate employee, daily wages shall be computed on the average of the total wages received by him for a period of three months immediately preceding the termination of his employment and for this purpose, the wages paid for any overtime work shall not be taken into account. |
| **Seasonal Employee** | An employee who is employed in a seasonal establishment and who is not employed throughout the year, the employer shall pay the gratuity at the rate of 15 days wages for each season to calculation in case of monthly rated employees.<br><br>In case of a monthly rated employee, 15 days wages shall be calculated by dividing the monthly rate of wages last drawn by him by twenty-six and multiplying the quotient by fifteen. |
| **Ceiling of Gratuity** | The total amount of gratuity payable shall not exceed Rs. 3,50,000/- (Section 4 (3)). |
| **Forfeiture of Gratuity** | The gratuity of an employee whose services have been terminated for any act of (i) wilful omission, or (ii) negligence, causing any damage or loss to, or destruction of, property belonging to the employer, gratuity shall be forfeited to the extent of the damage or loss so caused.<br><br>Where the services of an employee have been terminated:<br>(a) for riotous and disorderly conduct or any other of violence on his part, or |

(b) for any act which constitutes an offence involving moral turpitude provided that such offence is committed by him in the course of his employment. The gratuity payable to the employee may be wholly or partially forfeited, Section 4 (6).

Section 4-A provides for compulsory insurance for employer's liability for payment of the gratuity under the Act from the Life Insurance Corporation of India established under the Life Insurance Corporation of India Act, 1956 or any other prescribed insurer. However, employer of an establishment belonging to or under the control of the Central Government are exempted from the operations of these provisions. Further the appropriate Government may also exempt: *Compulsory Insurance*

(i) employers who have already established an approved gratuity fund in respect of his employees and who desires to continue such arrangement; and

(ii) employers employing 500 or more persons, who establishes an approved gratuity fund in the manner prescribed.

Each employee, who has completed one year of service, shall make nomination within such time, in such form and in such manner as may be prescribed. *Nomination*

Under Section 8 if the amount of gratuity payable under this Act is not paid by the employer, within the prescribed time, to the persons entitled there to the controlling authority shall on an application made to it in this behalf by the aggrieved person, issue a certificate for that amount to the Collector, who shall recover the same, together with compound interest thereon at such rate as the Central Government may, by notification, specify from the date of expiry of the prescribed time, as arrears of land revenue and pay the same to the person entitled thereto. *Recovery of Gratuity*

Quite apart from this Act prescribed punishment for violation of the provisions of this Act. *Penalties*

Voluntary Retirement is legally tenable and is an integral part of public policy. Immediately after liberalization the Government has created a special fund called National Renewal Fund and allocated nearly 90 per cent of the fund to voluntary retiree from the central public sector undertakings which are not commercially viable. The government service rules also provide for voluntary retirement of civil servants as a part of government policy to downsize the government. **Voluntary Retirement Scheme (VRS)**

In the public sector, the Dept. of Public Enterprise has framed guidelines which most public enterprises follow. The guideline followed in the 1980s and 1990s were

1. VRS open for employees who have completed 10 years of service or 40 years of service;
2. Management of the enterprise has the right not to consider any request under VRS;
3. Terminal benefits include
   a. Balance of provident fund accumulation;
   b. Leave encashment as per rules;
   c. Gratuity as per Gratuity Act;
   d. One/three months notice of pay as applicable;
   e. Ex-gratia payment equivalent to 45 days emoluments for each completed year of service or the monthly emoluments at the time of retirement or salary for the remaining period of service, whichever is less and
   f. Travel for self or family to the place of settlement as per leave travel entitlement.
4. Higher exgratia can be proposed only after the approval of the Dept of Public Enterprises;
5. The above rules apply to all categories of employees.

During the late 1990s, some public enterprises began to offer 3 months' basic and DA for every year of completed service. Some others extended membership of benefits like medial and holiday homes to voluntary retirees till the date of normal superannuation.

In the central public sector, SAIL has introduced a scheme in 1999 for those with a minimum of 20 years in SAIL or above 50 years of age. The monthly benefit, apart from other benefits mentioned under DPE scheme are: 100 per cent of last drawn basic pay plus DA for those who completed 55 years of age, 99 per cent to those above 52 years and below 55 years and 80 per cent to those at or below 52 years of age.

One of the most attractive VRS scheme in the private sector was introduced by TISCO in 1998. It is called Early Separation Scheme. If the scheme is voluntary, it should be voluntary for both employer and employee. If the scheme is called early retirement scheme, management can legitimise discretion of accepting or rejecting an application.

The essential features of the TISCO scheme are as follows: Employees separating before attaining the age of 40 years and who have not completed 10 years of service as on the date of separation, will be entitled to get a monthly pension equivalent to last salary drawn by them till their attaining the age of superannuation (60 years). Employees crossing the age of 45 years will get salary equivalent to 1.25 times of their last drawn salary till the age of 60 years. Voluntary retirees and their families are entitled to medical benefits till the age of superannuation and after attaining the age of 60 as per benefits available to retiring employees. Employees separating and desirous of starting some business are also eligible for a loan of Rs. 2 lakh or 50 per cent of the pension benefits, whichever is less.

As the financial outgoing on account of VRS is spread over several years the actual cost to the company is less than what it would have been had the company paid the entire amount in lump sum. From the employees' point of view, though the job is gone, income is protected till he attains the age of 60.

Cost Benefit analysis of VRS can be viewed from three points of view:
  (i) Cost and Benefits to the Company
  (ii) Cost and Benefits to the Employees
  (iii) Cost and Benefits to the Society
  1. The company introduces VRS with a view to reduce its surplus labour. If a company can reduce its workforce through retrenchment it has to pay compensation at the rate of 15 days' salary for every completed year of service. Companies employing more than 100 persons cannot retrench their employees without giving (i) prior notice (ii) consultation with union (iii) paying compensation under law and (iv) obtaining prior permission of the appropriate Government. Experience indicates that Government rarely gives permission to closure, lay off or retrenchment. Hence companies began to introduce schemes to induce workers to retire voluntarily. In monetary terms such inducement has to be much higher than the normal retrenchment compensation.

     It is observed that while in the public sector, VRS is usually voluntary it is not in most private sector enterprise. When a company introduces VRS or when it coerces some of its employees to take VRS compulsorily, it might affect the morale and motivation of the employees who remain in the company.
  2. For the high of skilled, high performers, VRS is a golden parachute. If they could invest the VRS amount which they get on monthly basic 60 to 70 per cent of their

previous income, their total earnings will be 30 to 40 per cent higher. If they become successful entrepreneurs, they not only improve their earnings but also provide job opportunities to others. But this is not always the case. A study by Gandhi Labour Institute, Ahmedabad showed that mill workers had to seek alternative jobs by becoming hawker on footpaths and in many unfortunate cases, women had to take to prostitution to save the family.

3. When a big company resort to downsizing through VRS, the costs to the society are very large due to widespread unemployment, social unrest, antisocial activities, prostitution and violation of law and other problems.

*Objective:*

(i) To achieve optimum human resource utilization.

(ii) To optimise return of investment in PSU.

(iii) In implementing the VRS scheme, managements shall ensure that it is extended primarily to such employees whose services can be dispensed with, without detriment to the company. Care shall be exercised to ensure that highly skilled and qualified workers and staff are not given the option. As there shall be no recruitment against vacancies arising due to VRS, it is important that the organization is not denuded of talent. The managements of the PSUs shall introduce the VRS with the approval of their Boards and the administrative departments. Under no circumstances shall grant of VRS be construed as a right.

## Test Questions

1. Why pension is provided to an employee? What are the two main types of pension schemes?
2. Write a note on (i) Employers' provident Funds (ii) Gratuity.
3. What do you mean by Voluntary Retirement Scheme (VRS)? What are its objectives?

# Reservation in Services

Reservation is given to Scheduled Castes (SCs), Scheduled Tribes (STs) and Other Backward Classes (OBCs) in services under the control of the Government Reservation is also provided to persons with disabilities and the ex-servicemen in certain categories of posts. The quantum of reservation for SCs, STs and OBCs in direct recruitment on all-India basis, by open competition is 15 per cent, 7.5 per cent and 27 per cent, respectively. In direct recruitment on all-India basis otherwise then by open competition, reservation is 16.66 per cent for SCs, 7.5 per cent for STs and 25.84 per cent for OBCs. In case of promotion SCs and STs get reservation at the rate of 15 per cent and 7.5 per cent respectively. There is no reservation for OBCs in case of promotion. Three per cent of vacancies are kept reserved for persons with disabilities. Ten per cent of the vacancies in the posts of the level of Assistant Commandant in all para-military forces, 10 per cent of the vacancies in Group-C posts and 20 per cent of the vacancies in Group-D posts are reserved for the ex-servicemen.

Articles 341 and 342 of the Constitution defines as to who would be the SC and the STs with respect to any State or Union Territory. The Government has prepared a list of OBCs. The inter-State area restrictions have been imposed so that the people belonging to the specific community residing in a specific area which has been assessed to qualify for SC, ST and OBC status only benefit from the facilities provided for them. Definition of 'ex-servicemen' for the purpose of getting reservation in services is contained in Ex-servicemen (Re-employment in Civil Services and Posts) Rules 1979 and conditions for reservation to persons with disabilities are given under the Persons with Disabilities (Equal Opportunities, Protection of Rights and Full Participation) Act 1995.

To ensure that reserved vacancies are filled by candidates belonging to appropriate category, certain relaxations and concessions like relaxation in upper age-limit etc. are provided. Liaison officers have been appointed for SCs/STs and OBCs in each Ministry to ensure proper implementation of the reservation policy for them.

The reservation of SCs/STs in Central Government. Services as on 1 January 2004 is given below:

| Group | Total | SC | percentage | ST | percentage |
|---|---|---|---|---|---|
| A | 80,011 | 9,744 | 12.2 | 3,311 | 4.1 |
| B | 1,35,409 | 19,602 | 14.5 | 6,274 | 4.6 |
| C | 20,40,970 | 3,44,865 | 16.9 | 1,36,630 | 6.7 |
| D (Excluding Sweepers) | 8,02,116 | 1,47,212 | 18.4 | 53,776 | 6.7 |
|  | 91,601 | 59,320 | 64.76 | 5,368 | 5.86 |
| Total (Excluding Sweepers) | 30,58,506 | 5,21,423 | 17.05 | 1,9,901 | 6.54 |

| | Total | SC | percentage | ST | percentage |
|---|---|---|---|---|---|
| Total (Including Sweepers) | 31,50,107 | 5,80,743 | 18.44 | 2,05,359 | 6.52 |

The scheme of reservation is being followed by public sector undertakings including nationalized public sector banks. State Governments have also provided for reservation of posts of SCs, STs and OBCs etc. and have taken steps to increase their representation in State services. Reservation in State Government Services, however, is under the exclusive jurisdiction of respective State Governments.

**Evaluation.** There was a strong reaction against the 27 per cent reservation quota in favour of the backward classes of SC/ST/OBC as espoused by HRD Minister Arjun Singh.

It is necessary to examine the legal, economical and logical aspects as to why these quota reservations could pose a major threat to the well being of our country.

Whereas Articles 15 and 16 ensure every citizen freedom and equality before law, the impractical provision for reservation only highlights the contradictions in the machinery of the Government.

Reservations were a part of the Constitution when it was released in 1950. However, that was supposed to be a temporary measure and was to last for 10 years only.

More than 50 years later, the reservation continue to exist and have only become higher with passing years. The politicians in an attempt to woo more votes from the public, continue to reserve more and more seats for SCs/STs/OBCs. This makes us feel as if the Governments covers up vested interests in the large clasp of democracy.

One important consequence of the reservation regime is that caste-hatred in the country will increase.

Youngsters will lose faith in the democratic system of the country. If vote banks are so important to our politicians then we can assure them that they would lose a considerable part of it. We will not stay unplugged.

The quota system, created to facilitate the poor, ends up wrongly being utilized by children of rich people, ministers and IAS officers belonging to SC/ST/OBC.

The important consequence of the quota reservation is Brain Drain. With the reservation being proposed, most of the parents are pushing their children to pursue their academics from institutions abroad sans the inequality and the so-called privileged treatment confined only to the 'depressed' classes. This will result in a major brain drain.

FICCI president said, "nowhere in the world is there reservation in the private sector."

Ratan Tata said, 'though I do not want to comment on reservation, it is bad in the same way, it will tend to divide the members of the country who will consider themselves unfortunate for not being tagged as 'depressed' classes. While uplift of socially backward classes is important, merit is an important aspect and should not be compromised."

Association President K. Sanghi said in 2004 "it will have a far reaching impact on the industry as it may completely destroy the meritocracy in such units and bring inefficiency."

FICCI President Y.K. Modi said in 2004 "we oppose it as the move is against industrialisation and will lead to job reduction."

## List of Scheduled Castes

1. Bagdi, Duley
2. Bahelia
3. Baiti
4. Bantar
5. Bauri
6. Beldar
7. Bhogta
8. Bhuiya
9. Bhuiya
10. Bind
11. Chamar, Charmakar, Mochi, Muchi, Rabidas, Rishi
12. Chaupal
13. Dabgar
14. Damai (Nepali)
15. Dhoba, Dhobi
16. Doai
17. Dom, Dhangad
18. Dosadh, Dushad, Dhari, Dharhi
19. Ghasi

20. Gonrhi
21. Halalkhor
22. Hari, Mehtar, Mehtor, Bhangi
23. Jaliakaibaratta
24. Jhalo Malo, Malo
25. Kadar
26. Kami (Nepali)
27. Kandra
28. Kanjar
29. Kaora
30. Karenga, Koranga
31. Kaur
32. Keot, Keyot
33. Khaira
34. Khatik
35. Koch
36. Konai
37. Konwar
38. Kotal
39. Kurariar
40. Lalbegi
41. Lohar
42. Mahar
43. Mal
44. Mallah
45. Musahar
46. Namasudra
47. Nat
48. Nuniya
49. Paliya
50. Pan, Sawasi
51. Pasi
52. Patni
53. Pod, Poundra
54. Rajbanshi
55. Rajwar
56. Sarki (Nepali)
57. Sunri (excluding Saha)
58. Tiyar
59. Turi

## List of Scheduled Tribes

1. Asur
2. Baiga
3. Bedia, Bediya
4. Bhumij
5. Bhutia, Sherpa, Tota, Dukpa, Kagatay, Tibetan, Yolmo
6. Birhor
7. Birjia
8. Chakma
9. Chero
10. Chik Baraik
11. Garo
12. Gond
13. Gorait
14. Hajang
15. Ho
16. Karmali
17. Knarwar
18. Khond
19. Kisan

20. Kora
21. Korwa
22. Lepcha
23. Limbu
24. Lodha, Kheria, Kharia
25. Lohara, Lohra
26. Magh
27. Wlahali
28. Mahli
29. Mai Pahariya
30. Mech
31. Mru
32. Munda
33. Nagesia
34. Oraon
35. Parhaiya
36. Rabha
37. Santal
38. Sauria Paharia
39. Savar
40. Tamang

## List of Other Backward Classes

1. Kapali
2. Baishsya Kapali
3. Kurmi
4. Sutradhar
5. Karmakar
6. Kumbhakar, Kumar
7. Swarnakar
8. Teli, Kolu
9. Napit
10. Yogi-Nath
11. Goa!a-Gope, Pallav-Gope, Ballav-Gope, Yadav-Gope, Gope, Ahir and Yadav
12. Moira-Modak (Halwai
13. Barujibi, Barui
14. Satchasi
15. Malakar
16. Jolah (Ansari -Momin)
17. Kansari
18. Tanli, Tantubaya
19. Dhanuk
20. Shankhakar
21. Keori/Koiri
22. Raju
23. Nagar
24. Karani
25. Sarak
26. Kosta / Kostha
27. Tamboli/Tamali
28. Roniwar
29. Christians converted from Scheduled Castes
30. Lakhera / Laahera
31. Fakir/Sain
32. Kahar
33. Tamang
34. Betkar (Bentkar)
35. Chitrakar
36. Bhujel

37. Newar
38. Mangar (Thapa, Rana)
39. Nembang
40. Sarnpang
41. Bungchheng
42. Thami
43. Jogi
44. Dhimal
45. Hawari
46. Bhar
47. Khandait
48. Gangot
49. Turha
50. Dhunia
51. Patidar
52. Kasai
53. Hela/Halia/Chasi-Kaibartha
54. Banshi-Barman
55. Nashya-Sekh
56. Pahadia-Muslim
57. Khen
58. Sukli
59. Sunuwac
60. Bharbhuja
61. Dewan
62. Rai (including chamling)
63. Shersha Badia (Bhatia / Badia)
64. Rayeen/Kunjra

## Test Questions

1. Reservation in services is given to SC, ST and OBCs. What would the consequence of reservation?
2. Reservation policy will have a far reaching impact on the industry as it may completely destroy the meritocracy in such units and bring inefficiency.
3. FICCI President opposes it as the move is against industrialisation and will lead to job reduction. Explain.
4. Do you support the Government's reservation policy? Discuss its consequences on the economy.

# 13

# Bonus

## Introduction

Bonus is one of the ways of sharing the profits of establishments. It is an incentive to increase production. It is neither an exgratia payment nor a matter of deferred wages. It generally represents the cash incentive given on some conditions, e.g., attainment of certain standards of attendance and efficiency. It contributes to the earning of the industrial concern and so labour should derive some benefit. However, under the Payment of Bonus Act 1965, it has now assumed a character of 'deferred' wage. Prior to 1965, the Full Bench of the Labour Appellate, in Millowners' Associations, Bombay v. Rashtriya Mill Mazdur Sangh, Bombay evolved the formula for determination of Bonus. According to that, the following prior charges were to be deducted from gross profits:

I. Provision for depreciation.
II. Reserve for rehabilitation.
III. Return of 6 per cent on the paid-up capital.
IV. Return on the working capital at a lower rate than the return on paid-up capital and
IV. Income Tax.

The balance, if any, was called 'available surplus' and the workmen were to be awarded a reasonable share out of it by way of bonus for the year.

## Beginnings of Bonus in India

It was during World War I that the practice of paying 'war bonus' started for the first time in the cotton textile industry in Bombay and in Ahmedabad. In July, 1917, an increase of 10 per cent in wages was granted to textile workers in Bombay to enable them to meet the rise in prices. A circular issued by the Bombay Millowners' Association in January 1918 announced that the war bonus of 10 per cent would be raised to 15 per cent with effect from 1 January, 1918. At the end of 1918, a strike was called at the Century Mill, which soon spread throughout the industry. The dispute was eventually settled, the employers agreeing to raise the war bonus from 15 per cent to 35 per cent. The amount was then termed a 'special allowance' on account of the high price of foodstuffs.

It may be noticed that these payments were, in fact, not bonus at all, in the sense in which it is understood today, but what is now called DA or dearness allowance to compensate workers for the rise in the cost of living.

On 1 December 1919, the employers sanctioned payment of a 'Bonus' to all operatives who were on the muster roll on 31, December, 1919, at rates varying according to the length of service. However a strike was called on 2 January 1920, in support of certain demands, one of which said that while the mill-hands were grateful to the employers for the bonus promised, they would request that for certain workers, more liberal terms might be granted. The Bombay Labour Settlement Committee, a committee of the mill owners, replied to the demand thus: "The Committee can make no definite announcements as regards the 'annual bonuses'. The question is one of profits and goodwill and no undertaking can be given". Nevertheless, on 20 October, 1920, the Committee of the Millowners decided to recommend payment of a bonus of one month's pay on the same scale as in the previous years. Bonus on similar terms was recommended in November, 1921 and again in November, 1922.

The bonuses declared in the four years during 1919 and 1922 were presumably profit bonuses as the mill owners had indicated in their notices of 24 January, 1920, that the question was "one of profits and goodwill". But the position was at best, vague, as the mill owners had indicated in their reply of 27 January, 1921, that in fact an annual bonus of one month's pay had been paid "whether the mill did well or not".

The mill owners announced on 23 July, 1923, that owing to bad trade they would be unable to pay bonus for 1923. This led to a general strike towards the end of January, 1924. On 22 February, 1924, the Government of Bombay appointed the Bonus Disputes Committees presided over by Norman McLeod, Chief Justice of Bombay. The Committee was asked (1) to consider the nature and basis of bonus which had been granted to the employees in the cotton textile mills of Bombay since 1919 and to declare whether the employees had established any enforceable claim, customary, legal or equitable and (2) to inquire into the profits made in each year since 1917 with a view to comparing these profits with the profits made in the year 1923 and to report on the contention of the mill owners that the grant of bonus similar to that paid in previous years was not justified by the profits of the mill industry as a whole in 1923.

The workers' case before the Committee was that, as the increase in wages allowed from the year 1917, owing to war conditions had been called 'war bonus' and as annual bonuses had been paid for five consecutive years, the mill workers had come to look upon the annual bonus as part of their wages and that, therefore, they had a just claim against the mill owners.

The Committee, however, came to the conclusion that the mill workers had not established any enforceable claim, customary, legal or equitable, to the payment annually of a bonus and that such a claim would not be upheld in a court of law. The Committee also found that the total profits before allowing depreciation amounted of Rs. 53 lakhs or Rs. 119 lakhs if the income tax on the profits for the year 1923 only was debited, that the amount required for depreciation amounted to Rs. 170 lakhs, and that the result of the working of the cotton textile industry as a whole showed that there was justification for the contention of the mill owners that the profits did not admit of payment of bonus.

The committee's first conclusion naturally tended to support the dictionary meaning of bonus, namely, that it was "a boon or gift over and above what is nominally due as remuneration to the receiver" (New English Dictionary), or a "gratuity to workmen beyond their wages" (Concise Oxford Dictionary) or again "payments made of grace and as of right" (Earl of Birkenhead in Sutton V. Attorney-General). The second conclusion suggested that such an exgratia payment could not be expected except when there were surplus profits remaining after meeting prior charges.

The Committee, nevertheless, threw out a hint as to the manner of meeting such claims – a method which was eventually to take bonus out of the category of exgratia payment. It said, ". . . it is question of bargaining between the workers and the employers in which consideration might be given to principles of equity. It is not a question of determining what is the contract between the parties."

In 1921, a dispute about bonus arose in the cotton textile industry in Ahmedabad. Pandit Madan Mohan Malaviya, who mediated in it, observed: "When a mill has made handsome profits, the workers who have by their faithful co-operation, enabled the mill to earn such profits should, as an ordinary rule, be given at the end of each year a bonus equal to one month's salary. When the profits have been extraordinarily handsome, mill owners might very properly and wisely give larger bonus to the workmen."

The late twenties and the early thirties were of depression and consequently there were no major bonus disputes during that period. Even so, bonuses continued to be given on an ad hoc basis in a few industrial undertakings.

## Bonus During and Immediately After the Second World War

Two developments which arose in the early stages of World War II served as the justification for the renewed spate of bonus demands made by workers practically in every industry. The first was the accrual of large profits to industries as a result of the war-time demand. The second, and chronologically later, development was the steady and substantial rise in the prices of essential consumer goods. As industrial disputes increased in number and threatened to affect the regular working of factories, the Government of India introduced the system of compulsory adjudication of disputes under Rule 81-A of the Defence of India Rules.

Workers in the cotton textile industry in Bombay have often taken the lead in extracting concessions from employers. In March 1940, there was a general strike in the textile mills in Bombay on the question of dearness allowance. The Government of Bombay, watching the progress of the dispute, felt that one of the causes of industrial unrest was the desire of workers to share in the profits. At the instance of the Government, the Bombay Millowners' Association decided that its member mills should grant their workers a cash bonus for the calendar year 1941 equivalent to 12½ per cent of their actual earnings exclusive of dearness allowance. Similarly for 1942 a bonus equivalent to one-sixth of the total earnings exclusive of dearness allowance was granted. Such annual payments continued till 1945.

Various other bonus disputes had necessarily to be referred to tribunals or courts for adjudication. Adjudicators, grouping for enlightenment without precedent or principles and lacking guidance, formed appellate or revisional courts, formulated their own ideas of social, legal or normal justice for granting or denying bonus claims.

Several adjudicators of the early period held that in the absence of a contract, express or implied, workers were not entitled to claim bonus as a matter of right and that in the absence of proof of excessive profits, it was not possible to allow bonus as an exgratia payment.

But there were others who were by no means certain of bonus being only an exgratia payment. This was a period of wavering and indecision – of doubt whether bonus was only a gift or whether it could amount to a right.

Some adjudications, not wishing to go quite so far as to decide that bonus could be claimed as a matter of 'right', met workers' claims half way by granting a limited amount of bonus on broad principles of equity, justice and good conscience. In one of the earlier cases, the adjudicator said that it was expedient from the point of view of the employers themselves that the workers in industries essential for the due prosecution of the war should be kept contented and happy and that if some concerns like that Standard Vacuum Oil Company and Caltex (India) Limited were making large profits, "it seems but fair to me that an infinitesimal fraction of these profits may well be given by way of bonus to the workers in these companies, without whose labour and co-operation these unusually large profits could not have been made available to these companies". On these considerations he awarded one month's wage as bonus.

In United Provinces Sugar Co., for their employees it was held that bonus as a share of profits could not be claimed as a matter of right every year but that if a concern had an unusually profitable year, some part of the extra profits should be distributed "as an award and encouragement to workers".

On this basis several adjudicators awarded one-twelfth or one-eighth of the total annual earnings as bonus.

## Bonus as a Matter of Right

Judicial decision was, however, not slow to come up to workers' expectations, probably because wages were still very low in those days and profits invariably very high. As early as 1942, Justice Chagla, adjudicating on a dispute between the General Motors (India) Ltd. and its workmen, said: "It is almost a universally accepted principle now that the profits are made possible by the contribution that both capital and labour make in any particular industry and I think it is also conceded that labour has a right to share in the increased profits that are made in any particular period. But the distribution of increased profits amongst workers is better achieved by the giving of an annual bonus than by a further increase in wages. Wages must be fixed on the basis of normal conditions". The adjudicator was obviously anticipating future trends, and perhaps influencing them, when he observed that it was also "conceded" that labour had a "right" to share in the increased profits.

These observations, which pleaded powerfully for recognition of labour's right to profit sharing, were quoted with approval in a large number of adjudications of that period.

By the end of World War II, the view that labour was entitled to a share in profits as a matter of right seems to have got more or less, well-established. Adjudicators were only searching for the right words to uphold the labour's right to bonus.

In a dispute between the Textile Labour Association, Ahmedabad, and the Ahmedabad Mill Owners' Association, the Industrial Court, Bombay, said that although bonus was an exgratia payment and could not be legally demanded, bonus was in the nature of a reward. It was a reward "for work already done by them, which has resulted in such high profits". The Court went on to say: "Such additional payment is not a pure gift because a gift may have no relation to any work done or to be done by the doer, but it is a reward in as much as it is asked for as an extra payment for work actually done". Though such a claim could not be enforced in a court of law, it could become the subject matter of an industrial dispute. Here the court was trying to justify bonus more as an extra remuneration or wage payment than as profit-sharing.

In the Lahore Electric Supply Company's case, the adjudication had no difficulty in justifying bonus as profit-sharing. Though bonus was not a legal right which could be enforced in a court of law, "the advancement of economic thought and industrial relations had led to a state of affairs where the workers claim for a share in the profits of industry may be legitimate and may have a certain normal and economic right".

In Indian Hume Pipe Co. Ltd., V.E.M. Nanavutty, the Bombay High Court ruled that payment of bonus could be demanded by workmen, "as of right, that is to say as a payment which should be made by the employer as extra remuneration for work done by the employees under a contract, express or implied".

In a dispute between 36 cotton mills in West Bengal and their employees, the Industrial Tribunal said that when bonus was demanded for work done, out of which the employers had made high profits "the demand is not for any payment gratis, but the price of labour". It added, ". . . the demand of bonus though not based on legal right raising out of contract, expressed or implied, has to be decided on broad principles of equity and justice".

It will be seen from the cases mentioned above that, adjudicators of this period – war and early post-war were wavering between treating bonus as extra remuneration for work done and viewing it as sharing in the profits jointly created by labour and management. But all were agreed on one point, namely, that a claim to bonus, while not enforceable in a civil court, could be adjudicated upon as a matter of right.

It was the Industrial Court, Bombay, which, in a series of cases, shaped the concept of bonus as we understand it today. In a dispute in 1947, between the Rashtriya Mill Mazdoor Sangh and Millowners' Association, Bombay, the Court observed: "The justification for such demands as 'industrial matter' arises especially when wages fall short of the living wage standard and the industry makes huge profits, part of which are due to the contribution which the workers made in increasing production. The demand for a bonus is, therefore, an industrial claim when either or both these conditions are satisfied."

In a dispute between the same parties relating to 1948 and decided in 1949, the Industrial Court, Bombay, reiterated the view it had expressed in 1947. As this case and the one relating to the bonus demand in the next year were the cases from which the Labour Appellate Tribunal evolved the 'Full Bench Formula' later on, we might notice the Court's observations at some length. The Court said: "Such a demand (for bonus) derives its strength, where the living wage standard has not been reached, from a feeling of deficiency in the means to attain the necessary standard of living. Therefore, bonus in such circumstances no doubt serves as a temporary satisfaction, wholly or in part, of his need. Theoretically, adequate wages and dearness allowance should be the first charge on an industry. . . . . .Labour as well as the working capital employed in the industry both contribute to the profit made and both are, therefore, entitled to claim a legitimate return out of the profit; and such legitimate return, so far as labour is concerned, must be based on the living wage standard. It is however, to be remembered that a claim to bonus might be admissible even if the living wage standard were completely attained. It may, therefore, be stated that so long as the living wage standard has not been attained, the bonus partakes primarily of the character of satisfaction, often partial and temporary, of the deficiency in the legitimate income of the average worker in an industry, and that once such income has been attained it would also partake of the character of profit-sharing. Owing to this dual character of bonus, it would be a mistake to regard a demand for bonus as a demand for profit-sharing pure and simple. Even if it be held, as the Committee on profit-sharing have held, that profit-sharing on a fifty-fifty basis would be equitable, it would be proper in our opinion, when the living wage standard has not been reached for labour to demand even a greater share after the gross profits have been reduced by depreciation, reasonable reserves and dividend and suitable provision for taxation".

## Payment of Bonus

This profit-sharing concept also resulted in a bonus being paid at the end of the year to the employees. Good companies began to pay up to three months' pay as bonus to their employees even in years which did not justify such a high bonus payment. This led to a belief in the mind of the worker that the employers were holding back a part of their wage and paying it at the end of the year under title 'bonus' as if it were an exgratia payment. Thus bonus began to be looked upon as a 'deferred wage'. This concept unfortunately was practically legalised by the payment of Bonus Act, 1965.

## The Payment of Bonus Act 1965

This Act came into operation on 29 May, 1965, replacing an ordinance. The scheme of the Payment of Bonus Act, 1965, has four objectives:

i) to impose statutory obligation upon the employer of every establishment covered by the Act to pay bonus to employees in the establishment;

ii) to define principle of payment of bonus according to the prescribed formula;

iii) to provide for payment of minimum and maximum bonus and link the payment of bonus with the scheme of 'set off' and 'set-on' and

iv) to provide for enforcement of the liability for payment of bonus.

### Scope of the Act

The Act covers all persons who are employed for hire or reward to do any work, skilled, manual, supervisory, managerial, administrative, technical or clerical work drawing a salary or wage not exceeding Rs. 3500 per month, in any factory or establishment employing more than 20 or more persons. The Act covers the probationer but does not covered the apprentice, as he is not included within the term 'employee'.

The Act applies to every factory and every other establishment in which 20 or more persons are employed on any day during an accounting year. However, the appropriate Government may extend the application of these provisions to any factory establishment employing less than 20 but not less than 10 persons during the accounting year.

### Act not to apply to certain classes of employees

Section 32 excludes the applications of the Payment of Bonus Act to:

i) employees employed by the Life Insurance Corporation of India;

ii) seaman as defined in the Merchant Shipping Act, 1958;

iii) employees registered under any scheme made under the Dock Workers (Regulation of Employment) Act 1948 and employed by the registered employers;

iv) employees employed by an establishment engaged in any industry carried on by the authority of any department of the Central Government or a State Government or a local authority;

v) employees employed by

    i) the Indian Red Cross Society or any other institution of a like nature;

ii) universities and other educational institutions;
iii) institutions established not for purposes of profit;
iv) employees employed through contractors on building operations;
v) employees employed by the RBI;
vi) employees employed by
   a) Industrial Finance Corporation of India;
   b) any Financial Corporation;
   c) Deposit Insurance Corporation;
   d) National Bank for Agriculture for Rural Development;
   e) The Unit Trust of India;
   f) The Industrial Development Bank of India;
   g) The National Housing Bank;
   h) any other notified financial institution.
vii) employees employed by inland water transport establishments operating to routes passing through other country.

## Calculation of Amount Payable as Bonus

The Act prescribes the procedure for calculating the amount payable to the employees. For this purpose, first of all, the available surplus in any accounting year is computed. Of this surplus, 67 per cent in case of company (other than a banking company) and 60 per cent in other cases shall be the 'allocable surplus' which would be available for payment of bonus to employees.

**Disqualification for Bonus.** An employee shall be disqualified from receiving bonus under the Act, if he is dismissed from service for
a) fraud or
b) riotous or violent behaviour while in the premises of the establishment or
c) theft, misappropriation or sabotage of any property of the establishment.

**Payment of Minimum Bonus.** Section 10 of the Payment of Bonus Act provides: Every employer is bound to pay to every employee in respect of the accounting year a minimum bonus which shall be 8.33 per cent of salary or wage earned by the employee during the accounting year.

## Payment of Maximum Bonus

Section 11 which regulates the payment of maximum bonus provides:

Where in respect of any accounting year, the allocable surplus exceeds the amount of minimum bonus payable to the employees, the employer shall, in lieu of such minimum bonus, be bound to pay to every employee in respect of that accounting year bonus which shall be an amount a proportion to the salary or wage earned by the employee during the accounting year subject to a maximum of 20 per cent of such salary or wage.

## Test Questions

1. Do you think that bonus is a "deferred wage"? It is said that bonus is neither an exgratia payment nor it is a matter of deferred wages. Discuss the statement.
2. Discuss that bonus is a matter of right.
3. Discuss the objectives of the Payment of Bonus Act. 1965. What is the minimum and maximum bonus under the Act?
4. Discuss the evolution of bonus is India since the first world war period with the practice of paying war bonus.
5. The Payment of Bonus Act 1965 has four objectives. Mention them.
6. Explain those classes of employees to whom the Bonus Act does not apply.

# Contract Labour In India

## Introduction

The system of employing contract labour is prevalent in most industries in different occupations including skilled and semi-skilled jobs. It is also prevalent in agricultural and allied operations and to some extent in the services sector. A workman is deemed to be employed as Contract Labour when he is hired in connection with the work of an establishment by or through a contractor. Contract workmen are indirect employees; persons who are hired, supervised and remunerated by a contractor who, in turn, is compensated by the establishment. Contract labour has to be employed for work which is specific and for a definite duration. Inferior labour status, casual nature of employment, lack of job security and poor economic conditions are the major characteristics of contract labour. While economic factors like cost effectiveness may justify system of contract labour, considerations of social justice call for its abolition or regulation.

The condition of contract labour in India was studied by various Commissions, Committees and also by the Labour Bureau of the Ministry, before independence and after independence. All these have found their condition to be appalling and exploitative in nature. The Supreme Court of India in the case of Standard Vacuum Refinery Company Vs. their workmen (1960-II-ILJ page 233) observed that contract labour should not be employed where:

(a) The work is perennial and must go on from day to day;
(b) The work is incidental to and necessary for the work of the factory;
(c) The work is sufficient to employ considerable number of whole time workmen and
(d) The work is being done in most concerns through regular workmen.

## The Contract Labour (Regulation and Abolition) Act, 1970

The concern for providing legislative protection to this category of workers, whose conditions have been found to be abysmal, resulted in the enactment of the Contract Labour (Regulation and Abolition) Act, 1970.

### Objects and Purposes of The Act

The Contract Labour (Regulation and Abolition) Act, 1970 was brought onto the Statutes Book to regulate the employment of Contract Labour in certain establishments and to provide for its abolition in certain circumstances and for matters connected therewith.

### Application

The Contract Labour (Regulation and Abolition) Act, 1970 and the Contract Labour (Regulation and Abolition) Central Rules, 1971 came into force on 2 February, 1971. The constitutional validity of the Act and the Central rules were challenged before the Supreme Court in Gammon India Ltd. Vs. Union of India 1974-1-LLJ. The Supreme Court upheld the constitutional validity of the Act & Rules and held that there is no unreasonableness in the measure. The Act & Rules were enforced w.e.f. 21 March, 1974.

The Act applies to every establishment in which 20 or more workmen are employed or were employed on any day on the preceding 12 months as contract labour and to every contractor who employs or who employed on any day of the preceding 12 months 20 or more workmen. It does not apply to establishments where the work performed is of intermittent or seasonal in nature. An establishment wherein work is of intermittent and seasonal nature will be covered by the Act if the work performed is more than 20 days and 60 days in a year, respectively. The Act also applies to establishments of the Government and local authorities as well.

### Appropriate Government

The jurisdiction of the Central and State Government has been laid down by the definition of the 'Appropriate Government' in Section 2 (1) (a) of the Act, as amended in 1986. The Appropriate Government, in respect of an establishment under the Contract Labour (Regulation and Abolition) Act, 1970 is the same as that in the Industrial Disputes Act, 1947.

As per the interpretation given by the Supreme Court through its judgment dated 30 August, 2000, in Steel Authority of India Limited and Ors Vs. National Union Water Front Workers & Ors., the 'appropriate government' in relation to an establishment would be the Central Government if (i) the concerned Central Government company/undertaking or any undertaking is included by name in clause (a) of Section 2 of the Industrial Disputes Act, or (ii) any industry carried on by or under the authority of the Central Government or by a railway company, or (iii) any such controlled industry as may be specified in this behalf by the Central Government, otherwise in relation to any other establishment, the Government of the State in which that other establishment is situated, will be the appropriate government.

## The Central and State Advisory Boards

The Central Government and State Governments are required to set up Central and State Advisory Contract Labour Boards to advise the respective Governments on matters arising out of the administration of the Act as are referred to them. The Boards are authorized to constitute Committees as deemed proper.

10.10 The Central Advisory Board – a tripartite Body was last re-constituted on 30 October, 1996. On expiry of the term of appointment of the Chairman, he has been reappointed on 16 November 1999 for a period of three years. The term of non-official members of the Board was three years but they will continue to hold office till their successors are appointed. The appointment of employer and employee members of the Board is under process. Fifty meetings of the Central Advisory Contract Labour Board (CACLB) have so far been held. The last meeting was held on 22 November, 2001.

The existing CACLB has held three meetings during the year under report and considered various issues relating to abolition of contract labour system in certain establishments. The working of the Act was also reviewed in these meetings. As a consequence, the Central Government on the recommendation of the Board, have prohibited employment of contract labour in various operations/category of jobs in various establishments.

## Registration of Establishment and Licensing of Contractors

The establishments covered under the Act are required to be registered as principal employers with the appropriate authorities. Every contractor is required to obtain a license and not to undertake or execute any work through contract labour except under and in accordance with the license issued in that behalf by the licensing officer. The license granted is subject to such conditions as to hours of work, fixation of wages and other essential amenities in respect of contract labour as laid down in the rules.

## Welfare and Health of Contract Labour

The Act has laid down certain amenities to be provided by the contractor to the contract labour for establishment of canteens and rest rooms; and arrangements for sufficient supply of wholesome drinking water, latrines and urinals, washing facilities and first aid facilities and have been made obligatory. In cases of failure on the part of the contractor to provide these facilities, the Principal Employer is liable to provide the same.

**Payment of Wages**

The contractor is required to pay wages and a duty is cast on him to ensure disbursement of wages in the presence of the authorized representative of the Principal Employer. In case of failure on the part of the contractor to pay wages either in part or in full, the Principal Employer is liable to pay the same. The contract labour who performs same or similar kind of work as regular workmen, will be entitled to the same wages and service conditions as regular workmen as per the Contract Labour (Regulation and Abolition) Central Rules, 1971.

**Penal Provisions**

For contravention of the provisions of the Act or any rules made thereunder the punishment is imprisonment for a maximum term up to 3 months and a fine up to a maximum of Rs. 1000.

**Other Provisions**

The Act makes provision for the appointment of Inspecting staff, for maintenance of registers and records and for making rules for carrying out the purpose of the Act. In the central sphere, officers of the Central Industrial Relations Machinery (CIRM) have been appointed as Inspectors.

**Prohibition**

Apart from the regulatory measures provided under the Act for the benefit of the contract labour, the 'appropriate government' under section 10 (1) of the Act is authorized, after consultation with the Central Board or State Board, as the case may be to prohibit, by notification in the official gazette, employment of contract labour in any establishment in any process, operation or other work.

Sub-section (2) of Section 10 lays down sufficient guidelines for deciding upon the abolition of contract labour in any process, operation or other work in any establishment. The guidelines are mandatory in nature and are: Conditions of work and benefits provided to the contract labour.

- Whether the work is of Perennial nature;
- Whether the work is incidental or necessary for the work of an establishment;
- Whether the work is sufficient to employ a considerable number of whole-time workmen and
- Whether the work is being done ordinarily through regular workman in that establishment or a similar establishment.

The Central Government on the recommendations of the CACLB, have prohibited employment of contract labour in various operations/category of jobs in various establishments. So far 48 notifications have been issued since inception of the Act.

## Exemption

The 'appropriate government' is empowered to grant exemption to any establishment or class of establishments or any class of contractors from applicability of the provisions of the Act or the rules made thereunder on such conditions and restrictions as may be prescribed. Nine notifications granting exemption to establishments in exercise of this power in the Central sphere have been issued.

## Enforcement

In the Central sphere, (CIRM) has been entrusted with the responsibility of enforcing the provisions of the Act and the rules made thereunder, through Inspectors, Licensing Officers, Registering Officers and Appellate Authorities appointed under the Act.

Regular inspections are being conducted by the Field Officers of the CIRM and prosecutions are launched against the establishments, whenever violations of the Act/Rules/notifications prohibiting employment of contract labour are detected. From time to time, instructions/directions have been issued to the field officers of CIRM and State Government for proper implementation of the Act.

A statement indicating the number of inspections carried out, prosecutions launched, licenses issued, establishments registered, etc. under the Act in the Central Sphere by the Industrial Relations Machinery is at.

A number of representations/petitions have been received by the Deputy Chief Labour Commissioner (Central) under Rule 25 (2) (V) (a) & (b) from the contract worker or their unions claiming that the contract workers are performing the same or similar work as performed by the workmen employed by the principal employer. Out of 83 cases received till 2000, orders have been passed in 33 cases and 50 cases are under investigation.

The Labour Bureau of the Ministry launched a survey on contract and the implementation of the Act in respect of the Cement Industry including related mines, FCI Depots and N.T.P.C Units in March, 2000. The report was brought out in July 2001 and by and large compliance with the provisions of the Act has been found.

## Important Judgments of The Supreme Court

Three judgments delivered by the Supreme Court in the cases of Gujarat State Electricity Board Vs Union of India, Air India Statutory Corporation Ltd & Ors Vs United Labour Union & Others and Steel Authority of India Ltd. & Others Vs National Union of Waterfront Workers and others on 5 May, 1995, 6 December, 1996 and 30 August, 2001 respectively are landmark judgments.

In Gujarat State Electricity Board case, inter-alia, the Supreme Court recommended that the Central Government should amend the

Act by incorporating a suitable provision to refer to the industrial adjudicator, the question of the direct employment of the workers of the ex-contractor in the principal establishments, when the appropriate Government abolishes the contract labour.

In Air India Statutory Corporation case, the Supreme Court held that though there exists no express provision in the Act for absorption of employees in establishments where contract labour system is abolished by publication of the notification under section 10 (1) of the Act, the Principal Employer is under statutory obligation to absorb the contract labour. The linkage between the contractor and employee stood snapped and direct relationship stood restored between Principal Employer and contract labour as its employees.

The Supreme Court in the case of Steel Authority of India Ltd. Vs National Union of Waterfront Workers & Others have held that neither Section 10 of the Act nor any other provision in the Act whether expressly or by necessary implication provides for automatic absorption of contract labour on issuing a Notification by the appropriate Government under sub section (1) of Section 10 prohibiting employment of contract labour in any process or operation or other work in any establishment. Consequently, the Principal Employer cannot be required to order absorption of the contract labour working in the concerned establishment. The judgment in the Air India's case was over-ruled prospectively.

## Streamlining Contract Labour Law

In the wake of economic liberalization as well as the judgments of the courts, proposals have been received from social partners to bring about amendments in the Contract Labour Act.

### Views of Employers' Associations:

- Since 1970, when the Contract Labour (Regulation and Abolition) Act was enacted, the economy has undergone a sea-change, from an era of protectionism to liberalization, from restricted domestic competition to international competitiveness.
- The system of contract labour offers tremendous opportunities for employment and allows the employers flexibility to choose what is best for them. This helps improve productivity and service competitiveness.
- The Act should be made applicable only to the main and core activities of the establishment in so far abolition of contract labour system are concerned.
- Supportive or allied activities of an establishment like maintenance or house keeping should be outsourced and the Act should only provide for regulating the working conditions and wages.

- The Principal Employer should, however, have to ensure payment of wages to contract labour as laid down under the law in force as also other basic amenities and social security benefits.
- Work requiring specialized skills unavailable within the establishment.
- If the contract labour system, which is cost effective, is not allowed to continue, industries may go in for technological restructuring with less number of workers leading to reduction in employment.

## Views of the trade Unions

The Trade Unions are totally opposed to the idea of contracting of services and in job which are perennial in nature for following reasons.

- Reduction of regular employment;
- The contract labour generally belongs to weaker sections of the society and will be deprived of the benefits that accrue to regular employees.
- Efficiency will decrease as the establishment will be deprived of experienced staff.
- Co-ordination of activities of large number of contractors/sub-contractors will prove to be more time consuming and costly than in-house activity.
- What is required is not privatization but in-house improvements and restructuring.
- Outsourcing will only lead to a type of employment founded on discrimination and exploitation of contract labour in regard to wages paid, working conditions, etc.
- The Second National Labour Commission has been entrusted with the task of rationalization of labour laws and hence its report should be awaited.

The Government, at the moment, has undertaken a thorough review of the Act, keeping in view the aforesaid views of the employers' association and that of the trade unions. The changes to be made in the law are still being worked out.

## Test Questions

1. Describe the objectives and purposes of the Contract Labour.... (Regulation and abolition) Act, 1970.
2. Discuss the views of Employers' Association and Trade Unions on the Contract Labour Law.
3. What are the objectives of the Contract Labour (Regulation and abolition) Act 1970.

# 15

# Tax Planning

The system of direct taxes in India provides a variety of tax shelters which can be utilized to reduce the tax liability of taxpayer. Every employer has therefore an opportunity to design the compensation package so as to minimize the tax liability of the employee without infringing any provision of law. It should be made clear that tax planning is not the same as tax evasion.

Tax planning is a conscious and well thought out process of arranging one's financial and economic affairs in a manner that enables him to take advantage of all deductions, exemptions, allowances and rebates available under Income Tax laws with a view to reducing his tax liability to the minimum. In relation to salary and wages, tax planning is important from the point of view of both the employer and the employee. It enables the employer to ensure compliance with income tax laws and related provisions while at the same time ensuring the maximum possible post tax income to the employee corresponding to a defined compensation package. Maximization of post tax income has direct relationship with motivation and is therefore mutually beneficial to both the employer and the employee.

Tax planning includes all financial arrangements which allow a tax-payer to reduce to the minimum his tax liability without violating any legal provision and without resorting to any colourable device. Any tax planning arrangement which involves any overt or covert intention of defeating the spirit behind the legal framework will amount to colourable device. Tax planning is legitimate only to the extent that it is within the framework of law and conforms to the spirit behind the legal framework. Any tax planning done with the intention to defraud the revenue will amount to tax evasion even if all transactions entered into by the assessee taken individually could be legally correct. All such methods which are resorted to deceive revenue, impairing the true spirit of the statute with what would be termed as colourable devices.

## Tax Planning for Employee Compensation

The basic purpose of tax planning exercise is to minimize the incidence of tax to both the employer and the employee. It is therefore necessary that the design of compensation should meet the following objectives.

(a) All constituent parts of employee's remuneration are deductible as business expenses to the extent possible. If this requirement is not met, the compensation package will put an avoidable financial burden on the employer and will thereby reduce the profitability of his business.

(b) Remunerations received by the employees should qualify for concessional rate of taxation so that their post tax income is maximized. This is an important consideration because the post tax income is perceived as the real income by the employee and therefore has significant implications for his morale, motivation and commitment to the organization.

**Composition of Compensation Package.** The compensation package generally consists of the following components.

(a) **Salary.** Salary is a fixed payment made periodically to a person as compensation for regular work or remuneration for services rendered.

Salary has been defined as the recompense or consideration paid or stipulated to be paid at regular intervals, especially to holders of official executive or clerical positions. The definition of salary includes wages and conceptually there is no difference between the two; both being a recompense for work done or services rendered. In general, the word salary is used for payment of services of a higher class and wages is confined to earnings of labour. Before any payment made to a person is treated as salary or wages, it is essential that the amount payable must be quid pro quo for services rendered by him as an employee. The test of what is or is not a salary or wage is whether a particular payment is in the nature of a personal gift or compensation for the work done is in accordance with the contract of employment. In the former case, the payment is not taxable as salary, but in the latter case it is. The question depends upon the fact whether or not a relationship between the person who pays and the person who receives is that of an employer and employee. The sine qua non any income coming with the meaning of salary is that there must exist a relationship of employer or employee.

(b) **Allowances.** All payments made by the employer by way of allowances to the employees for the personal benefit of the latter will form part of the salary and hence will be chargeable to income tax.

(c) **Perquisites.** The third component of employer's remuneration is perquisites. A perquisite is defined as a gain or profit incidentally made from employment in addition to regular salary or wages. It signifies such benefits in addition to the amount that may be legally due by way of contract for rendering service. Perquisites are normally in the nature of voluntary payments attached to an office or employment. Their main characteristic is that they are payable only during the continuance of employment and directly dependent on the service. When employment comes to an end, perquisites cease to be payable.

## Tax implications of employee compensation package to the employer

Tax provisions which have implications to the employer in respect of various components of compensation package should be kept in view while deciding on compensation package. It should be clearly understood that the principles of carrying on any business or profession should not be sacrificed solely for the purpose of achieving the objective of reduction in tax liability of the employee. In other words, the decision on tax planning for employees is subordinate to the needed and exigencies of business. The scope of tax planning in respect of salaries and perks is considerably limited as the law specifically provides for the treatment of each component of the compensation package. Income Tax makes provisions for the following deductions in respect of employee remuneration:

i) Payment of salary/allowances and perquisites.
ii) Insurance premium on health of employees.
iii) Bonus and commission.
iv) Employer's contribution to the staff welfare fund.
v) Family planning expenditure.
vi) Entertainment expenditures.

The employer has to ensure that tax is deducted at source.

## Tax implications of compensation to the employees

(a) **Salary.** The term 'salary' for the purpose of income tax has been defined to include within its scope (i) wages; (ii) any annuity or pension; (iii) any gratuity; (iv) any fee, commission, perquisites or profits in addition to any salary or wages; (v) any advance of salary. All such payments made by the employer by whatever name these are called, fall within the meaning of salaries and would be taxable.

(b) **Allowances.** All allowances granted by the employer for the personal benefit of the employee will form part of his salary for the purpose of assessment of income tax. There are, however, some special allowances which fall within the scope of Section 10 (4) of the Income Tax Act, and hence entitle the employee to the benefit of total exemption from income tax. To qualify for exemptions, it is necessary that such allowances are granted specifically to meet the expenses incurred wholly, necessarily and exclusively in the performance of the duties of an office.

   (i) **House Rent Allowance.** Tax exemption for HRA is available only if the same is received as reimbursement for payment of rent in respect of accommodation occupied by the employee as a tenant. HRA qualifies for total exemption only to the extent it exceeds 10 per cent of the employee's salary and does not exceed 60 per cent of salary at Delhi, Bombay, Calcutta and Madras and 40 per cent of salary where accommodation is situated at any other place.

  (ii) **Conveyance Allowance.** Conveyance Allowance is exempt from income-tax to the extent that it is actually utilized for performance of duties of an office.

 (iii) **Travelling Allowance and Expenses.** Any such allowance whether granted on tour or for the period of journey in connection with transfer to meet the travelling expenses incurred by the employee on account of absence from his normal place of duty is exempt from income the income tax.

(c) **Perquisites.** As a general rule, a substantial part of salary is in the form of perquisites.

   (i) **Rent-free Accommodation.** The perquisite value of rent-free accommodation at Delhi, Bombay, Calcutta and Madras is taken at 10 per cent salary so long as the rent of the accommodation does not exceed 60 per cent of salary. In respect of any other place, the ceiling of fair rent for the purpose of assessment of perquisite value of rent-free accommodation is 50 per cent of salary.

  (ii) **Provisions of company owned car.** The perquisite value of this benefit is nil when the car is used wholly for the private purpose of the employee, the amount of expenditure actually incurred by the employer for the maintenance and running of the car is also included for calculating the expenditure incurred on running and maintenance of the car.

 (iii) **Leave Travel Concession.** The exemption in respect of leave travel concession is available to any place in India to the extent specified below:

(a) Amount equivalent to air-conditioned second class fare by the shortest route or the amount spent whichever is less where journey is performed by rail. In case the place visited is not connected by rail, first class or deluxe fare in any recognised public transport by the shortest route or the actual amount spent whichever is less.

(b) The above exemption is available in respect of employee and his family comprising his spouse and children. The definition of family also includes parents, brothers and sisters if they are wholly or mainly dependent on the employer.

(v) **Medical facilities.** The benefits derived by employees from medical facilities are not a payment for services rendered and hence do not constitute part of the salary. These facilities cover the employee and the members of his family and are either in the nature of reimbursement of expenditure actually incurred on the treatment. The benefits derived do not constitute a part of remuneration and are therefore tax free.

(vi) **Other non-taxable perquisites.** In addition to major perquisites already discussed, the following perquisites are non-taxable.

(i) Refreshment provided by the employer during working hour in office premises.

(ii) Subsidised lunch or dinner provided in the company's canteen.

(iii) Recreation facilities.

(iv) Goods manufactured by the company sold to the employees at concessional rates.

(v) Subsidized transport to cover journeys between office and residence.

(vi) Employees' contributions to group insurance scheme.

(vii) Payment of premium for personal accident policy.

(viii) Education allowance to the extent of Rs. 50 and hostel allowance of Rs. 150 per month per child subject to a maximum of two children.

The primary purpose of designing a compensation package is to ensure that the employee gets a fair return for the contribution he makes to the employer's business.

## Tax Planning

**Solved Problems:**            **Exercise**

### Gratuity

1. Mr Akash retired from service on 15th June, 2011 after serving 24 years and 7 months and received gratuity of Rs 5,45,000. He is covered by Gratuity Act, 1972. At the time of retirement his Salary was- Basic Rs 12,300 p.m., DA 60 per cent of Basic. Calculate taxable gratuity.

**Computation of Taxable Gratuity for the Assessment Year 2012-13**

| Details | Rs | Rs |
|---|---|---|
| Gratuity received | | 5,45,000 |
| Less: Exempt u/s 10(10)(i), least of the following | | |
| (i) Actual gratuity received | 5,45,000 | |
| (ii) Maximum limit | 10,00,000 | |
| (iii) 15 days wages for every year of completed service | 2,83,846 | |
| (Rs 19,680×15/26×25) | ---------- | 2,83,846 |
| Taxable Gratuity | | 2,61154 |

2. Mr. Sagar retired from service on 1st August, 2011 after 25 years and 11 months of service and received gratuity of Rs 3,42,500. He is not covered by 1972 Act. At the time of retirement his Salary was - Basic Rs 7,300 p.m., DA Rs 3,400 p.m. Determine taxable gratuity.

**Computation of Taxable Gratuity for the Assessment Year 2012-13**

| Details | Rs | Rs |
|---|---|---|
| Gratuity received | | 3,42,500 |
| Less: Exempt u/s 10(10)(i), least of the following | | |
| (i) Actual gratuity received | 3,42,500 | |
| (ii) Maximum limit | 10,00,000 | |
| (iii) ½ month Salary for every year of completed service | 1,33,750 | |
| (Rs 10,700×15/30×25) | ---------- | 1,33,750 |
| Taxable Gratuity | | 2,08,750 |

## Leave Salary:

1. Mrs Anindita has retired from service on 24th June, 2011 after 23 year and 9 months of service and received Leave Salary of Rs 2,34,000. She is entitled to get 24-days leave every year. At the time of retirement her Salary was: Basic Rs 4,500 p.m., DA 60 per cent, Commission on Sales Rs 6,000 p.a. Calculate taxable leave salary.

### Computation of Taxable Leave Salary for the Assessment Year 2012-13

| Details | Rs | Rs |
|---|---|---|
| Leave Salary received | | 2,34,000 |
| Less: Exempt u/s 10(10AA) (ii), least of the following | | |
| (i) Actual Leave salary received | 2,34,000 | |
| (ii) Maximum limit | 3,00,000 | |
| (iii) 10 months average salary (Rs 7,700×10) | 77,000 | |
| (iv) 30 days leave for each year of completed service (23 × 24/30 × Rs 7,700) | 1,41,680 | 77,000 |
| Taxable Leave Salary | | 1,57,000 |

2. Mr. Arup has retired from service on 30th April, 2011 after 25 year and 7 months of service and received Leave Salary of Rs 3,43,000. He is entitled to get 35 days leave every year. During service he already encashed 120 days leave. At the time of retirement his Salary was: Basic Rs 7,500 p.m, DA Rs 4,300 p.m., Commission on Sales Rs 12,000 p.a. Calculate taxable leave salary.

## Test Questions

1. What is the objective of Tax Planning? Is the Tax Planning same as Tax Evasion?
2. Discuss (i) Tax implications of employee compensation to the employer and (ii) Tax implications of compensation to the employee.
3. In relation to salary and wages, tax planning is important from the point of view of both the employer and the employee. Discuss this statement.

# 16

# Oustees from Dam: Resettlement of Project Affected People

The country does not have a national policy on re-settlement and rehabilitation of oustees from projects like Tehri and Narmada. The fact is that even after more than half a century of our Independence, we have none. In fact, to begin with, in the heady days of Nehru's temples of modern India, the days of large basic infrastructure projects, not much thought was given to the problems of the ousted people, majority of whom happened to be extremely poor and very often tribal people, who themselves had no voice. Everybody was in a euphoric condition of creating the commanding heights of Indian economy. The standard thing to do in those early days was to pay cash compensation under the Land Acquisition Act of the British vintage, that is, 1894. It was amended only in 1984 to provide for an alternative, i.e., the Government could provide land in lieu of cash compensation or alternative land it could be given to only those families who had land title, the patta issued by the revenue administration in the districts. Neither landless nor those cultivating land for years without having the pattas could get any benefits. In the event, it was left to the concerned State Government to take care of the landless families to whatever extent these Governments could. The case of Dumbur Hydel Project illustrates such an effort. Some State Governments managed to obtain few jobs within the project establishment for one member of each of an oustee families but such an effort was greatly handicapped on account of extremely low levels of skills or technical and educational facilities in such areas. Even in the case of better-off families who got either cash or land in compensation, without talking of the other and larger group not entitled to cash or land compensation, there was hardly any considered policy, guidelines or directions to take care of socio-economic concerns as also sustained rehabilitation of the uprooted families.

It is only recently that a draft of the National policy was prepared by the Department of Social Welfare in the Government of India but it is still at the stage of consideration by different Ministries in the Central Government and till it is finalized, it is only a piece of paper with the concerned Ministry under whose administrative control a particular project falls going about this vital question of the very livelihood of the ousted families in their ways. In any case, this draft policy is the only available touchstone against which the policies adopted can be tested and it will be useful to just mention the salient features that are likely to be covered within the framework of such a national policy:

1. There should be detailed planning for resettlement and rehabilitation of all the families that will be uprooted by a project.
2. The policy should provide for defining various groups of displaced persons so that major sons, adopted sons/daughters, widows, unmarried daughters etc. are adequately covered by resettlement and rehabilitation programmes.
3. The policy should clearly lay down the principles and aims of displacement and rehabilitation process so that programmes could be formulated to achieve such aims and objectives.
4. The policy should also enumerate various stages of implementation of the policy. It must guard against earlier than required evacuation, or taking the families to the rehabilitation sites without advance preparation etc.
5. The National Policy should enumerate the elements of rehabilitation package with the ultimate objective of improving or at least regaining the standard of living prior to displacement.
6. The policy must also direct itself to provide for the other related matters like availability of social and physical rehabilitation infrastructure at the new location.

As a result of Tehri-Dam project, 9290 rural and 4561 urban families were affected. A Rehabilitation Policy was devised only in 1995, the basic features of which are as follows:

(i) Rural oustees to be compensated through allotment of agricultural land or cash lieu thereof. District Administration shall take over the direct responsibility for the entire Rehabilitation task to be carried out directly by its officers under the overall supervision and control of Commissioner, Gerwal Revenue Division. Funds for rehabilitation would, however, be made available by Tehri Hydro Development Corporation to the State Government.

(ii) The rural oustees should be settled in large blocks so that the fabric of their social life remains intact.

(iii) Oustees or their representatives be involved in selecting the rehabilitation centres.

(iv) Community facilities be provided at each of the rural rehabilitation centres at the cost of project even if they did not exist in their earlier settlement.

(v) Minors under the category of land owners are also given the benefits of fully or partially affected families.

## Rural Rehabilitation Package

As per demand of oustees, efforts are being made as far as possible to rehabilitate them in the district of Dehradun and Haridwar or nearby areas by developing rehabilitation sites with all civic facilities and amenities like electricity, irrigation, drinking water, roads, school, dispensary, community centre etc. The affected families are classified either under fully affected or partially affected families. A family whose more than 50 per cent land is under submergence, is being treated as a fully affected family and is to be settled at new rehabilitation sites. The family whose less than 50 per cent land is coming under submergence, is being treated as partially affected family and will be rehabilitated in their own area. The important Rural Rehabilitation packages are

(a) Entitlement of rural families for rehabilitation benefits is determined as on the date of Section-4 notification under the Land Acquisition Act.

(b) Each displaced landowner family to be provided with minimum of 2 acres of developed irrigated land, cost of which would be adjusted against the compensation.

(c) Landless agricultural labourers of fully affected areas are also given 2 acres of land free of cost or half acre of developed irrigated land adjacent to the Municipal limit of Dehradun or Haridwar city subject to availability.

(d) The minimum cash compensation in lieu of land allotment is Rs. 2 lacs.

(e) Compensation of land to the oustees is given as per Land Acquisition Act + ex-gratia at the rate of Rs. 12,000 per acre for irrigated land and Rs. 6000, Rs. 4000 for Class I and II, respectively for unirrigated land.

(f) A house plot of 200 sq.m. on payment of cost at rural resettlement sites.

(g) Rehabilitation grant for shifting of household effects is Rs. 5000 and grant for purchase of seeds and fertilizers is Rs. 4000. An additional incentive grant of Rs. 15,000 per displaced family would be admissible to those who shift to new rehabilitation sites by the end of September, 1999, or within six months from the date of award of compensation of land or date of allotment of land, whichever is later.

(h) Compensation for acquiring a house is paid at PWD schedule rate at the time of acquisition at depreciation value with solatium charges at 30 per cent of deprecated value plus an ex-gratia payment equal to the depreciation amount subject to maximum of Rs. 50,000 while the minimum amount of compensation payable for house structure was Rs. 40,000 from 1 January, 1995.

(i) Stamp duty, if any, will not be borne by the Project-affected person effective from 1 January, 1995. Registration charges, if any will be paid by affected persons.

A Socio-economic survey of Project Affected People (PAP) was carried out by the Administrative Staff College during 1993, to study the condition of PAPs already rehabilitated and those yet to be settled. The study showed that:

(i) The persons engaged in agriculture increased from 24.2 to 30.3 per cent and no one is engaged as agricultural labour after rehabilitation.

(ii) There is harmonious relationship between new settlers and old inhabitants.

(iii) The value of assets of the oustees has increased after they got rehabilitated.

(iv) The average income from agriculture has increased by about 50 per cent after rehabilitation.

(v) The annual income of the household has raised by 34.67 per cent while the annual average expenditure per household has a growth rate of about 60 per cent.

(vi) As per study of 10 per cent of the sample households, one member from each family is employed by Tehri Hydro Development Corporation/Uttar Pradesh Irrigation department. (This gives an extremely rosy picture as an employed person would be of great help but it must be mentioned at this juncture itself, that this survey was conducted only in one Resettlement & Rehabilitation site and in case of employment, only 10 per cent of sample households were taken up).

(vii) The new settlements are provided with pucca buildings with furnishing and electricity in schools as against inadequate educational facilities provided earlier.

(viii) The resettlement sites are provided with medical facilities, which were not available in the submergence sites.

(ix) The new houses are bigger and modern. The agricultural land is allotted in consolidated holding, as against fragment-holding earlier.

(x) The supply of drinking water and LPG connections have been provided/made available as against the traditional collection of water from springs and wood from forests.

This almost ideal picture brought out by the report of the State's own Administrative Staff College seeks to indicate as if there should be absolutely no problems left for the oustees. The report must therefore be seen against persistent grievances and even agitations carried out by the displaced families after 1993 and reports prepared by various NGOs.

The Status Report (May, 2000) showing position as on December, 1999 prepared by R&R Directorate, Central Water Commission, New Delhi is the latest available status on resettlement and rehabilitation of Tehri Project oustees. The extracts relating only to the rural oustees (to the exclusion of essentially urban/town oustees) is proposed to be included here.

(xi) Arrangements are still being made for acquiring additional land.

(xii) 13841 families inclusive of urban/town areas have already been resettled in 8 resettlement sites of Dehradun, Rishikesh and New Delhi township according to their choice.

(xiii) Infrastructure facilities like post office, police station, seed store, electricity, primary middle/high school, primary health centre/dispensaries, drinking water, approach and internal road, panchayat ghar etc., which existed in the affected area are provided in resettlement sites. Seventeen tube wells for irrigation have also been provided.

(xiv) One shopping complex in Bhaniawala relocation site has been provided comprising ten shops.

(xv) State Government has transferred electricity/water supply, roads, irrigation tube wells to THDC for maintenance.

(xvi) Sewing and knitting machines have also been provided along with training at the site visited (Pathri Block site) to augment income of families.

(xvii) Enquiries made by the survey team with the displaced families indicated improved living conditions at the Pathri Block site.

(xviii) The PAPs of Pathri Block site are demanding land rights and declaration of the site as a Revenue village, as in the absence of land holding in their name, it is very difficult to obtain loans.

(xix) The agricultural families informed that the supply of water to their fields is not sufficient and some tube wells of Pathri Block are not functioning properly. They are demanding to connect their guls viz. small traditional irrigation channels, to Ganga canal by constructing the branch canal.

(xx) One settler complained of non-payment of compensation for the submerged land while another complained that the land allotted to him is less than 2 acres. Two settlers complained that in spite of having deposited money towards cost of a residential plot, they have not yet been given possession of the same.

**Confusing Reports.** An overview of the resettlement and rehabilitation of rural oustees of Tehri dam as brought out in the socio-economic survey conducted by the Administrative Staff College in 1993 and the Status Report of May, 2000 by the Central Water Commission indicate that the resettlement and rehabilitation is progressing satisfactorily. If these are compared with the reports of independent NGOs there appears a lot of confusion about even basic facts, total disregard to Government's own orders and sometimes the inhuman attitude of the project authorities towards affected human beings making huge sacrifices to the 'national cause' and the strong smell of fishy and corrupt practices.

It is shameful for an organization that it does not know how many people it is required to look after. Even after 27 years of the Tehri Dams start-up, Tehri Hydro Development Corporation does not seem to be sure of the number of Project Affected People. The Environmental Impact Assessment for the Project (1990) estimates 97,000 R PAPs but current data of Tehri Hydro Development Corporation adds up to only 67,500. In the circumstances, it is natural for affected people to doubt the credibility of THDC from the very start. The project therefore, failed to inculcate a feeling of trust and partnership with the local people. A difference of 29,500 human beings on a base of 97,500 is no small matter to ignore. If such a large proportion of people are being denied Resettlement and Rehabilitation facilities, it is a matter of serious human rights violation.

Another shocking aspect of RR progress is that in four years between 1997 and 2001, the project authorities have made actually negative progress in land acquisition for rehabilitation of affected families. The World Commission on Dams remarked that at least 75 per cent of some 40 million people displaced by large dams in India over the past five decades have never been resettled.

## Test Questions

1. A National Policy is needed for the resettlement and rehabilitation of families that will be affected by a Project.
2. Point out the case for the Rural Rehabilitation Package for people ousted from Dam.
3. Cash compensation should be given to the people ousted as a result of land taken from them for construction of Dam. Justify the demand of such people.
4. Do you support the government policy for taking agricultural land from the cultivators? Give your arguments.

# 17

# Equal Pay For Equal Work

The problem of equal wage presents itself as a special case of wage-differentials which have assumed various forms between regular and overtime hours; the sexes, races and age groups; various occupations; industries; districts and regions within the country and lastly between different nations. The principle of 'equal pay for equal work' has been taken to imply (i) equal pay for equal effort and sacrifice, (ii) equal pay for equal product and (iii) equal pay for equal value to the employer. These differences are given in the interpretation because of the vagueness in the term 'equal work'. The first interpretation is unsatisfactory, for effort and sacrifice cannot be precisely measured. The more common interpretation is the second one which takes into account the amount and quality of the output as the measure of equal work. The third interpretation is given by the employers. For them the output per worker for a given 'unit' of work is not a satisfactory index of value, because the employment of women involves special overhead charges, and hence the 'overall value' of women's outputs is diminished. The above differentiations are, however, not generally accepted. The most familiar is the interpretation given by the Trade Unionists which is accepted by the Royal Commission on Equal Pay. It is in terms of 'the rate for the job' and as very seldom the two jobs are quite the same in all respects 'equal work implies work not only in the same job but also in similar and comparable jobs'.

The main source of difficulty with regard to these definitions is the meaning of the term 'equal work'. The Royal Commission expressed its doubt as to whether 'very diverse activities' could be regarded as 'similar and comparable'. We take it that in the context of our enquiry, equality signifies at least some degree of similarity between employments; but we are unable to discover any general principle in the light of which to decide what degree of similarity is required in order that the work done in two employments may be described as either being unequal or as being equal'.

Moreover, even in case of jobs which may fairly be considered as providing 'similar work' the phrase 'equal work' is vague; for it may imply either (i) similarity in the nature of the work, or (ii) work of equal value to the employer.

The two jobs providing 'equal work' may be of unequal value to the employer firstly because of the differences in the quality and quantity of the product, and therefore, the 'equal work' for which equal pay is claimed must be work not only of the same kind but of the same amount. When 'the rate for the job' is a time-rate the claim implies that differences in output are inconsiderable, or at least not greater between man and woman than between man and man. Even when 'the rate for the job' is a piece-rate, though earnings per hour will now vary with output, the slower worker is still worth less because he raises cost per unit of output. Secondly, they may be of lower 'overall value' to the employer due to the special overhead charges being incurred on account of them. But taking the principle to imply 'rate for the job,' the inequality in respect of 'overall value' is to be left out of account and to this extent the principle will not imply the same thing as 'equal pay for equal value to the employer'.

## I. Causes of Inequality

The recognition of the principle of Equal Pay has been based mainly on considerations of social justice. Before analyzing the basis of claim for Equal Pay and considering the implications and probable consequences of removing the inequality in pay for different sexes in the same occupation, it is necessary to classify the cause of such an inequality. This problem may be discussed under the following heads:

**Economic Factors**

Firstly, it is contended that because of the lower physical strength of the female workers, they are not suited to many of the industries requiring hard work and, therefore, there may be fewer remunerative jobs left for them. This statement does not imply that women are, 'in any absolute sense, less efficient than men'. It has been found that the 'productive efficiency' of the female workers (as compared to male workers) varies from occupation to occupation. In some, such as nursing and cotton spinning, it is much greater than others like coal mining and iron moulding. Nevertheless, the occupations left open for women workers is still very narrow and 'the range of occupations in which strength and endurance are of preponderant importance is still great enough to exert a strong influence upon the relative intensity of the demand for men's labour and women's labour in general,' and so upon the relative rates of remuneration.

Secondly, it is maintained that because of the lower productivity of women workers, the production cost is increased. The British Employers' Federation, in its memorandum to the Royal Commission on Equal pay asserts that the output of women workers is in general lower than that of men and that even in cases where men and women workers are employed at identical piece-rates, the earnings of men are in general greater than those of women 'thereby increasing, the number of workers required for a given amount of production and overhead costs involved in respect of accommodation, machinery, supervision, inspection and administration of labour generally'. The enquiry conducted by the Royal Commission on Equal Pay also confirms the lower productivity of women. The claim is, however, disputed by the Trade Unionists. Certain investigations in Canada and USA show that women often produce as much or more than men. It has also been argued that the lower productivity of women is due to the fact that they are compelled to enter occupations having a low value output, owing to the more limited range of occupations open to an appreciable number of them. Since 'equal pay for equal work' refers to a given category of work, *ex-hypothesis* the question of differential productivity does not arise. On a different assumption (although there is insufficient evidence in support of the view that female labour is less productive), however, the employment of female labour will raise the production cost and consequently prejudice the employment of women and depress the demand for their labour.

Thirdly, to young women with prospects of early marriage it is less worthwhile than the men to acquire proficiency and skill, because they do not follow any occupation as a regular vocation throughout their life. On the other hand, a labour force composed of male workers considers its occupation as more or less permanent. The employers, therefore, regard less useful a labour force which is subject to 'rapid depletion and new recruitment' than one which considers its occupation as a more or less permanent employment. In India, however, this factor is less effective as 50 to 60 per cent of the female workers in different industries are married.

Fourthly, the higher rate of absenteeism among women is alleged to be another factor causing the wage-differentials. The Royal Commission considered that 'it must be a factor in reducing the overall efficiency of women'. But the information collected by the Government of India, Ministry of Labour does not show any significant difference in the magnitude of absenteeism between men and women workers, and as there is no sufficient evidence of a higher rate of absenteeism for women it cannot be regarded a factor 'in reducing the overall efficiency of women'.

Fifthly, most women normally do not have to support a family or dependants and they regard their *income as supplementary* to the family income rather than essential. But there are also less fortunate women responsible for the entire family. As 'the claims for the women as a whole are governed by the *needs* of those who have themselves to support', it will be interesting to study the marital status of the women workers. The data collected by the Government of India, Ministry of Labour, in the eight important industries (Cotton Textile, Silk, Jute, Coal Mines, Municipalities, Paper Mills, Chemicals and Steel) indicate that the unmarried women (who may be regarded as free from financial responsibility for family) were, except in the silk industry (28.4 per cent) in Bombay and Cotton Textiles (25.3 per cent) in Coimbatore, employed in very insignificant numbers. Considerable proportions of women workers are either married or widowed. The married women (whose earnings may broadly be regarded as supplementary to the family income) formed roughly 50 to 80 per cent of the women workers, whereas the widowed women (whose earnings may broadly be regarded as essential to support a family) formed 20 to 50 per cent of the women workers. And it is the number of these women which is of decisive influence on the labour market. Supply of these women workers is inelastic in the sense that they will be prepared to accept lower wages because of the greater intensity of their family needs.

Further, as a majority of the women workers do not expect to support a family, it has been argued that if minimum wages are to be calculated on the basis of family requirement there is every justification for rating standard family at lower number of consumption units in case of female workers. The Royal Commission has held the view that there was no antithesis between the wage claims based on productivity and on the family needs. It has broadly agreed with the demand for their labour being a more important factor in the wage determination than the family needs. It is evidently impressed by the fact that 'virtually all men are and always have been and always will be in the market for employment', and that the proportion of women workers seeking employment is variable due to the influence of social forces.

Sixthly, in India, as elsewhere, there is a traditional division of labour based on sex. Certain occupations have been considered suitable for men and some others for women. For example, in mining, women are usually employed only on surface and open working. In the cotton and jute mills their employment is confined to a few departments. In cotton mills they are employed mostly in the reeling and winding departments. Similarly in the Jute Mills industry they are employed mostly in the batching, preparing and finishing department. It has been observed that '....due to employment of women in certain occupations for a long time, a sort of convention has developed whereby these occupations have come to be known as "*maghi*" jobs or women's jobs'. This traditional distribution of labour on the basis of sex has created separate labour markets for men and women with the result that the movement of labour from one labour market to another has been very limited, thus depressing the demand for women's labour by restricting their employment opportunities. In addition to this immobility of labour from one labour market to another, there is also the fact of mobility differentials as between men and women. Mostly, the mobility of men has been reported to be higher than that of women.

Lastly, in so far as the inequality in wages is due to imperfect competition, it can be removed by suitable measures, without creating any economic dislocation and will be in accordance with social policy. It is important, therefore, from the point of view of policy formation to analyse the competitive process and its effects on wage-differentials. This analysis cannot be undertaken here. It may, however, be pointed out that mainly because of domestic responsibilities, collective bargaining is less developed among women workers than it is among male workers. This factor operates as a defect in the competitive process. The organized employers resist an increase in the supply price of women's labour and the women, being unorganized, are unable to take advantage of the potentially favourable conditions of demand for their labour.

## Social Factors

Prof. R.F. Harrod maintains that the economic system which has resulted in unequal pay has been maintained due to its having served certain deeper social purposes and gives two social causes for unequal pay. Firstly, 'to secure that the position of the national income flowing into the hands of parents is not unduly restricted'; he therefore advocates unequal pay on the ground that 'the proposal to raise the rates of women to equality with those of men is the same as a proposal to reduce the income of parents'. This argument is based on the assumption of a larger proportion of unmarried women being occupied in the labour market-which is true in case of the British occupational structure; it will not hold in the Indian context where a large proportion of employed women being either married or widowed – who are helping in or wholly bearing the family responsibility – the social purpose or advantage to parents will certainly not be hindered but furthered by equal pay.

Prof. Harrod's second argument is based on the social role of motherhood. He says, 'to secure that motherhood as a vocation is not too unattractive financially compared with work in the profession, industry and trade'. He justly advocates that the highest priority should be accorded to parenthood in the context of a rapidly declining birth rate in the UK. In India, however, equal pay will further the social purpose by providing indirect incentive to family planning.

## II. Wage-Differentials in India

The level of wages of the women workers in relation to those for men in the various industries and regions has been discussed in the *Economic and Social Women Workers in India*. The differences are analysed below.

According to the Bombay Textile Labour Enquiry Committee, in 1937, women winders in the cotton mills at Bombay and Ahmedabad were in receipt of an average wage of Re. 0-9-11 and Re. 0-8-5 per day while men employed in similar jobs were getting an average wage of Re. 0-11-7 and Re. 0-9-11 per day. Similarly, women workers received lower wages in the reeling department at Ahmedabad (Re. 0-8-7 per day) as compared to men workers (Re.0-11-6 per day). However, in the drawing tenters section of the cotton mills at Ahmedabad and Sholapur women workers received daily wages (Rs. 1-0-2 Re. 0-9-9, respectively), nearly as much as the men workers (Rs. 1-0-4 and Re. 0-9-8, respectively).

**Cotton Textiles**

A comparison of the average earnings of men and women workers in the Cotton Textile Industry made by the Labour Investigation Committee (1944-45) shows that although the wages of women in general were lower than those of men at the various centres, the differences were not much pronounced. In a few centres and units of the industry like Coimbatore and West Bengal, however, women received much lower wages than men.

According to the Labour Investigation Committee, 1944-45, the differentials in the basic rates of wages and average earnings for men and women workers were not pronounced. In many instances women were paid equal basic wage-rates with men. The differences were further narrowed down as a result of the fixation of wage rates by the Industrial Tribunal without making any discrimination on the basis of sex. Thus although men and women employed in similar occupations were paid at almost equal rates of wages, the annual earnings of men and women employed in the Jute Mill

**Jute Mill Industry**

Industry on the whole for the year 1951 show that annual earnings of female workers (Rs. 507) were only three-fourths of the annual earnings of male workers (Rs. 672), which is presumably due to the fact that 'the employment of men in skilled and semi-skilled jobs for which wage rates are comparatively high, is relatively more than that of women'.

### Other Factory Industries

The average annual earning for men and women workers in 10 other factory industries, as given in the above-mentioned report for the year 1948, shows large differences. The earnings were remarkably lower in iron and steel, match, engineering and vegetable oil industries for women (being Rs. 557, Rs. 272, Rs. 494 and Rs. 200, respectively) as compared to men workers (being Rs. 1,273, Rs. 949, Rs. 824 and Rs. 545, respectively). These differences are mostly due 'to the concentration of women in the lower paid unskilled jobs and larger percentages of men employed in the skilled and semi-skilled jobs' and do not necessarily imply differences in the rates of wages paid to men and women for similar work.

### Coal Mines

A survey of the average daily earnings of men and women working on the surface in the Jharia and Raniganj Coal Fields during the last decade indicates that the earnings of women workers have throughout, been lower than those of male workers. In December, 1942, the daily earnings of female workers working on surface in Jharia and Raniganj were only Re. 0-5-3, and Re. 0-4-9 as compared to Re. 0-8-3 and Re. 0-7-3, respectively for the male workers and this difference had not been reduced up to December, 1950 when the earnings for women workers were Rs. 1-3-0 and Rs. 1-2-0 as compared to men workers being Rs. 1-10-9 and Rs. 1--11-3. In 1952 in Madhya Pradesh, Orissa and Bikaner States the average weekly cash earnings of women workers were even less than half (being Rs. 4-10-6, Rs, 3-7-5 and Rs. 4-1-6, respectively) of the earnings of the male workers (being Rs. 9-5-1-, Rs. 8-4-6 and Rs. 8-12-8, respectively). Since 1947, however, the wages of colliery workers have been gradually standardised as a consequence of the awards of the Conciliation Boards in different States so far as piece-rates are concerned and the Conciliation Boards have not discriminated between men and women workers; time-rates, however, vary in different States. Whereas in Bihar and West Bengal coal fields, equal minimum basic wages have been fixed by awards, a lower wage for women workers has been fixed by award in the case of Madhya Pradesh, Assam and Hyderabad coal fields.

## Plantations

The average monthly cash earnings of male and female workers in the tea plantations in Assam show large differences. In 1929-30 the earnings of women workers was only Rs. 8-5-2 per month whereas for the male workers it was Rs. 10-2-5 per month. This difference has not been reduced in the subsequent years and up to 1949-50 the earnings of female workers (Rs. 15-15-1 per month) was only three-fourths of that of the male workers (Rs. 21-12-5 per month). The difference was largely because of the lower rates of wages paid to the women workers and also due to the higher degree of absenteeism of women workers in the plantations.

In the Public Works departments of the Central and State Governments, the rates of wages paid to men and women workers also show wide differences. The minimum daily rates of wages fixed for the Central Public Works Department in 1951 shows varied differences for the male and female workers in the different States. In the Ajmer State it was only Re. 0-13-0 for female workers as compared to Rs. 1-8-0 for male workers whereas in Delhi it was as high as Rs. 1-8-0 for the female workers as compared to Rs. 1-12-0 for the male workers.

The daily wages paid to the women workers employed in River Valley Projects are also very low as between the male and female workers. In the Hirakud and Bhakra Nangal, the daily wages of unskilled women workers were Re. 1-0-0 and Rs. 1-12-0 only as compared to Rs. 1-8-0 and Rs. 2-0-0, respectively for the male workers.

### III. Movement for Equalisation

With a steady expansion in the number of industries and occupations in which women are employed in doing identical or almost identical work done by men, the problem of equal pay for equal work has received increasing attention. It has been the subject of investigation or negotiation in a number of countries. The principle has been incorporated by the International Labour Organization in a Convention, the various recommendations and a number of resolutions adopted by its various bodies. As early as 1919, in Article 41 of its Constitution the ILO affirmed 'the principle that men and women should receive equal remuneration for work of equal value'. The recommendation (No. 3) concerning the application of the Minimum Wage Fixing Machinery adopted in 1928 reaffirms this principle incorporated in the original Constitution. The recommendation (No. 71) concerning the employment organizations in the transition from war to peace, adopted in 1944, calls for 'the establishment of wage rates based on job content, without regard to sex, in order to place women on a basis of equality with men in the employment market'.

The ILO in the preamble of its amended Constitution adopted in 1946, recognized the principle of equal remuneration for work of equal value as one of the means by which labour conditions could be improved. Convention (No. 82) concerning the social policy adopted in 1947 states that 'it shall be an aim of social policy to abolish all discrimination among workers on grounds of race, colour, sex . . . . . . in respect of wage rates, which shall be fixed according to the principle of equal pay for work of equal value in the same operation and undertaking.....'. It formed the topic of a resolution adopted by the Economic and Social Council of the United Nations (10 March 1948) on the basis of the memorandum on equal pay submitted to it by the World Federation of Trade Unions. The Memorandum to the Commission on the Status of Women for further consideration was transmitted by the United Nations Economic and Social Council to ILO. This memorandum formed the basis for the Equal Remuneration Convention, 1951 (Article 2, ILO) which singles out a legally established or recognized machinery for wage determination as a means by which this principle may be applied.

Until recently the principle of equal pay had not found general acceptance in India. Although the Constitution of India, in its Directive Principles of State Policy, has recognised the principle of equal remuneration for workers without discrimination of sex, there are some industrial awards and certain provisions in the Minimum Wages Act which come in conflict with the Directive Principles. Recently some industrial tribunals have, however, made awards in favour of equal pay for men and women. Thus the Labour Appellate tribunal reversing the decision of the Industrial Tribunal (January 1957) regarding Calcutta Coal Mines, made an award to the effect that for the same category of work there should be no disparity between the male and female workers as to wages.

It is rather odd that there should exist a serious gap between some of these industrial awards on the trend and the provisions regarding equal pay contained in the Directive Principles of State Policy. Constitutionally it is, of course, eminently desirable that immediate steps should be taken to remove this anomaly. From an academic point of view, it is, however, most necessary to examine the socio-economic implications of the principle of equal pay before it is taken as an axiom of social policy.

The Royal Commission on Equal Pay has carefully gone into this question. In the following section we discuss this question in the context of Indian socio-economic conditions.

## IV. Socio-Economic Consequences

It is not easy to form a clear picture of the possible socio-economic consequences of Pay Equalisation, for the various factors bearing on the problem may combine or interact in ways which cannot always be foreseen. It may, however, be useful to workout some of the consequences arranged under different headings. These headings refer to different spheres in which the consequences occur; they, however, by no means represent independent categories. We have, therefore, tried to indicate the possible interaction among the effects in these different spheres. This analysis is, however, not as definitive and comprehensive as one might desire.

**Psychological Effects**

Mainly, these will be determined by the prevailing beliefs among the workers about the relative status of the sexes. In case the general belief is favourable to the doctrine of the equality of the sexes, the effects would be most beneficial and would contribute to the lessening of friction and the improvement of the efficiency of women workers by removing their sense of inferiority and grievance against male domination. The men workers too, would feel better since equalization would eliminate their fear of being undercut.

On the other hand, if it is assumed that the attitude of the male workers is not favourable to the doctrine of sex-equality, the effects on them would be far from beneficial. It would engender in them a sense of injustice which would be strengthened by their argument that they had family responsibilities from which women were relatively free. In such a case, the increased efficiency of the males and friction between the sexes will increase rather than decrease. It should, however, be added that the actual consequences will be greatly modified by the relative strength of the beliefs of the two sexes.

It may not be universally correct to assume that women workers believe in the doctrine of sex-equality. Where this belief is absent or weak and the level of wages sufficiently high, pay equalization may not have any beneficial effect on women workers.

**Effects on Health and Efficiency**

The actual effects of this type will largely depend on the changes occurring in the mental attitudes of men and women. If the mental health aspects of pay equalization are all right, it stands to reason that the health of women and therefore their efficiency will also improve, for they would have more spending power. A counteracting fact may, however, not necessary that this increase should take place and there is no factual evidence to support the theory of increased strain of competition with men, unless it is already assumed that the working capacity of women is always lower than that of men.

## Effects on Marriage and Birth Rate

There are two possible consequences. Pay equalization may encourage earlier marriages on the part of women by improving their financial position for it. If this is the case, it may also mean an increased birth rate. Secondly, it may mean postponement of marriage and lower births, for the increased earnings may go towards improving the standards of living. So far as the first possibility is concerned, it is subject to the operation of other socio-economic factors. It assumes a sufficiently high level of real wages, an absence of rural link and a modern western form of marriage institution. In the Indian context, therefore, this possibility is not quite relevant. In any case, early marriage is universal in India. The second possibility depends on the assumption that standards of living are not sufficiently high or that improvement in the standard of living regularly takes precedence over the need for marriage. In both cases the prevailing social attitude is the most important factor.

## Economic Consequences

In economies where the private sector is dominant and the employers believe that the actual output of women is less in comparison to that of men, equalisation of pay is most likely to result in lowering the level of women's employment, though it cannot go beyond the point where it can induce a rise in the wages of men workers. (It is assumed that the initial level of employment is not too low). On the other hand, pay equalisation will always increase the cost of production: however, in planned economies the employers can be made to bear it and thus it need not lead to a price rise and off-set the increase in female labour earnings. It may, however, be urged against this that pay equalization is a further addition to the cost of employing women, for the employers (and the State) have to pay them maternity benefits, etc. This is clearly a short-sighted approach, assuming that population-planning, maternity and such other benefits cannot be regarded as additional cost, since motherhood is a vital service to the economy (and the society).

## Test Questions

1. The ideal of equal pay is based on considerations of social justice. What are the causes of inequality?
2. What are the economic and social factors responsible for inequality in wages?
3. Discuss wage differentials of women workers in relation to those for man in various industries and regions in India.
4. Bring out the socioeconomic consequences of Equalization of Pay.
5. Explain wage differentials in India between men and women.
6. Describe regional differences in wages in different parts of India.

# 18

# Methods of Wage Payment

There are two method of wage-payment — time-rate and piece-rate. These two systems differ in their incentive effects and in their effect on production cost. To overcome difficulties of simple piece rates, premium bonus system was introduced. Nature of progressive system of payments by results has been indicated.

## Time-rates and Piece-rates

The two commonest forms of wage-payment to be found are time-rates and simple piece-rates. Under the former, the worker is paid according to the time for which he works, usually on the basis of so much per hour, but sometimes by the week or month (or for salary-earners even longer). Piece-rate payment is when the worker is paid in direct proportion to the amount of work he turns out. For this to be possible, the work must be easily measurable, consisting of standard 'pieces' which can be counted (e.g., in dozens or hundreds or by gross) or else of output that can be measured by length (like cotton yarn and cloth) or by weight (like coal and ore). The work done must not be continually changing, i.e., it must consist of fairly long-runs of standardized output, to make a system of piece-rates easy to operate; and considerations of quality must not be dominant. In nearly all types of work some minimum standard of quality has of course, to be observed; but in many cases this can be taken care of by an adequate system of inspection, discarding any work that falls below the required minimum. It is only in cases where requirements of quality or precision are too complex or exacting to be handled in terms of a minimum standard that they constitute and obstacle to the operation of a piece-rate system, which places a premium on quantity at the expense of quality. This is why some of the most skilled work, especially of older types where manual skill is mainly involved and the work is little mechanized and unstandardized, is usually paid on a time-rate basis.

The two systems differ markedly in their incentive effect and in their effect on production cost. The first is obvious enough: if what one earns in a day or a week rises with one's output, one will have more inducement than under time-rates to step-up one's rate of output, at any rate up to the point where the extra strain and fatigue of working more intensively makes the extra payment no longer worthwhile. This is recognized by the common assumption based on fairly wide experience that output on piece-rates is higher by a quarter or a third than comparable work paid by time-rates. Piece-rates have, therefore, been a traditional method whereby employers have secured higher speeds of work from their employees and hence (given the price of out-put) more profit per man employed. When we come to the effect on employers' costs per unit of output, however, the position is not that simple as might seem at first sight. If the employer by putting his men on piece-rates secures, say, a 30 per cent increase of output, he has also to pay a 30 percent higher wage-bill in order to get it; and accordingly, so far as wages go, his cost per unit of output will be the same as before, and if his capital were to consist solely in outlay on wages, his profit as a ratio to capital would not be any higher than before. Where he would gain would be with regard to various fixed costs which did not vary with output, such as plant and equipment and buildings and administration; these would now represent a lower figure when averaged out over total output. Accordingly, there is likely to be a special inducement to adopt piece-rates (or some other system of payment by results, which we would discus in this chapter) where fixed costs bulk large in total costs.

The output-rate may not, however, differ only because of the worker's own exertions or skill; and it is a common fallacy to believe that this is the main reason for high or low output. In most cases it depends to a much larger extent on the machinery with which the worker is working, on the manner in which the works organized (e.g., whether the operation involved is complex or simple, whether the work consists of long runs of standardized output, or a series of short runs of different things requiring frequent adjustment of machinery and work-rhythm). Where such conditions differ between different firms in the same industry, under a system of uniform piece-rates these differences will cause the worker's earnings to vary according to whether he is employed in a relatively efficient or an inefficient firm. The firm's costs, on the other hand, so far as these consist of wages, will be standardized and will be the same per unit of output for the efficient and the inefficient firm. Again, if a firm in the course of time improves its efficiency by new machinery and organization, and thereby raises its output rate, it will not as a result get any reduction in benefits by spreading certain fixed costs over a larger output. Under a time-rate system of payment, by contrast, the higher the output-rate, the lower the cost per unit of output to the firm, while the worker will earn the same (given uniform hours per week) whether he is employed by an efficient and up-to-date or an inefficient and old-fashioned firm.

It is for this reason that where conditions of the kind we have spoken about differ at all appreciably between different firms or different sections of an industry, or are likely to change in the course of time, allowance is commonly made for this in the way that a piece-rate system is applied. In such cases it is very rare to have a piece-rate system unrelated to a standard of normal time-earnings. For example, it may be that, instead of a uniform piece-rate over a whole industry or occupation irrespective of circumstances, the piece-rate is fixed at a different level for different districts, or even for different firms, according to the particular circumstances governing the output-rate. This is the case, for instance, under the national wage-agreement between trade union and employers' federation in the boot and shoe industry in Britain; the national agreement stipulating that piece-rates shall be so fixed by local negotiation in each locality as to enable a 'normal worker' to earn a given amount each week. In some cases there may even be a machine-rate as well as a job-rate: that is, a special piece-rate for a worker doing a job on a particular type of machine; and it is quite common to find it stipulated in wage-agreements (e.g., in the British engineering industry) that when the machinery or methods of production change, the piece-rate for the job can be altered. How much alteration there is in such a case will be, of course, a matter of bargaining prevailing or if the matter goes to arbitration, the question of principle is raised as to how far the results of higher productivity due to improved methods of production should accrue to wages or to profit (or in a State-owned industry, perhaps to consumers of the product in lower prices).

Another example is the traditional systems of payment that have prevailed in the cotton industry. In cotton spinning, the amount spun varies both with the quality of the yarn and with the nature of the machine (whether slow or fast) also with the quality of the raw material, which affects the number of breakages of thread in the course of spinning. The strain on the worker as a machine-minder varies with the number of spindles he has to tend and the tendency for breakages to occur. It is usual for the piece-rate paid per amount of yarn spun to be adjusted automatically, under the so-called 'lists' of prices, according to some if not all of these factors: for example, according to the 'count' or quality of the yarn, if not according to the spinning-speed of the machinery. Similarly, in weaving, the length of cloth woven depends not only on the efficiency of the loom and the width of the cloth, but also on the complexity of the weave; and allowance for such factors is commonly made in the piece-rate lists that govern payment per unit of length woven.

In other cases, both the type of job and the conditions under which it is done, are sufficiently standardized to make possible the drawing up of standard piece-rate lists for various jobs. In such cases, the piece-rates can be negotiated by trade union with collective bargaining for a whole industry and laid down in a comprehensive list for all jobs. But this may not always be the case. Work may be insufficiently standardized for this to be done. Jobs may not be capable of precise definition or may vary from time to time. Trade unions may oppose the introduction and use of piece-rates, because time-rates can easily be made the subject of a collective bargain covering the whole trade, whereas a piece-rate system cannot and will either render collective bargaining impossible or leave numerous loopholes and possibilities of evasion in any negotiated list of piece-rates.

There are other circumstances that determine the comparative effects of the two methods of payment on the interests of the two sides. Where the speed of work is predominantly a matter of the worker's own effort, the incentive-force of piece-rates will be greatest and this method of payment is most likely to be favoured by employers. Under conditions of modern technique, however, an increasing amount of work is of such a kind that output-speed is governed by the pace of machinery, as for example in automatic production processes of all kinds. In such cases, payment on a time-basis is common. Indeed, it may happen that in some cases of this kind, when the speeding up of the mechanical process lays a greater strain on the worker, it is the trade union side that presses for payment to be proportional to output in order that the wage-earners may be compensated for the strain of higher speeds.

Another circumstance affecting the advantage of piece-rates from an employer's standpoint may be the ease or difficulty of supervision. Where work is concentrated within a comparatively small area, it may be easy to supervise, and an employer may find it cheaper to engage some extra foremen and supervisors to obtain the output standard he requires than to put all his workers on piece-rates. Where, on the other hand, work is individualized and more scattered (e.g., in a mine), constant supervision is either impossible or would be too expensive. When work takes the form of group-work or gang-work, individual piece-rates may not be possible, because there is no way of distinguishing individual contributions to the total result. But here, some system of group piece-rate or bonus-system based on group-output is measurable and there is some easy basis for allotting collective payment among the individual members of the group.

A fear that is often expressed by workers is that, if under the inducement of an attractive piece-rate they speed-up their work and earn more, the rate may then be cut by the employer, leaving them in the end working harder but earning no more than they did originally. This fear of 'rate-cutting' has often been the basis of workers' hostility towards conversion of any rate to piece-rate. It is most likely, of course, to happen where workers are unorganized and lack the protection of a trade union agreement, and is less likely to be an objection where workers are protected by a strong trade union organization. It may also be the fear of such rate-cutting that encourages concerted 'go slow', or tacit agreement among workers to put a 'ceiling' on the output-rate, to prevent earnings going so high as to cause the management to think that the piece-rate has been set too generously and ought to be revised.

Another case where payment by results is apt to be distrusted by workers is where interruptions of work or breakdowns are likely to occur at intervals (whether due to interruptions in supply of raw materials or arrivals of orders and blue-prints from the office or to failures of power or machinery). This will cause earnings to fall through no fault of the workers. In mining, however on a difficult seam, one may find coal-getting interrupted for long stretches owing to the amount of preparatory work needed in opening up the seam. It is in such cases that trade unions generally demand, as a protection, a minimum time-rate below which earnings shall not fall, as a floor to the operation of a piece-rate system; a piece-rate thus being combined with a minimum time-rate.

## Bonus Based on Standard Time

In an attempt to get around some of the difficulties involved in simple piece-rates, some employers have devised more complex bonus systems by setting a certain time for a job and giving a bonus if the job takes less time than that. This method was, indeed, anticipated when piece-rates took the form, not of pricing each operation or 'piece' of output (into which a complex job might not necessarily be divisible), but of allotting a certain 'time allowance' for the job as a whole and paying for the job at the time-rate of the 'time-allowance'. Thus, a certain, job (e.g., plastering the walls and ceilings of a house or dockers unloading a cargo) might be given a 'time allowance' of, say, 10 hours, and when finished the job would be paid at 10 times the hourly time-rate, irrespective of the actual time taken over it.

Thus, if the workers finished the job in, say, 8 hours, they would be paid at the time-rate equivalent to 10 hours and would receive in effect a bonus of 2 hours; and provided that work was plentiful they could, after finishing one job, start another and so earn more in each week. But of course they would get paid exactly the same in proportion to the effort expended, whether they finished the job in 6 hours or in 8 or 10 or 12.

The dividing line really came when a bonus was started being given for the time saved on the standard time. In what are known as Premium-Bonus Systems, the basic payment is the time-rate for the hours actually worked (and not for the time allowed); and onto this, a bonus is added if the actual time taken is less than the standard time. There are several ways in which this may be done. The two systems that are best known are the Halsey-Weir and the Rowan; the difference between them being that, under the former the bonus consists of a certain proportion of the time-rate for the time saved, while under the latter the bonus is expressed as a percentage depending on the ratio of the time saved, to the time allowed. Thus under the Halsey System (which was first introduced in Canada in 1890), if the time-allowance is 10 hours and the job is done in 8 hours, the worker gets paid the normal time-rate for the 8 hours worked with a bonus equal to half the time-rate for the 2 hours saved. It will be obvious that this is less favourable to the worker than the piece-rate based on paying for the time allowed for the job. Under Halsey-Weir bonus, payment increases less than in proportion to the increased speed of work it induces; for which reason it is sometimes spoken of as an example of regressive payment by results. For this reason it was strongly opposed by the engineering trade unions in England when it was first introduced, passing a resolution against it. The Trade Union Congress of 1909. Professor G.D.H. Cole in his 'Payment of Wages' said: 'This system has only the merit of simplicity' (p. 50). At the same time its effect on costs will be to reduce the wage-cost per unit of output with higher speed of work. This was no doubt one of the reasons why it acquired a measure of popularity among employers. What was officially said in its favour was that it avoided the difficulties arising from fixing piece-rates too high.

Under the other system, the Rowan (first introduced in a Glasgow firm of marine engineers in 1898), if the standard time is 10 hours and the job is done in 8 hours, the worker again gets paid the normal time-rate for the 8 hours worked, but the bonus added on to this basic payment will be 20 per cent (which is the ratio of the two hours saved to the standard time of 10). Had the job been done in as little as 5 hours, the bonus would have been 50 per cent on top of the basic payment for the 5 hours worked. It is again less favourable to the workers than a simple piece-rate; but it will be more favourable to them than the Halsey-Weir bonus for comparatively small increases in the output-rate; but as the output-rises (and the 'time saved' increases) it becomes progressively less favourable than the other type of bonus.

A great deal depends, of course, on whether the standard time for a job under such systems is set leniently or severely, at the level of the majority of workers, of the average or of the fastest; and it is for this reason that trade unions are apt to be particularly suspicious of or hostile to such methods if the calculation is left to the management or even to outside 'experts'. They regard control over the setting of such standard times as being of equal importance as control over a list of job-prices under a piece-rate system. It was largely because collective bargaining over such matters was difficult and the introduction of such payment systems was apt to mean reversion to individual bargaining, that their introduction was for so long opposed by trade unions in the British engineering industry, although with greater trade union strength and greater standardization of engineering products and methods, trade union's acceptance of payment by results has in the past few decades, become more general.

## Differential Piece-rates and Progressive Bonus Systems

Finally, we have a group of payment systems which yield a more than proportional increase of earnings for increases in output beyond a certain minimum or standard output-rate. We may accordingly speak of them as 'progressive' systems of payment by results, by contrast with the 'regressive' type of which we spoke above. In view of what we said about the advantages of the latter to an employer, it might seem hard to believe that 'progressive' systems could even be to an employer's advantage, since their effect is to increase the wage-cost of a unit of output, the more successful they are in stimulating, more output. Clearly, they are only likely to be favoured where either there are very large fixed costs, whose fall per unit of output more than compensates for the rise in unit wage cost, or where they are considered to have some special advantage such as setting new efficiency standards or 'skimming the cream of the labour market' by offering better earning-opportunities than other firms or industries to fast workers.

One form of this is the Differential Piece-Rate, under which the actual piece-rate paid per unit of output is itself raised as the output-rate rises (and correspondingly lowered for low output-speeds). A fast worker is thereby doubly benefited, by being paid more for more output and being paid for the whole output at a higher rate, and a slow worker is doubly penalized. This type of payment was associated with the introduction of the Taylor-system of so-called 'scientific management' in America and had as its aim the popularization of the new work-methods and the attraction of the most efficient workers to the firms adopting them. Critics of the scheme alleged that it was a device for attracting younger and healthier workers, working them out earlier and then throwing them on the scrap-heap.

Another form is a system of bonuses whereby, the bonus for additional output gets greater, the higher the output-rate above a certain 'norm' or standard. For example, a 10 per cent increase in output above standard may bring a 15 per cent rise in earnings above the basic wage, a 20 per cent increase in output a 30 per cent rise in earnings, a 30 per cent increase in output a 45 per cent rise in earnings, and so on (it is clear that there can be a great number of different relationships between the increases of output and of earnings). This kind of progressive bonus system has been widely used in the industry of the socialist countries, being associated in particular in the USSR in the 1930s with the Stakhanovite Movement, and its attempt to encourage emulation among workers in acquiring new standards of efficiency. The output-norms on the basis of which the bonus-system operated were fixed each year in relation to the new output-targets of the annual plan. One recent example from enterprises of the Ministry of Machine tool Construction (UK) is as follows:

Standard Percentage of increase in earnings above.

| output | basic-piece-wage |
|---|---|
| 1–10 | 30 |
| 10–25 | 50 |
| 25–40 | 75 |
| 40 and more | 100 |

More recently the system has come under criticism on the ground that it has made a disproportionately large part of normal earnings consisting of bonus, so that if through interruption of work for any reason the output rate falls, and workers fall back on the 'basic wage' and, they are disproportionately penalized. This is, of course, the danger in some degree of any 'progressive' system (unless it is prevented by the setting of a fairly high 'floor' below which earnings cannot fall). In view of such criticisms recent changes in the socialist countries seem to have been in the direction of raising the basic wage and reducing the steepness of the progressive bonus increase, thereby bringing basic wage and average earnings closer. This may reduce its force as a production-incentive, but at the same time reduce the number of grievances and disputes arising from anomalous cases and inequitably large fluctuations in earnings.

## Test Questions

1. What are different methods of wage payment? Discuss their relative merits and demerits.
2. Why the trade unions oppose piece-rates? Do you think that their apprehension is based on wrong thinking?
3. Discuss the principle of bonus based on standard time.
4. Briefly explain the progressive systems of payment by results.

# 19

# Job Evaluation

Job evaluation is concerned with assessing the value of one job in relation to another. It helps in securing internal and external consistency in wages and salaries. Job evaluation depends on job analysis and job description. Four methods of job evaluation are (1) Ranking system, (2) Job classification system, (3) Points rating and (4) Factor comparisons system. Conditions for the success of job evaluation are (1) Participation of unions, (2) Simplicity, (3) Joint implementations, (4) No pre-emption of collective bargaining, (5) Wage survey and (6) No reduction of existing wages.

Cases of job evaluation are (1) it is a means of determining internal pay structure, (2) instrument of company's pay policies, (3) control over wage and (4) a realistic foundation for gearing company pay scales to those of competing companies.

## Job Evaluation Methods

Some form of job evaluation is invariably part of a formal wage and salary programme. The objective of job evaluation is to price the job rather than the man. Job evaluation is concerned with assessing the value of one job in relation to another for it is only when each job has been properly evaluated, that a sound wage structure can be built. The British Institute of Management had defined job evaluation as the process of analysis and assessment of jobs to ascertain reliably their relative worth, using the assessment as a basis for a balanced wage structure. The ILO defines job evaluation as an attempt to determine and compare the demands which the normal performance of particular jobs make on normal workers without taking account of the individual abilities or performance of the workers concerned. Individual abilities or efforts may, of course, also be taken into account and reflected in the workers' earnings, for example, under a system of payment by result or of merit rating but this is something entirely different from the rating of the job. Job evaluation rates the job, not the man.

Job evaluation is a fairly recent method of wage and salary administration. Formal job evaluation techniques have been in use only since World War I. Originally used for determining the wage of hourly paid workers whose jobs can be relatively accurately described, these techniques are now widely used for determining wages in industry and government.

Job evaluation helps in securing internal and external consistency in wages and salaries. Internal consistency is a matter of a rational relativity of wages within the enterprise. A job requiring a high degree of skill should not normally be rated lower than one requiring a lesser degree of skill. Again, a supervisor should be paid higher than a person he supervises.

External consistency demands that jobs in one firm should not be paid lower than what is paid in comparable jobs in firms in the same area. The principle of external consistency is at times carried to a great extent by the trade unions and workers. The job-evaluation process aims at eliminating wage inequalities which are not related to skills and responsibilities of the workers.

Job evaluation systems are better applied to manual or blue-collar jobs than to white-collar jobs. Managerial jobs, where the discretionary content of the work is high and jobs which cannot be broken up easily into their constituents in a quantifiable manner, are generally kept out of job evaluation processes.

All job evaluation systems depend be heavily on job analysis and job description.

## Preliminary Steps—Job Analysis and Job Description

Job analysis indicates the specific duties to be performed by the worker and the circumstances under which these duties are to be performed. "Job analysis is the process of getting information about jobs; specifically, what the worker does, how he gets it done, why he does it, skill, education and training required; relationships to other jobs; physical demands and environmental conditions".

In other words, job analysis is concerned with assessing the worth of one job in relation to another. It thus places each job in its position in its larger job structure. Analysis of assigned job duties is the first step in the job evaluation process. Evaluation plan would be useless in measuring job worth unless the job duties were accurately determined through job analysis. Information obtained from the analysis of the job duties is recorded in the job description. Job descriptions reflect all the information which is obtained in job analysis. In addition to compiling the factual data regarding job assignments, analysts are called upon to specify the basic requirements necessary to carry out the assigned tasks. When this is incorporated into the job descriptions, the results are commonly referred to as job specifications. Specifications involve judgments regarding the amount of experience and education required, the extent of responsibility involved, the importance of initiative etc.

The information regarding the job is collected by (i) observation, (ii) interviews with the operative and his supervisor, (iii) questionnaire and (iv) a written description obtained from the operative. Under Indian conditions, the last two methods would generally be ineffective and reliance has to be placed on the first two methods.

Job descriptions are prepared primarily to serve as the basis for job evaluation. If the job descriptions correctly indicate an outline of assigned job duties, they may be used by the manager in planning the work of his group. The listing of assigned duties in a job description helps managers to determine reasonable standards of performance for the job and such standards plus the listed duties themselves can help the manager in appraising individual performance. Job description can be useful in analyzing manpower utilization. The manager can consult each description and eliminate time-consuming tasks which are below the general level of work assigned to a job. Less skilled work may then be reassigned to lower paid jobs. Moreover, the manager can study duties in terms of work load to determine how many man hours are required. With this information, he can determine how many employees are really needed for each phase of the work. Finally, job descriptions are useful as a basic management tool. A study of job descriptions may show possible improvements in operating methods by indicating duplication of work, by indicating a better flow of work or by suggesting better use of specialization. Thus job descriptions can be a major management aid if they are carefully prepared.

## Job Evaluation in India

Job evaluation techniques are used in India in the organized sector of industry, but do not generally enjoy the support of trade unions. In the government jobs, the techniques have not yet been systematically employed. The Third Pay Commission had only a sample evaluation done by the Administrative Staff College and have recommended its application, where necessary, by the staff inspection Unit of the Ministry of Finance. What the INTUC stated in a communication to the ILO in 1956, remains, by and large, the true attitude of the trade unions in India even today. The INTUC had found the scheme, as applied to Indian Industries, to be defective because of the absence of consultation with the workers in the evaluation of a scheme, the failure to inform them of the details of the scheme, the absence of union co-operation in the conduct of job evaluation, the failure on the part of the evaluator to carry out essential foundational procedures such as job analysis and description, the failure to evaluate conditions and hazards and the assumption of differentials instead of their ascertainment as a result of job evaluation. Generally, trade unions in India do not welcome job evaluation studies—either because of distrust of employers or lack of technical competence to participate in the process or for fear that the application of the technique might upset the traditional wage structure which, however unscientific, the workers have got used to.

On the other hand, the demand for job evaluation is quite often heard from aggrieved individual workers. There are also a few examples of the successful application of job evaluation techniques in Indian industries carried out with the co-operation of recognized trade unions. For example, the collective agreement dated 8 January, 1956, between the TISCO and the Tata Workers' Union (INTUC) provides that a joint committee consisting of an equal number of representatives of the company and of the union shall be appointed with an independent expert as chairman for the work of job evaluation. The parties agreed that the joint committee shall be accepted by both parties as forming the basis of the future structure of wages and their emoluments. Thereafter, the parties shall negotiate the rates of the future structure of wages and emoluments. The TISCO evaluation system is effective even today.

In India, the Wage Boards which have standardized the wages in most of the major industries have not, at any stage, resorted to the job evaluation system for determining wage relativities or differentials.

## Methods of Job Evaluation

Four principal systems of job evaluation are (1) Ranking system, (2) Job Classification System, (3) Points Rating and (4) Factor Comparisons System.

**(1) Ranking (or Grading) System:** This is a very simple method of job evaluation. Under this system the job raters simply rank one job against another without assigning point values. Jobs within the organization are arranged in some order, from the most difficult to the simplest or in the reverse order. It does not measure the values of jobs but establish their ranks only. When this method is employed, the job rater simply compares two jobs, one against another and asks which of the two is more difficult. Once that question has been settled, another job is compared against the first two and a similar determination is made. This process is repeated until all jobs from the job of the greatest difficulty down to the job with least difficulty have been assigned relative positions. Job ranking is preceded by systematic job analysis and job description. Sometimes job titles and brief job descriptions are recorded on cards and the raters are asked to arrange the cards in the order of importance. The hourly rates to be paid of different jobs are suggested by raters without any consideration to the existing wage rates.

The ranking systems of job evaluation are generally used in small organizations where all jobs are well known to the job rates. The simplicity of this system is its greatest asset. Little preparation as well as little investment is required.

The very simplicity of the system is also its greatest weakness. The system does little to guide the judgment of the raters. Without a formal yardstick, there is a tendency to judge each job on the basis of its dominant factor. The ranking system is extremely difficult to explain to employees because there is no objective norm to guide the judgment of evaluators. Lastly, the ranking system can only tell us that one job is more difficult than another without indicating how much difficult it is.

**(2) Job Classification System:** The job classification system is one of the oldest methods of evaluating jobs and emphasizes allocation of jobs to classes. Job classification system begins with an overall comparison of all jobs on the basis of common sense and experience. The job structure is divided into a number of classes. For each class a general specification is prepared indicating the nature of work and responsibility that are included. Each class is assigned a salary range with maximum and minimum limits. After that, actual jobs are fitted into these predetermined classes. Thus according to this system, the menials may be put into one class, clerks in another, supervisors in a higher class and higher executives on the top class. This system is best suited to small organizations. This is also used in government services. But this is not suitable for a large organization with complicated class specifications.

**(3) Points Rating System:** This is a widely used system in modern business. It is based on the assumption that it is possible to assign points to the different factors as well as to each degree of each factor involved in jobs and that the sum total of the points will give an index of the relative value of jobs. The first step is to decide the factors or elements which cover all the jobs such as, skill, effort, responsibility, working conditions, etc.' and each factor is given a maximum points value. The degree of each factor is determined and these degrees determine the number of points to be assigned to the job. The total of the points assigned for all factors establishes the point value of the job and its value is translated into terms of money on a predetermined formula.

Some firms are using values and points developed from their own experience while others use the system developed by industry-wide organizations.

The points rating system has many advantages over ranking and classification systems. The use of fixed and predetermined factors forces the evaluator to consider the same job elements when rating jobs. The systems have the advantage of forcing job raters to consider individual factors rather than the job as a whole. Moreover, the assignment of point values indicates not only which job is worth more than another, but how much more it is worth. Finally, a clear record of the judgments of the evaluator is later available for explaining the results of the evaluation to superiors and employees alike.

Though this system is commonly used in industry in the UK, it has its limitations. The listing of factors may omit some elements that are important in certain jobs. It is obvious that arbitrary weights are attached to various degree and to the factors by specifying maximum and minimum points. The same points systems cannot generally be used for production and office jobs. Lastly, this system is inflexible.

**(4) Factor Comparison System:** This system is similar to the points rating system and is widely used in business. This method begins by finding out the major factors which are present in varying degree in all the jobs in a particular organization. Usually the most common factors are mental effort, skill, physical effort, responsibility and working conditions. These are not predetermined but are chosen on the basis of job analysis. The second step is to select a number of key jobs – ten or twenty – which can be used for comparing all other jobs. For example, key jobs may be fitter, machine operator, watchman, driver, etc. The money rates of each of these key jobs are already known. This means that the accuracy of the evaluation methods depends to a large extent on whether the key jobs selected for comparison are themselves properly paid or not. In the third step, each of the key job's current rate of pay is analyzed to suggest what per cent of the total rate is attributable to each job element. Thus, it may be found that if a fitter is paid Rs. 10 per day, the first element may be assigned a value of 10 per cent, the second 20 per cent, the third 40 per cent, the fourth 10 per cent and the fifth 20 per cent. When all key job rates have been thus analyzed, averages of the percentage thus obtained, are accepted as weights for the elements. At the final stage all other jobs are appraised and assigned a value on each factor by comparing them with key jobs. Thus for each job to be evaluated a particular key job is found to which it is very similar. Under this system it is the task of the evaluators to analyze all jobs and then to rank them in terms of one factor. If, for instance, the factor being considered is technical skill, the evaluators will first rank all jobs in this respect, from those which require the most, down to those which require the least technical skill. After this step is completed, evaluators will then rank all jobs in relation to a second factor and so forth, until separate rankings have been established for each of the factors involved. As point values have already been assigned, it is only necessary to total point values in order to get the overall relative worth of that job.

The system has two distinct advantages. First, it uses the job-by-job comparison technique which is a far more accurate method of measurement. Secondly, the weights selected are not entirely arbitrary but reflected existing wage and salary practice. The difficulty of the system is that it is very expensive and complicated and cannot be readily explained to the workers.

When job evaluation is completed, the relative difficulty of jobs within the company is determined in terms of point rankings. Thereafter it is easy to assign money value to these jobs in some direct proportion to the points assigned under evaluation.

**(5) Business Criteria evaluation for management posts:** A technique which has developed for evaluating management jobs or for comparing and validating the grading of senior posts can be termed Business or Functional Criteria Evaluation. This is a form of factor comparison where the factors are for specific groups of senior positions, usually in one function at a time.

When considering grading within a group of jobs such as general managers, the basic procedure is to identify all the main criteria which are relevant to evaluation of the group of posts under review. We then assess the relevant level of each job against the criteria, either in ranked order or against weighted scales for the criteria. A simple weighting can be used to arrive at a points score. It is easy to develop use and explain.

**(6) Profile Method of Job Evaluation:** An evaluation technique which has been in use in the USA for a considerable time and which is now finding increased favour in the UK is generally known as the Profile System of job evaluation. It is used mainly for evaluating high-level management jobs.

Basically, it is a points system, but is distinguished by the apparently small number of factors employed, often only three. These factors, however, are multidimensional in that having made a decision on, say the amount of knowledge a job calls for, the experience rating for the job, then has to be read off. Where the degrees of the two factors meet, a point's score for that overall factor then has to be read off. As in many other evaluation systems, if this approach helps the person concerned to think about the job and to analyze it in relation to other jobs, thus arriving at an appropriate grade or salary range, then it has achieved its objective—to grade and price the job in relation to other company jobs under study. The system is just as subjective as any other and has no particular magic.

| Knowledge//Experience | 1-2 Yrs | 2-4 Yrs | 4-8 Yrs | 8-12 Yrs | Over 12 Yrs |
|---|---|---|---|---|---|
| 1. Good basic education without specialization | 10 | 20 | 40 | 80 | 160 |
| 2. Proficiency in a technical subject without professional qualification | 20 | 40 | 80 | 160 | 320 |
| 3. Professional qualifications | 40 | 80 | 160 | 320 | 640 |
| 4. Higher professional qualification | 80 | 160 | 320 | 640 | 1280 |
| 5. Complete professional knowledge of scientific/ management function Profile Method of Know-how | 160 | 320 | 640 | 1280 | 2560 |

## Use of Job Evaluation

Job evaluation is the cornerstone of a formal wage and salary programme. Without determining a relative job's worth into a reasonably defensible manner, it would be difficult to establish a formal programme. Job evaluation process plays a key-role in wage and salary administration in the following ways:

1. Job evaluation is the most effective means of determining internal pay relationships for most types of job.
2. Job evaluation can be used as an instrument for implementing the company's basic pay policies.
3. Equitable base-pay relationships set by job evaluation serve as a foundation for incentive or bonus plans. Through job evaluation, the company is able to establish the standard job value upon which extra incentive earnings, bonus payments or merit increase can be established.
4. Job evaluation provides a reasonable basis for personnel moves. Unless relative classes of jobs are established in the first place, managers will not know whether a personnel move represents a promotion, a demotion or a transfer.

5. Useful controls over wage and salary costs can be greatly aided by job evaluation.

6. Job evaluation provides a realistic foundation for gearing company pay-scales to the pay-scales of competing companies. This, in turn, gives reasonable assurance that the company will get the numbers and types of persons needed to operate the business and, at the same time, maintain wage costs at a competitive level.

7. Job evaluation assists managers in meeting day-to-day pay problems. This in turn contributes to the reduction of employee grievances, to higher employee productivity through higher morale and to more turnover.

Thus, the advantages to be gained from job evaluation are significant. But the establishment of a job evaluation programme may involve a substantial increase in costs. These will include the salaries of the staff devoted to the job evaluation process and the administrative cost inherent in a formal job evaluation programme. Management must weigh these costs against the potential benefits.

## Some conditions for the successful conduct of job evaluation

1. *Participation of recognized unions:* The existence of a strong, recognized union is an essential requirement. In an atmosphere of trade union rivalry, the recognized union may not feel secure enough to agree to participate in any kind of job evaluation.

2. *Simplicity and Clarity:* The scheme adopted should be a simple one and clearly understood by the workers.

3. *Joint implementation:* The system should be implemented jointly by the management and the union. Suitable procedures should be evolved to ensure consultation and participation at all stages and for modification. Even the job description should not be revised without an agreement with the union.

4. *No pre-emption of collective bargaining:* The union should be assured that wage rates for jobs remain negotiable even after job evaluation which only classifies and analyses the jobs in an objective manner and provides a basis for collective bargaining.

5. *No reduction in existing wages:* Normally no worker's wages should be reduced and no individual worker should be down-graded as a result of job evaluation. Existing workers' wages should be protected.

6. *Wages and Salary Surveys:* Before undertaking job evaluation, the management should ensure that wage and salary surveys, at least for the key jobs in the organization, are conducted and relevant information collected.

## Test Questions

1. What do you mean by job evaluation? What are its objectives?
2. Describe job analysis and job description as the basis of job evaluation.
3. What are the conditions for the success of job evaluation? State its issues.
4. Describe the methods of job evaluation.

# 20

# Incentives

Incentives involve a system of payment by results under which, the amount payable to a person is linked with his output. Incentives may be financial and non-financial. Executive compensation practices in India are delineated. Fringe benefits and promotion policies are looked upon as motivators. Major Incentive Plan e.g., Halsey Premium, Rowan Premium Bedeaux's Point, Taylor's differential piece rate, Merris system, Gnatt Task on Bonus and Emerson Efficiency Plan have been identified for calculating incentives.

**Incentives**

Incentives may be defined as a system of payments under which the amount payable to a person is linked with his output. Such a payment may also be called payment by results.

Incentives are of two types: (1) Financial incentives and (2) Non-financial incentives. In the light of the need hierarchy concept, in case of persons operating at the lower level, where the physiological needs are not yet fully satisfied, money can be a very powerful motivator of human conduct. However, as one rises higher in the management hierarchy and therefore in the need hierarchy, money may still be important in view of rising prices and inflation in India, but its importance diminishes and other non-financial incentives becomes more powerful.

There is no escaping the fact that it is necessary to have an adequate compensation programme which will attract and retain key people of superior caliber in the organization. Such a programme would also stimulate such persons to improve their performance. Monetary compensation can be used to reward significant achievements made by them.

**Compensation Programme**

An effective compensation programme would have a base pay and an incentive element besides fringe benefits. The base pay must be equitable when compared with salaries prevailing outside and within the organization for similar jobs. The importance of base pay lies in that it determines many other payments such as the bonus payable and certain fringe benefits. The base pay represents the long-term value of the position whilst the commission and bonus type of payments are the short-term values. The incentive aspect of pay can be used to secure the desired conduct from employees. For example, for salesman, different rates of commission can be given on different types of products. A higher rate should be given for selling a product which is more difficult to sell, but which provides the company with a higher margin of profit. Thus an adequate compensation structure can be devised to motivate the employee in the desired direction by integrating the employee's goals with those of the company.

Fringe benefits like provident fund, free medical treatment etc. do not generally motivate an individual. This is because, after some time these are taken for granted. At the most, they may generate loyalty towards the organization. This is because such benefits, unlike commission, are not directly dependent on increased production or performance.

## Executive Compensation Practices

In India, a survey was conducted during October, 1970, to February, 1971, covering eighteen companies representing a cross section of technologies like textiles, petroleum products and automobiles, having varying sizes and management styles. Attempt was not made to collect data on compensation practices for specific executives such as the company secretary or the marketing manager. Instead, data were collected on compensation package applicable to nine salary levels. The compensation package was divided into several fringe benefit groups. Analysis indicated that the number of items included in the compensation package rose as one ascended the management hierarchy. The increase in the mix of benefits was abrupt at around Rs. 1,600 which the author described as the 'select executive group'. In most of the companies, provision was made for transportation, medical assistance and housing assistance. A very few made allowances for children education or permitted family allowance. Pension was popular at the salary levels exceeding Rs. 1,000.

## Personalized Compensation Plan for Executives

At times it is suggested that in order to motivate executives, a specially tailored compensation plan would be more effective. The compensation paid would naturally depend on the type of industry, the size of the organization as well as the executive's educational level and contribution to the organization. In spite of this, universal scales for compensation are generally used for most executives on the same type of pay scales without taking into consideration the individual's needs and abilities. A personalized compensation plan is therefore suggested in place of such an approach. This type of approach would first "evaluate each key man's contribution to the firm; determine his work pattern and the impact of his services on the profit and growth of the company". In the second step, a financial profile of the employee is made indicating his income and expenses and the extent to which the company's compensation plan meets his requirements. It is suggested that a personalized compensation plan should then be developed on this basis for each executive combining many diverse compensation techniques like salary, bonus and fringe benefits. In this way, it is claimed that the executive would be adequately motivated and would resist the temptation of leaving the organization. On the other hand, it must be realized that preparation of a plan of this type is not an easy matter as equity in compensation has to be maintained. Besides, if this information leaks out, as is very likely, it can result in considerable heart burning and constitute a disincentive instead of an incentive to effective performance.

## The Cafeteria Approach in Salary Fixation

At times, in relation to the personalized salary fixation approach, it is suggested that since the benefits have uniquely to fit the executive's needs, the selection of the mix of benefits should be left to the executive concerned, the only limitation being that this should not exceed the amount allowed, say, as his salary increase. Such an approach would individualize the system. As the choice here is left to the executive, it can be called 'the cafeteria approach.'

## Do Fringe Benefits Motivate Employees?

Some people seem to suggest that apart from the question of compensation in terms of monetary rewards geared directly to an employee's performance, even fringe benefits including bonus motivate an employee. For Example, M.L. Bhatia suggests that apart from legal requirements the employer should take into account the preferences and the perceptions of the employees. He stresses that the "motivational value of a particular item of fringe depends on how it is perceived by the employee to satisfy his particular need or needs". He thereafter gives the result of research studies in the USA. For example, he states the finding of a research that longer vacations come higher than a pay raise in most employees' judgments. Analyzing this aspect, one would like to ask the question as to whether an employee who is given one month's vacation will produce less than an employee who receives two months' vacation. In fact, the longer vacation may make the employee lazy and the laziness he will bring to the work situation on his return. What is to be remembered, to create a motivational situation through a compensation plan, is the fact that unless the payment or offer of any benefit is geared directly to the performance of the employee, it is not likely to result in better or increased performance. Well-perceived fringe benefits can only make the employee more loyal. Why should he not be loyal to such a generous employer who is willing to give benefits not geared to his performance?

## Non-Financial Incentives

Whilst money is an important motivator of human behaviour, in terms of the need hierarchy, it can help satisfy only the 'physiological' needs of the human being. This brings into focus the importance of non-financial incentives of psychic wages aimed at satisfying the other needs in the hierarchy. The psychological need for 'safety or security' can be satisfied by the psychological climate or environment of the work place. Some organizations are noted for their policies of hiring and firing at will, whereas in other organizations a person can retire in old age, although inefficient. Thus a balance has to be struck so that sufficient sense of security is created without encouraging complacency. The human being's need for belongingness and love in the work situation can be met by providing appropriate interaction. In this area, participative management techniques can make a valuable contribution.

As one moves up the employee hierarchy of the management ladder, the needs higher up in the Maslow's Need Hierarchy come into operation. For example, a high level executive has his 'esteem' needs which can often be satisfied by giving him an air conditioned cabin, a motor car and other benefits of this nature which increases his prestige and satisfies his ego.

The employee must be made to feel that he has achieved something through his contributions. Such a feeling of achievement can motivate him to extra effort. Ensure others to know of their accomplishments. Therefore, the person who has achieved something should be praised in public and given recognition in that manner.

The need for self-actualization is present in almost every human being and should be stimulated by providing opportunities for growth and promotion. The only limitation would be that his activities must be directed towards the achievement of appropriate organizational goals.

Some of the non-financial incentives, in brief, are as follows:
(1) Providing responsibility through job enlargement;
(2) Providing involvement or participation;
(3) Creating a sense of achievement;

(4) Providing recognition for accomplishment and

(5) Offering inducement of promotion and growth as a result of effective performance.

## Promotion Policies as Motivators

Adequate policies must be laid down regarding promotion to generate continued motivation of the employees. Promotion refers to assignment to an individual of a position of greater responsibility or increased authority. It normally involves ascending in the management hierarchy or at least an increase in the pay or status or both for the employee concerned. It can be used to supply the employee's need for self actualization and thereby motivate him. In addition, promotion can make the organization more effective by using more productively, the employee's skills. Promotion should also be used as a recruitment source for higher appointments. This would provide a motivational environment.

An adequate promotion policy providing effective motivation would be one which offers the employee a career within the organization itself. A climate has to be created that promotion is not merely based on seniority but that merit plays an important role. To enable an organization to offer such opportunities, it is necessary to initiate adequate succession planning.

## The Chief Incentive Plans

### 1. Halsey Premium Plan

This is a time-saved bonus plan which is ordinarily used when accurate performance standards have not been established. Under this plan, it is optional for a workman to work on the premium plan or not. His day's wages is assured to him whether he earns a premium or not, provided that he is not so incompetent as to be useless. A standard output within a standard time is fixed on the basis of previous experience. The bonus is based on the amount of time saved by the worker. He is entitled to a bonus calculated on the basis of 33 1/3 per cent of the time saved. He thus gets wages on the time rate basis. If he does not complete the standard output within the stipulated time, he is paid on the basis of a time wage. The plan is a combination of the day wage and the piece wage in a modified form.

(a) The merits of the plan are:

(1) It guarantees a fixed time wage to slow workers and at the same time, offers extra pay to efficient workers.

(2) The cost of labour is reduced because of the percentage premium system; the piece-rate of pay gradually decreases with increased production.

(3) The plan is simple in design and easy to introduce.

(4) As the wages are guaranteed, it does not create any heart-burning among such workers are unable to reach the standard.

The disadvantages of the plan are (i) It depends upon past performance instead of making new standards and (ii) From the stand point of the administration, the policy is one of drift for, in this plan, the worker is left alone to decide whether or not to produce more after the standard has been reached.

## 2. Rowan Premium Plan

This plan differs from the Halsey Plan only in regard to the determination of the bonus. In all other respects, the two are the same. In the Rowan Plan, the time saved is expressed as a percentage of the time allowed and the hourly rate of pay is increased by that percentage so that the total earnings of the worker are the total number of hours multiplied by the increased hourly wages. The plan aims at ensuring the permanence of the premium rate, which is often cut by the employer when the worker's efficiency increases beyond a certain limit. The premium is calculated on the basis of the proportion which the time saved bears to standard time.

The Rowan plan has all the merits and demerits of the Halsey Plan except that, because of the limitation on earnings, it does not provide an incentive, for maximum productivity, Moreover, the complex method of premium calculation is generally unintelligible to the worker. He cannot, be expected to take much interest in the plan.

These premium plans may be classified as differential piece work systems and have been evolved with a view to giving the benefit to both parties. They are based on the fundamental principle that a worker's earnings should increase when his production rises above a pre-determined target. As his extra earning is not in proportion to his usual wage rate, the overall production cost per piece falls when the output increases.

## 3. The Bedeaux Point Plan

This plan is used when carefully planned performance standards have been established. Every job is expressed in terms 'B's which means that a job should be completed in so many minutes. If a particular work is rated at 60 Bs, the worker is allowed one hour for its completion and receives a bonus of 75 per cent for the number of Bs, i.e., time saved. Suppose that a worker earns 600 Bs in a day; if the rate per point is Rs. 0.01, his total earnings would be.

Rs. $4.80 \times 0.01 + 3/4 \,(600-480) \times 0.01 = 4.80 + $ Rs. $0.90 = $ Rs. $5.70$

The chief advantage of this plan is that it can be applied to any kind of a job. It is particularly suitable for plants in which workers are assigned diverse kinds of jobs and are shifted from one job to another. All the points which a worker earns in a day are recorded and the bonus is calculated on that basis.

**4. Taylor's Differential Piece-Rate Plan:** This system was introduced by Taylor with two objects: First, to give sufficient incentive to workmen to induce them to produce up to their full capacity; and second, to remove the fear of wage cut. There is one rate for those who reach the standard; they are given a higher rate to enable them to get the bonus. The other is the lower rate for those who are below the standard, so that the hope of receiving a higher rate (i.e., a bonus), may serve as an incentive to come up to the standard. Workers are expected to do certain units of work within a certain period of time. This standard is determined on the basis of time and motion studies. Such scientific determination ensures that the standard fixed is not unduly high and is within the easy reach of workers. The system is designed to encourage the especially efficient worker with a higher rate of payment and to penalize the inefficient by a lower rate of payment.

**5. Merrick's Multiple Piece Rate System** This system too is based on the principle of a low piece rate for a slow worker and a higher piece rate for higher production but the plan differs from Taylor's plan in that, it offers three graded piece rates instead of two. The first step is at 83 per cent of the standard, on task production and the second at the task point.

**6. The Gnatt Task and Bonus Plan** This plan has been devised by H.L. Gnatt and is the only one that pays a bonus percentage multiplied by the value of standard time. Under this system, fixed time rates are guaranteed. Output standards and time standards are established for the performance of each job. Workers completing the job within the standard time or in less time receive wages for the standard time plus a bonus which ranges from 20 per cent to 50 per cent of the time allowed and not time saved. When a worker fails to turn out the required quantity of a product, he simply gets his time rate without any bonus.

**7. Emerson Efficiency Plan** Under this system, a standard time is established for a standard task. The day wage is assured. There is no sudden rise in wages on achieving the standard of performance. The remuneration based on efficiency rises gradually. Efficiency is determined by the ratio between the standard time fixed for a performance and the time actually taken by a worker.

**8. Profit Sharing** Profit sharing is regarded as a stepping stone to industrial democracy. It is an arrangement by which employees receive a share fixed in advance of the profits. A profit sharing scheme is generally introduced to achieve the following objectives:

(i) To promote industrial harmony and stabilization of the workforce;
(ii) To eliminate waste in the use of materials and equipments;
(iii) To instill a sense of partnership among employees and employers;
(iv) To attract desirable employees and retain them, thereby reducing the rate of turnover;
(v) To encourage employee thrift;
(vi) To provide a group incentive for a larger output;
(vii) To ensure employee security and
(viii) To demonstrate some measure of social justice to employees.

## Test Questions

1. What do you mean by incentives? What are its types?
2. Do you think that fringe benefits motivate employees?
3. Do you think that non financial incentives motivate employees? What are such incentives?
4. Discuss critically three incentive plans.
5. What do you mean by the cafeteria approach in salary fixation?
6. Describe some non financial incentives.
7. What are the objectives of introducing project sharing plan?

# 21

# Wages and Productivity

Production is not the same as productivity. Productivity is the ratio of output to the corresponding input of labour. Productivity and real wages move in the same direction. Productivity is one of the several criteria in wage fixation. Gains in productivity should be shared among employers, employees, consumers and shareholders.

**Wages and Productivity**

Higher production has to be distinguished from higher productivity. Labour Productivity has been defined as the ratio of output to the corresponding input of labour. It can be expressed by a formula $P = O/M$, where P is the productivity of labour, O is the unit of output and M, the input of labour.

Production and productivity are two different concepts and should not be confused. A large volume of production has no connection with a high rate of productivity. They do not necessarily go hand in hand in all cases. Increased production does not necessarily mean increased productivity, though higher productivity leads to higher production. If the same volume of production can be obtained by the application of lesser inputs, that is also a case of increased productivity. Increased production is brought about by investing more capital and employing additional labour. But increased productivity is only possible through the making of larger production by using the same capital investment and labour. If a firm by using the same materials, machines and man-hours produces 150 units now as compared to 100 units before, its productivity is said to have gone up by 50 per cent. Thus productivity is concerned with the efficiency of production.

A steady rising level of productivity of the economy as a whole is the source of real improvement in the level of living of people, particularly of wage earners in the economy. There is a fairly close relationship between the rate of change of productivity of the economy as a whole and the rate of change of real wage level, but that relationship is valid only over a long period of years and not on a short-term basis. Over the long periods of years both productivity and real wages would be found to have moved up pari passu.

Productivity in the manufacturing sector can rise in two distinct ways. First, it can rise through more intensive effort on the part of the worker and the acceptance by him of a higher work-load than before. The second way of raising productivity does not depend primarily on greater effort on the part of the worker. Large industry-wide increases in productivity have accrued in the past from new capital investments, greater mechanization and automation, advancing research, and improved technology, intensive specialization, better management and above all a clear recognition by workers that higher standards of living are possible only through rising levels of productivity over the entire economy.

*Productivity—only one of several criteria in Wage Fixation—* Productivity has been considered to be only one of several criteria employed in wage determination. In India, the Committee on Fair Wages, 1949, suggested that in fixing the 'fair wage', with its lower limit at the level of the minimum wage and its upper limit set by the capacity of the industry to pay, the following factors should be taken into consideration: (i) productivity of labour, (ii) the prevailing rates of wages in the same or similar occupations in the same localities, (iii) the level of national income and its distribution and (iv) the place of the industry in the economy of the country.

However, though the Supreme Court, as the ultimate authority in matters pertaining to the statutory adjudication of industrial disputes, has emphasized only three criteria, namely the industry-cum-region basis of wage fixation, comparison and capacity to pay. The Supreme Court has made only casual references to productivity. The Wage Boards too have not found it possible to take the productivity criterion into account in the settlement of the wage structure. Thus productivity has not figured as a criterion of any importance in wage fixation in India.

*Limitation to the Use of the Long-term Wage-Productivity Relationship—* The only wage-productivity relationship that is completely valid is that for the economy as a whole, real wage earnings rise more or less at the same rate as the overall increase in output per man-hour or labour productivity, both rates of increase being recommended on a truly long-term basis. In the broad form in which it has been stated, this is not an operational criterion. To be meaningful, a number of qualifications are necessary. First, the long-term rate of increase in output per man-hour is a mere statistical average and has no relationship to the actual short-term changes in labour productivity in the economy. The year-to-year or short-term changes in labour productivity in the economy may not be uniform, being influenced by various economic factors. Moreover, the changes may not be in the same direction.

Secondly, if the long-term trend in productivity of the economy has to be applied in a period of temporary curb on wages and other incomes, it should be borne in mind that because of the need to step up savings and capital formation, in a growing economy like that of India, the whole long-term gains in productivity is not available for increased current consumption. Curbs on the consumption of profit earners are generally applied through suitable measures of taxation, but in the case of wage earners the only method of providing for savings is to ensure that the increase in the wages allowed are somewhat lower than the full extent warranted by the increase in productivity.

Thirdly, increase in money wages in all sectors of the economy at the same rate, namely, the long-term average rate of change in productivity in the economy as a whole will amount to unwarranted interference with the economic forces that ordinarily influence and determine wage levels in particular industries. Uniformity in wage changes over the entire economy would be undesirable from the point of view of ensuring the optimum allocation of resources. Some industries would be expanding while others will be contracting in response to economic pressure. Capacity to pay will necessarily vary from industry to industry. In these circumstances a dead level of uniformity in wage increases can only be at the risk of interfering with the inevitable process of progress or decline of particular industries necessitated by market conditions and prevailing economic trends. Consequently, even in the special circumstances in which State interference in terms of an incomes and price policy might be justified, a single productivity rate, derived from long-term trends in the economy as a whole, cannot be applied blindly to all industries and other sectors of the economy.

*Productivity and Wage Changes in Particular Industries* – If the long-term economy-wide productivity rate is not an operational standard for regulation of wage rates on a short-term basis, the rates of changes of output per man-hour in particular industries are even less suitable for the purpose. There are many reasons why wages in particular industries should not be raised in line with increases in the output per man-hour in those industries. Output per man-hour in individual industries varies very irregularly from year to year even in a developed economy. The short-term gains have little relation to the long-term trend. In a period of rapid industrial development, as is the case in India, the variations in productivity from time to time in different industries might be so great that they cannot be said to have any meaningful relation to the long-term trend. It is obvious that no wage structure can be subjected to such violent year-to-year variations.

A more serious objection to relating wage changes in particular industries to changes in output per man-hour in those industries is that such a process will introduce unjustified inequalities into the wage structure. Prof. Summer Slichter said, "If wages were increased in those various industries in proportion to the rise in productivity, the wage structure would have soon little relationship to the skill and responsibility required of the workers or to the relative attractiveness or unattractiveness of working condition".

Yet another objection is that large wage increases in line with advancing productivity in progressive industries would contribute to wage inflation as such increases will, sooner or later, be transmitted to the less productive sectors of the economy where price rises would become inevitable.

*Sharing the Gains of Productivity* — What has been said so far about the relationship between productivity and wages is largely of a negative character, namely, that though a close relationship exists between the long-term trend of the rate of increase in output per man-hour for the economy as a whole and the long-term trend of the rate of increase in real wages and incomes in the economy, no operational formula has so far been evolved whereby wage changes could be linked to productivity changes from time to time. The long-term trend of productivity in the economy as a whole is pressed into service as a broad guide to regulate current wage adjustments only in emergencies when the state of the economy calls for the imposition of restraints on incomes through an officially-sponsored incomes and prices policy. At other times no such conscious effort can be made to equate the one with the other. Market forces, supplemented by collective bargaining or governmental intervention in the form of fixation of minimum wage rates are supposed to ensure a fair distribution of the gains of productivity as between workers on the one hand and stockholders on the other, besides providing for price reduction in certain circumstances.

When one speaks of the sharing of the gains of productivity, it is necessary to emphasize that one is concerned not with the gains of productivity obtained through incentive systems of payment but with the increase in productivity of an industry, the bulk of which arises from technological advance. On technological productivity, the consumers at large and the Government have also justifiable claims, the former, in the shape of reduced prices of the products of the industry and the latter in the form of higher taxes imposed on higher earnings of employees and stockholders. In fact, a large volume of opinion is in favour of reduction of prices as the principal method of spreading the benefits of rising productivity among as large a proportion of the population as possible.

While there are distinct advantages in keeping the wage level more or less steady and in reducing prices out of the gains of productivity, some economists suggest that in order to give greater stimulus to new investment, it would be better to ensure stability of prices and simultaneously to raise money wages as productivity increases. Reduction of prices, they argue, might discourage investment and lead to unemployment.

Let us assume that the gains of rising productivity have to be shared concretely between the three principal claimants, namely workers, stockholders and consumers. Is there any rational way of making this distribution, and can any formula be evolved which will reduce the tensions inevitable in the bargaining of shares at periodic intervals? Apart from annual improvement factor based on the estimated long-term gain in national output per man-hour, we know of no formula which even advanced countries have been able to evolve to apportion the gains of productivity among the claimants. Discussing the principles of distribution of the benefits of higher productivity, the ILO says, "These arguments do not answer the question—what is labour's 'reasonable share' of the benefits of higher productivity in any particular case. Nor do they settle the question of the form which this share should take. It says, "these are clearly questions to which there are no simple universal answers. Each case must be decided on its merits".

***Indian Efforts to Evolve a Formula for Sharing*** — Though experts in advanced countries have not found it possible to evolve any formula for sharing the gains of productivity, this has not deterred India from making attempts to work out a mathematically precise formula for the purpose. The National Productivity Council constituted an expert committee in 1960, to examine the principles which should govern the distribution of the gains of productivity. The Committee under the chairmanship of Leslie Sawhny, suggested, that 20 per cent of the gains should be used towards lowering prices to the consumers and 20 per cent should be distributed as additional dividend on the capital. The remaining 60 per cent is to be utilized partly for paying productivity bonus to labour and partly for capital reinvestment for development. The precise break-up of the total for these two purposes is to depend on the extent of the free reserves of the firm in relation to its equity capital. If the free reserves are below 50 per cent of the equity capital, 30 per cent should be allotted to capital for reinvestment. If, however, free reserves are more than 50 per cent of the equity capital, the share of labour is to be raised gradually to a maximum of 40 per cent and the share of capital for reinvestment correspondingly reduced to a minimum of 20 per cent. Thus, out of the 80 per cent remaining after deduction of 20 per cent. from the total gains for reduction of prices, labour is to get as, productivity bonus 30 to 40 per cent and capital for dividend and re-investment, 50 to 40 per cent.

*National Commission on Productivity and Wages* – The National Commission on Labour has made observations on certain aspects of productivity and wages which are relevant to both the problem of sharing of gains and the relationship, if any, between wage changes and productivity trends.

Briefly the Commission's suggestions can be summed up as follows:

(1) The value added by manufacture per worker increased from Rs. 2113 in 1952 to Rs. 4621 in 1964. After adjustment for price changes during this period, this means that production by worker increased by about 63 per cent between 1952 and 1964. A part of the increase must have been contributed by labour whose real earnings have remained almost static during the period.

(2) Money wages as a percentage of total output dropped from 13.7 to 11.4 between 1952 and 1958. Between 1960 and 1964 the drop was from 10.9 to 9.7. The decline varied from industry to industry but was registered in all cases except in matches. Even after adjustment for prices, there was a fall in the share of wages in the output between 1952 and 1964.

(3) The percentage of wages to the value added by manufacture showed a decline from about 50 per cent in the period 1949-50 to about 40 per cent in 1958. Wages as a percentage of value added declined from about 40 per cent in 1960 to 36.5 per cent in 1964. Even if the money value of benefits and privileges is taken into account, the conclusion remains the same though the decline then becomes less sharp.

(4) To sum up, increases in money wages of industrial workers since Independence have not been associated with a rise in real wages nor have real wage increases been commensurate

with improvements in productivity. Simultaneously, wage costs as a proportion of total costs of manufacture have registered a decline, and the same is true about workers' share in value added by manufacture. "Wage disputes under these conditions have continued to be the single most important cause of all industrial disputes".

The National Commission's assessment on the growth of money and real wage levels in the context of productivity does not sufficiently take into account the factors that are responsible for inflation and hence for a corresponding decline in real wages. The Commission makes three statements in the concluding portions of the chapter of wage policy, e.g., (1) wage policy should aim at a progressive increase in real wages, (2) sustained improvement in real wages cannot be brought about without increasing productivity and (3) the real wages of any group of workers cannot be unrelated to their productivity.

**Test Questions**

1. Distinguish between production and productivity. How can productivity rise?
2. Besides productivity what other criteria are employed in India in wage determination?
3. What are the limitations to the use of long-term increase in production as a basis for wage increase?
4. How the gains of productivity should be shared between the principal claimants?
5. Discuss the National Commission on Labour's suggestions for sharing the gains of productivity and wages.

# Executive And International Compensation with a Reference to Executive Compensation in India

In the contemporary society there is a feeling that the amount of compensation of the top executives is unrealistically high. In his book, *In Search of Excess: The Overcompensation of American Executives*, Graef S. Crystal, has attacked executive compensation packages.

In defense of executive compensation packages, top management, members of the board of directors who approve these packages state that, these components are needed and useful to attract and retain management personnel of outstanding ability and to encourage excellence in the performance of individual responsibility. They state that these awards recognize the ability, efficiency and loyalty of these executives whose efforts contribute to the success of the organization.

Let us consider the major components of an executive incentive package. The following are the major components of an executive compensation plan:

1. Base salary
2. Short-term performance bonuses
3. Variety of equity (stock ownership) and equity-related components.
4. Long-term performance bonuses
5. Severance Package (golden parachutes and other severance plans)
6. Retirement Programs
7. Wide variety of benefits and perquisites

1. *Base Salary:* Senior management is responsible for the proper organization and operation of the firm. In a small organization, senior management may consist of only the owner or the president. In a larger organization, it will consists of executives and senior managers – those who have responsibility for setting the objectives of the organization, establishing its operating policies and defining courses of action through the strategies they develop and approve.

   In 1976, approximately 135,000 employees in American business could truly be identified as policy making executives. Given a work force at that time of approximately 85 million; this executive group consisted of approximately one-sixth of 1 percent of the total workforce. The highest-ranking officer of this group who may be the chief executive officer (CEO) or the president is responsible for all operations.

   By the late 1980s, many of the top executives of the major corporations in the USA began to receive annual salaries in excess of a million dollars. By 1992, the average salary of those top CEOs exceeded $1.5 million. These million-dollar plus salaries are only the tip of the iceberg of executive compensation.

2. *Short-term Bonuses:* To augment the base salaries of executives of major corporations, short-term bonuses have ranged from 50 per cent of base pay to 10 or more times base pay when their respective organizations have had a good year according to some kind of financial indicators.

   Here are some examples of incentive plans designed to stimulate specific employee behaviours.

   (i) *Attendee Bonus:* A serious cost and quality problem that faces many organizations is absenteeism. This problem is widely prevalent in the automobile assembly plants. High rates of absenteeism required US automobile manufactures to hire large numbers of extra workers to substitute for absentees. The replacement workers frequently did not perform a specific assignment as well as the permanent job holder. When sufficient numbers of regular workers report to work, there is no need for replacement workers who are receiving a full day's pay for standing by. Reduction of absenteeism has been a major goal of all automobile manufactory. General Motors instituted an attendance bonus programme. An employee with no unexcused absence during the quarter received a $50 bonus.

(ii) *Length-of-Service and Seniority Rewards:* Although seniority rewards are normally a direct part of the compensation system, some organizations recognize long service through some form of recognition awards (gold watch, for example).

The most recent view is that seniority or length of service rewards should not be part of the base pay programme, but rather an additional element in the total compensation reward system. Many people believe that seniority is the one stabilizing factor available to all employees. It enables employees to know where they stand in relation to coworkers, where they have been and where they are going. It makes the future easier to live with and more acceptable. It is still possible to recognize to some degree the importance of seniority through a separate year of service bonus.

(iii) *Referral Awards:* Employees who refer applicants who accept employment and become fulltime employees receive a small cash award for their efforts. This award generally is used only in tight labour market conditions; it is rarely a permanent part of a compensation programme.

(iv) *Patent Awards:* Employers tap the intellectual capabilities of each employee. Most jobs require employees to think about a variety of things and then relate these thoughts to work situations for a long time; organizations have recognized and rewarded intellectual contributions. One way an organization rewards its best 'thinkers' is through promotion, but promotion is not always a practical option. For the most creative of employees whose inventions result in patents, organizations provide patent awards. For the professionals who work in the research and development field, awards are usually provided for issued patents. A few firms are now offering the scientists who develop patentable ideas a percentage of all royalties generated, as long as the individual remains with the company.

(v) *Suggestion Plans:* Although only a small number of employees may have the spark of genius that result in a patent, within the brain of every employee is the capacity to develop suggestion that can lead to profitable innovations. Ever since the 1880s, when the suggestion box was introduced into US organizations, employee suggestions have been a major factor in improving operations, products and services. In India, suggestion plans operate in many organizations.

In 1985, General Motors paid out approximately $64 million for approximately 369,000 suggestions and Eastman Kodak spent approximately $4.6 million for approximately 87,000 ideas.

Practically every incentive plan recognizes the importance of the suggestion and provides rewards to stimulate employee creativity and innovation. The suggestion system is a major element in any employer plan that encourages greater employee involvement.

(vi) *Special Achievement Awards:* There are organizations which recognize outstanding employee contributions through special awards. In USA, formal cash awards offered to outstanding contributors may range from $500 to $100,000. The number of prizes offered annually depends on corporate policy and the size of the prizes awarded. The special awards usually are granted to a small number of employees on an annual basis.

(vii) *Contest Bonuses:* Many organizations develop contests, games or promotions to stimulate extra effort. These special goals can focus on productivity or quality improvement, development of a better safety record or reduction of costs, absenteeism or tardiness.

Most contests encourage some type of individual effort and foster a spirit of competition.

A study of executive compensation revealed that almost all companies in all industries have incentive plans for their executives. Incentive opportunities were provided not only to top managers and sales representatives but also to middle managers, key professionals and technical staff.

(3) *Equity and Equity-Related Components:* Perhaps the major wealth building opportunity available to executives of US corporations is through the acquisition of stock in the organization or some combination of money and stock that relates to the improved price of organizational stock.

(4) *Long-Term Performance Bonuses:* Long-term performance bonuses are cash payments similar to the short-term bonus awards provided to corporate executives. The major difference is that the receipt of the award is 2 years or more into the

future and the size of the award is based on multi year achievement of established performance-related goals. When establishing these kinds of performance standards or goals, the actual size of the bonus often relates to achieved levels of performance.

(5) *Severance Packages:* Many executive compensation components include features designed to keep the involved individual in the Corporation and at times 'non complete' requirements severely penalize financially an executive who leaves the organization and goes to work for a competitor. These severance packages specify awards to be provided if the employee is required to leave the organization under specific circumstances. A major part of a severance package may be an employment contract.

Golden parachutes are Change In Control (CIC) agreement. These agreements identify the executives to be covered, the effective period of the agreement and the kinds of triggers that would initiate the payment of the incentives. A golden parachute can permit the payment of long-term incentives in the year of the CIC. It may also contain pension enhancements and the continuation of health, life and medical benefits.

The term 'golden parachute contracts' vary significantly but generally they guarantee the contract holder (1) continuation of base pay for 1 to 5 years – it may be paid as a lump sum or over a specified period of time, (2) any bonuses that would normally have been granted during the time, (3) supplemental benefits and frequently (4) immediate vesting of any stock option. The contract normally establishes a minimum level of income the recipient will receive during the term of the contract.

(6) *Retirement Programmes:* Corporate executives are provided with an array of supplemental retirement programme that ensures that they receive equal retirement benefits than those offered to the other key officials of the firm; a bias against those senior jobholders becomes evident.

(7) *Special Package of Benefits and Perquisites:* Executives have available to them, all of the benefits the organizations provide to their employees. A special group of benefits that has been provided mainly to executives is called perquisites (perks). The following brief description of some of the common perks:

   (i) *Company-provided Car:* The employee is able to use the car for business as well as personal use.

(ii) *Chauffeured Limousine:* Normally provided only to the CEO or key officials. The chauffeur can also act as a bodyguard.

(iii) *Kidnap and ransom protection:* A service of recent vintage aimed at protecting key officials who may be victims of such action.

(iv) *Counselling service:* Includes financial and legal services. Tax-related expenses are tax deductible; cost of non-business related services is considered taxable income.

(v) *Attending professional meetings and conferences:* Opportunity to enhance professional knowledge and enjoy activities at selected sites.

(vi) *Spouse travel:* The company pays for expenses incurred in taking the spouses of key officials to a convention or on a business trip.

(vii) *Use of the company plane and yacht:* Opportunity to make use of the company plane and yacht for personal enjoyment and business purposes.

(viii) *Home entertainment allowance:* Executives who do considerable entertaining are frequently provided with a domestic staff for given a home servant's allowance, the allowance can include cost of food and beverages and payment of utility bills.

(ix) *Special living accommodations:* Executives required to perform business activities at odd hours or at a reasonable distance from home are provided with an apartment or permanent hotel accommodations.

(x) *Club membership:* Country club and luncheon club memberships are provided to executives who use such facilities in the performance of their jobs.

(xi) *Special dining rooms:* The business provides special dining facilities for key officials and their business guests.

(xii) *Season tickets to entertainment events:* The executive has free use of season tickets for family and business associates to a variety of entertainment events.

(xiii) *Special relocation allowance:* A variety of relocation allowances is provided only to key officials. This includes low interest loans to purchase a new home and complete coverage of all relocation expenses.

(xiv) *College tuition reimbursement for children:* Special programmes that provide for college tuition.

(xv) *No and Low interest loans:* Executives are provided funds at no interest or at interest rates well below market.

Some corporations in India grant executives amount of money to pay for income tax.

## International Compensation

Compensation managers of many organizations face an entirely different set of problems in designing managing compensation of employees who work for the company in a foreign nation. The unique compensation issues are in these areas are

1. Incentives provided to stimulate movement or expatriation to a foreign location or host country.
2. Allowances for repatriation to home country.
3. Additional tax burdens placed on employees working in a foreign location.
5. Cost of living allowances in the host country.
6. Home country and host country currency fluctuation.
7. Formal and informal compensation practices unique to the host country.
8. Determining home country rates for setting base pay of third country nationals (TCNs)

Many reasons exist for sending employees to a foreign worksite. The most common are the following:

1. Existing or potential employees who live at the foreign worksite do not have the necessary knowledge, skills and related work experience.
2. Existing or potential employees who already live at the foreign location do not have the necessary knowledge of the business, its operations, plans, policies and strategies.
3. The organization wants to develop a global perspective among employees and make it part of a career development program.

*Home Country Employee:* An organization operating in one or more foreign countries may draw employees from three different places of residence: (i) the nation or host country where the operation is located, (ii) the home nation of the parent operation and (iii) foreign countries other than the site of the operation.

The title given to those employees whose basic residence or home is the host nation is nationals or locals. Those who come from the home country of the operation are expatriates and those whose nation of residence is neither the host country nor the home country are third country nationals (TCNs).

The compensation provided to locals, expatriates and TCNs can vary considerably. Normally, the total compensation package provided to locals is the least costly, whereas that provided to expatriates is the most costly. From strictly a cost point of view, the more locals are employed at the worksite, the lower the labour cost and the greater the return on invested capital. The expenses involved in stimulating an employee to move to a foreign site, the payment of relocation costs and finally the additional tax burden incurred by having expatriates and at times, TCNs in foreign operations are substantial. These expenses often result in an excessive drain on the profitability of the foreign operation.

*Attracting Individuals to a Foreign Work Site:* Recruiting new employees with the requisite knowledge and skills or influencing current employees to move to a foreign site requires a wide variety of compensation-related incentives. The kind of compensation components offered and the amount of components available vary according to the desirability of the location.

*Site Desirability:* Each site has its unique strength and weaknesses and the perception of these strengths and weaknesses varies by individual employee. Some of these strength and weaknesses relate to geographical location and climate and others relate to social and political conditions.

*Transfer Incentives:* The first compensation issue that faces the compensation manager is the amount of additional pay required to induce an employee to move from the present job site to the new one in the foreign country. In some cases the site may be so desirable that almost any job candidate would find it sufficient if the organization guaranteed that the individual would be financially rewarded in the host country as at home. In most cases, however, the person asked to move to a foreign site will demand some premium over that earned in the present assignment.

The next set of compensation issues resolves around present housing. In many cases, the employee owns a house and looks to the employer to cover some or all of the expanses involved in selling it. These sale-of-residence expenses may include sufficient money to guarantee the employee no financial loss in the house sale or even some percentage of the profit. Because a house, in many cases, is currently one of the best investments a person can make, organizations now provide home rental assistance and absentee ownership management services for the home owner who rents rather than sells while on foreign assignment.

In most cases, the organization takes care of all moving expenses to the new site. In these cases in which it is impractical to move the family, special consideration must be granted for their maintenance at the present residence. In case in which spouses or families do not make the move, the transfer probably will be for a limited period.

*Developing a Compensation Programme for Expatriates:* Establishing a compensation plan for a job in a foreign location begins with the determination of base pay. The market or going rate of pay for a comparable job in the home country at the time of expatriation is normally used for setting this rate.

After setting base pay comes the determination of a Foreign Service Premium (FSP) which is an incentive bonus for performing the assignment in the host country. The FSP usually is expressed as a percentage of base pay and is part of the total pay received by the employee each pay period. Some organizations are now granting expatriates lump-sum bonuses in lieu of FSPs. These lump-sum payments are made at the time of expatriation and repatriation.

To maintain the employees' present standard of living in the foreign location, organizations provide a number of allowances to keep them 'whole'. A major one provides money for additional living cost (food, housing and transportation in the host country). Compensation managers obtain ballpark figure from various sources on additional living costs to be incurred, in moving an employee to a foreign location.

In a host country where conditions are undesirable, a 'hardship' allowance is added to base pay. Most pay plans include a cost-equalization allowance that includes cost of living and housing allowances. The equalization allowance consists of the difference between the costs of food, other consumable items, services and housing in the home country and the cost of those items in the host country. In many cases the cost of living allowance is tied to a change in the currency exchange rate, tied to a change in the currency exchange rate between home country and host country.

Many organizations also provide tax equalization allowance. In computing such an allowance, the first step is to determine the hypothetical tax liability incurred by the employee. This is done by assuming that the employee still is working in the home country and receiving the established base pay for a comparable job. Using the base pay and appropriate home base income tax rates a hypothetical tax liability is established. Then the organization computes all tax liabilities of the expatriate for all income earned on the job. From those total tax liabilities of the expatriate for all income earned on the job. From those total tax liabilities, the hypothetical tax, the expatriate would normally have paid on a comparable job in the home country is subtracted. This is the amount of tax burden assured by the employer on the tax equalization allowance.

To minimize problems related to exchange of currency and to protect the employee, many organizations now split an expatriate's compensation between home country and host country compensation packages. A split-pay plan is one in which a certain amount of total pay received by the expatriate is paid in home country currency and credited to a designated account in the home country. The expatriate receives the remaining pay in the host country in host country currency.

A procedure often used for determining the amount of the split that goes into the home country or domestic account and the amount that goes into the host country or foreign account takes this approach. First, a spendable income for the employee in the home country must be established. Spendable income is that amount of pay that is spent on goods, services and housing. It represents total pay minus taxes, savings, investments, health and life insurance premiums and any contributions made by the employee to benefit components.

Supplementing the spendable income are house and cost of living allowances to ensure the expatriate the same standard of living in the host country as that enjoyed in the home country at the time of expatriation. These disposable income and living adjustment allowances are further supplemented during the period the expatriate is in the host country by the spendable portion of any pay increase granted and by any cost of living changes that occur.

The domestic account consists of pay plus premiums minus spendable income and an amount set aside for hypothetical income tax. It also includes that part of any pay adjustments granted to the individual or adjustment granted to the individual or all employees of the organization not set aside for spendable income.

In addition to the aforesaid compensation items, a number of payments and services are provided to employees willing to accept a foreign assignment. These payments and services can be included in the following two groups:

I. *Life style enhancement services.* These programmes make living more acceptable and enjoyable at the foreign site. These include:

1. Provision for employee and family to learn the local language.

2. Education and training of employee and family on local culture and social customs.
3. Counselling service for employee and family.
4. Assistance in finding a house at the foreign work site.
5. Assistance in finding schools for children.
6. Company car, driver and domestic staff.
7. Subsidized health care services.
8. Assistance in joining local, social and professional organizations.
9. Assistance to spouse in finding suitable and acceptable employment.

II. *Service allowances and premiums include the following:*
1. Temporary living allowance.
2. Hardship premium.
3. Currency Protection.
4. Mobility premium.
5. Home-leave allowance.
6. Stopover allowance.
7. Assignment extension bonus.
8. Emergency Loans.

## Executive Remuneration: Indian Perspective

It is a fact that there is a wide disparity in compensation prevailing in India. There is a peculiar co-existence of enormous riches and abysmal poverty in society.

Trade unions have all along been highly critical about high salaries and perks enjoyed by the top executives in the private sectors while some of the basic needs of the workers are not satisfied. The top executives have introduced 'five star' culture in the industrial sector which has created tension among the employees who are even denied a living wage. Again, there is resentment among managers in public enterprises that for discharging the same kind of managerial responsibilities, they are paid much less than managers in comparable private enterprises. One dimension of the industrial relations problems in India is the wide cultural, social and financial gap between the higher levels of management and the lower level of employees.

Compensation has an impact on attracting, retaining and motivating the executive. Disparities in compensation pattern often leads to dissatisfaction among executives. To make the executives comfortable to the extent possible and further to keep them from turning hostile, private companies have been giving in recent years, bigger and more frequent rises in salaries. Companies have started looking at executive compensation more proactively so that they can expect better performance from them.

Executives play a major role in looking after the economic health of the company and are important for the success, growth and profitability of an organization.

Compensations at the top management level appear to be influenced by factors like size of the organization, specific type of industry and contribution of the individual executives to the process of decision makings. The larger the company, the greater is the amount of salary paid to individual executives at the top level group.

Compensation has an impact on attracting retaining and motivating the executive remuneration particularly for private sector executives who have assumed significant importance in recent years. Salaries, commissions and perks to the executives in the private sector organization are fantastic and this sudden spurt in managerial remuneration is the result of economic liberalization, privatization and globalization of the Indian economy.

Workers' wage and salary system is treated distinctively from managerial remuneration system. The elements of managerial remuneration are not identical with those of wages. The remuneration of an executive includes the five elements – salary, bonus, commission, long-term incentives and perquisites.

1. *Salary:* Salary is the first component of executive compensation. Salary is determined through job evaluation and is the basis of other type of benefits. But job evaluation is not everything – executives must be paid for their performance skills rather than what the job demands. Salary is not very significant as a component of total remuneration because it is subject to deductions at source and is also subject to government regulations. It is for this reason executives are offered hefty incentives and attractive perks.

2. *Bonus:* Besides salary, bonus is an important component of employees' earnings. Most of the companies these days are using bonus as a form of executive remuneration. Executive bonus is subject to the judgment of the board of directors. Executive bonus is a share of the surplus of the company. Executives deserve bonus because the company can earn bonus because of organizational success. Organizational success is mainly the result of executive success.

3. *Commission:* Some private companies pay commission to their executives and commission may be a significant portion of executive remuneration. As per Companies Act, an organization may pay 11 per cent of its profits as commission. Kumar Mangalam Birla of the Aditya Group received a commission of Rs. 1.02 crore in 2003-04. At Crompton Greaves, two non-executive directors received commission of Rs. 32.85 lakh each in 2003. Public sector companies do not generally pay commission. Directors are entitled to a performance-linked bonus. At AOC, chairman M.S. Ramachandran received Rs. 10.69 lakh in 2002-03.

4. *Long-term Incentives:* Incentive plans motivate employees to show superior performance. As long-term benefits, stock options are offered to executives. Companies allow executives to purchase their shares at fixed prices. Stock options are valuable as long as the price of share goes on increasing. Stock options are very attractive to shareholders. An option is not a bonus. Executive will purchase the stock with their own resources. Options are a form of profit sharing which links the executive's financial success to that of the shareholders. Stock options are one of the methods to offer larger rewards to executives.

5. *Perquisites:* Perks constitute a major source of real income for the executive. Tax considerations have led to the introduction of perks such as allowance for repair and maintenance of flats, entertainment and club allowance. Rent subsidy, medical facilities, superannuation benefits and leave travel allowance are differently structured and are given on a more liberal basis. Dearness allowance, overtime and incentive bonus which constitute the bulk of worker's remuneration are rarely admitted to managers.

*Special Features of Executive Remuneration:* Executive remuneration has certain unique features:

1. The elements of managerial remuneration are not identical with those of wages. Workers' wage and salary system is treated separately from managerial remuneration system.

2. Secrecy is maintained in respect of executive remuneration. What X receives is not made known to Y and what Y gets Z cannot know. Secrecy is maintained because no two executive in the same grade receive the same remuneration. Remuneration depends upon many factors.

3. Executive remuneration is subject to statutory ceilings. As per latest guidelines, the monthly salary varies from Rs. 40,000 to 87,500 including perks.

4. Executive remuneration is not supposed to be based on individual performance but rather on organizational performance.
5. Theoretically the executive remuneration is supposed to be guided by job descriptions, job evaluation and salary survey. But in actual practice, these norms are completely thrown to winds and fantastic amounts are paid to decision makers in the organization which cannot be justified.
6. With globalization and emergence of global corporate citizen, compensation strategy in the environment has acquired increasing importance. In general what multinational corporations are offering to their executives must have some impact on the remuneration to be offered by the Indian companies.

The Remuneration of some Top Indian Executives are given below.

| Company | Name | Designation | Amount (2003-04) (Crores) |
|---|---|---|---|
| Hero Honda Motors | BML Munjal | Chairman | 11.71 |
| Reliance | Mukesh Ambani | Chairman | 11.62 |
| Hero Honda Motors | Pawan Munjal | MD | 11.53 |
| Cadila Health Care | Pankaj Patel | MD | 8.40 |
| Wipro | Vivek Paul | | 5.70 |
| Ranbaxy | D.S. Brar | | 4.05 |
| Nestle | Carlo MV. Donati | | 2.75 |
| ITC | Y.C. Deveshwar | | 1.87 |
| Hindustan Lever | M.S. Banga | Chairman | 2.47 |
| Apollo Tyres | Onkar Kanwar | Chairman | 5.12 |

## Test Questions

1. Explain the major components of an executive compensation plan.
2. A special group of benefits that are provided mainly to executives called perks. Give a brief description of some of the common perks.
3. Do you think that in contemporary society the amount of compensation to top executives is unrealistically high? Explain the statement.
4. Explain the Special Package of Benefits and Perquisites which are provided to top executives.
5. Develop a compensation program for expatriates.
6. One dimension of industrial relations problems in India is the wide financial gap between the higher levels of management and lower levels of employees. Justify the statement.
7. Explain the special features of Executive Remuneration in India.

# National Wage Policy

**What is a Wage Policy?**

The ILO defines the term 'Wage policy' to mean "legislation or government action calculated to affect the level or structure of wages, or both, for the purpose of attaining specific objectives of social and economic policy." The objectives here referred to are those relating to national interests and not to sectional interests. Workers and employers have their own legitimate sectional interests to sustain and safeguard interests which need not necessarily coincide with national interests as a whole, as interpreted by those responsible for the governance of the country for the time being. While sectional interests tend to pull in their different directions, it should be the aim of a national policy to advance the interests of the country as a whole. A national policy is, in effect, an essay in balancing sectional interests and in reconciling them with national interests to the greatest extent possible.

A wage policy seeks to influence the level or structure of wages or both. This can be done either by formulating broad guidelines for the fixation or revision of wages in the economy generally or by laying down a detailed scheme for the regulation of wages in individual industries or in the economy as a whole in terms of precisely formulated norms and standards. Detailed regulation involves decisions on a wide variety of subjects, such as the restriction on consumption required to provide for a desired level of savings and investment, the average annual rate of increase in the general wage level sustainable, the range and structure of different kinds of wage differentials, the method or system of payment, etc. A wage policy aims at imposing a discipline on all wage payments in the economy so that excessive, inadequate or inappropriate wage payments may not come in the way of the fulfilment of the objectives, economic and social, which the country has set for itself in pursuit of steady national development.

## Objectives of Wage Policy

As an instrument of economic policy, wage policy was referred to, inter alia, as a means of promoting (i) investment; (ii) internal price stability; (iii) worker efficiency; (iv) a more effective distribution of the labour force; (v) the international competitiveness of the economy and (vi) an influx of foreign capital.

As an instrument of social policy, it was variously acclaimed as (i) an alternative to social security systems; (ii) a means of achieving industrial peace and (iii) a vehicle for securing social justice.

The impacts of wage policy on the level of employment and on the distribution of income, two variables which have both economic and social implications, were also emphasised by participants.

A wage policy which sought to take account of all or even a majority of these goals would be impossible and would encounter internal conflicts. There was, therefore, general agreement with Prof. K. Austin Kerr's plea that the number of objectives posed for wage policy should be reduced. Which of the objectives should be pursued and which ignored would depend on the country's needs and conditions.

The objectives which are generally considered unsuitable for wage policy were (i) improvements in minimum living standards and (ii) pursuit of a disinflationary economic policy.

Minimum wage regulation could do little to redistribute income and raise minimum living standards, partly because the proportion of the working population who were wage-earners was frequently small and partly because large rural groups who endured the lowest living standards could not be helped much because of lack of minimum wage coverage or of ineffectiveness in enforcement of minimum wage regulations.

On the other hand, fiscal policy could be more effective in raising the lowest living standards. Social investment policies (provision of education, accommodation health facilities etc.) and social security provisions (sickness and unemployment benefits, children's allowances, pensions etc.) which could be financed by raising adequate revenues, would be the best means of quickly raising the lowest living standards. Moreover, this would be a surer way of raising the worker efficiency than by granting a wage rise. The argument that elaborates and has far-reaching social security provisions might be prejudicial to the cause of productivity and would apply with much less force to social investment projects.

The wage policy should have both economic and social goals. Social goals were important not merely because of their intrinsic desirability but because they ensured support for the policy of the community at large. Nevertheless, that the primary goal of wage policy in developing countries should be the promotion of economic development, pervaded the whole proceedings.

*Why a Wage Policy at all?*

"No Government can avoid having a wage policy. Even non-intervention is a policy. Since Governments must be concerned about the general level of economic activity, they must also be concerned about the general wage level".

It is not in the purely technical sense of even non-intervention amounting to a policy that the question of evolving a wage policy is being considered here. Wage policy should be an active and vigorous instrument for the purpose of achieving the economic and social goals set by the society.

The role of wage policy in contributing to society's economic and social goals is somewhat different in developed countries from what it is in developing countries. Broadly speaking, wage policy assumes importance, if not concern, in a developed country only during an economic or national emergency, such as, for instance, a serious adverse balance of payments or a severe inflation, particularly during war. The state then tries to cope with the emergency by applying a wage policy which might place severe restraints on excessive wage increases for a limited period. Often such a policy forms part of an overall incomes and prices policy, controlling also non-wage incomes and price increases. Concern over balance of payments was responsible for the restrictive wage policies in the past in the Netherlands, Norway, Sweden, and occasionally in the UK, while the need to contain inflation was at the bottom of wage policies adopted by several countries during World War II and by the United States during the Korean War. The somewhat stringent wage controls imposed in the US in 1971, and in the UK in 1975, aimed at moderating inflation. In normal times wage fixation in these developed countries is through free collective bargaining. Any restrictive wage policy would, therefore, have to interfere with the normal course of wage fixation and is viewed with disfavour except in a national emergency. Says B.C. Roberts "In Britain and America intervention has been looked upon as a regrettable necessity rather than as a desirable activity of the part of the Government".

Not so in Australia and Holland, where, wage policies are of the essence of all economic planning.

In a developing country like India, all the compulsions behind the institutions of wage policies that exist in advanced countries are present along with several others. Inflations and balance of payments difficulties, despite substantial inflow of foreign capital, are continuing afflictions of the Indian economy. Besides, the urgent need to increase the volume of annual investment from the country's internal resources has serious implications for the rate of growth of consumption and hence for the rate of growth of wage incomes. The mounting unemployment in the economy makes the adoption of labour-intensive schemes on the widest possible scale a vital necessity. This, in turn, imposes substantial limitations on increases in the general wage level.

Professor H. A. Turner of the Cambridge University, while contributing a paper to the Egelund Symposium, comes to the conclusion "that the tendency towards Government-promoted or imposed 'wage and incomes policies' in the less developed countries will accelerate and that public agencies will accept (if they do not demand) an increasing influence on the level, structure and trend of wages". He gives five reasons why the question of a formal wage policy cannot be avoided in these countries. In the first place, any system of dispersed wage determination has grave risks for social well-being or national economic welfare. The development of sectional collective bargaining "clearly involves the risk of inflation for the modern sector as a whole, of unnecessary under-employment in the traditional sector, and of the appropriation of the major gains of development to organized minority groups". Secondly, the Government and other public bodies are involved as major employers in the whole process of wage fixing. Thirdly, economic planning processes involve important considerations of cost. Decisions on investments to create employment, on the attraction of overseas capital, on the encouragement of exports, etc. are concerned with questions of wage policy. Fourthly, the Governments of under-developed countries may find it difficult to correct the developments leading to tensions by indirect methods, namely, monetary and fiscal policies, and may have to exert direct influence on income distribution.

The Ceylon National Wage Policy Commission supporting the case for a clear-cut and well-defined wage policy, says that though wages boards, industrial courts, remuneration tribunals and arbitrators working in the country have had an opportunity of fixing wages on the basis of economic and social principles, "they have had no positive directives to do so". They do not indicate whether their awards are based on any principles, and in some cases, "the decision may represent nothing more than a compromise between two rival points of view". Consequently, the wage structure in the country resulting from such methods of wage fixing "does not, therefore, reflect the pursuit or such methods of wage fixing "and also does not, therefore, reflect the pursuit of any conscious, consistent overall economic and social objectives".

In India, in all the Five Year plans, the National Commission on Labour freely refer to the 'wage policy' as if it were an existing, concrete, and well-accepted instrument of planned development but they seldom proceed to clarify in precise terms what that policy is or how it will contribute to the achievement of prescribed economic and social objectives. While the development of wage policy in India will be the subject matter of the next section, it may be mentioned here that though the desirability of evolving a wage policy is admitted by all and there are elements of such a policy scattered all over the relevant documents, there is little evidence of any cogent policy, building up towards declared objectives, having resulted from the labours of the highest planning and policy making bodies.

In this symposium, a kind of consensus emerged in respect of some fundamental issues:

*International Symposium on Wages in 1967*

1. It would be necessary for the Government to formulate and implement a wage policy. Its evolution could not be left to the market forces. Such Governmental intervention is called for in the interest of economic planning, which many countries have adopted also to remove the existing social and economic inequities preserved in the wage structure from a colonial past or by tradition. Otherwise these inequities would generate conflict and hamper development.

2. Wage policy should be an instrument of economic policy as well as an instrument of social policy. In its former role it should encourage investment, internal price stability, worker efficiency, better distribution of the workforce, international competitiveness (so that exports could develop) and influx of foreign capital. In its latter role, such a policy should secure social justice, help to achieve industrial peace and provide an alternative to social security systems where those do not exist or cannot be provided.

3. There was a general agreement that a low wage policy would be suitable for developing countries than 'a high wage' approach. There were complaints that 'high wage islands' created by foreign firms, particularly multinationals in these countries, created problems for other industries. A low wage policy restrained consumption, promoted capital formation and reduced the wide gap between urban wages and rural wages.

4. About minimum wage, the general view was that minimum wage as an instrument of wage policy had serious limitations in a developing economy. Once the desired equilibrium in the wage differentials between the rural and urban employment was achieved, minimum wage regulation could be a more effective instrument.
5. As for collective bargaining, it pre-supposed that both employers and employees are equally strong. Decentralised i.e., plant-level bargaining would be generally less preferable to centralised or national-level bargaining for the administration of a wage policy.
6. While it was the general feeling that the wage policy could be formulated better by experts (generally economists) rather than by consensus, since the different interest groups wanted to participate in the formulation of wage policy, the consensus approach, although the 'second best' solution, would have a greater chance of success.
7. It was realised that a wage policy in a developing country is a long-term process. First, the undesirable inequalities have to be removed, then, the desired equilibrium between wages, incomes and prices has to be attained, and it is only after that, that a permanent wage policy can be formulated.

## The National Commission on Labour (1969) on Wage Policy

While the NLC did not think that the fixation of a national minimum wage was feasible for the whole country, the Commission was firmly of the view that the first claim of the workers was for a basic minimum wage, irrespective of any other consideration. This is consistent with the Supreme Court pronouncements on the subject. Now this basic minimum wage is the wage that is fixed under the Minimum Wages Act. According to the Supreme Court, no industry has the right to exist if it cannot pay this basic or subsistence wage. This wage has nothing to do with the need-based minimum wage. The basic recommendation of the National Commission on Labour (1969) is that the National Wage Policy has to be framed taking into account such factors as the price level which can be sustained, the employment level to be aimed at the requirement of social justice and capital formation needed for future growth.

The National Commission has also stated that:

i. The main aim of the wage policy should be to ensure rise in real wages. The real wages of a group of workers, above the basic minimum level, should be related to their productivity – otherwise inroads into the sphere of other groups will be made. In other words, other workers will pay for this group of less productive workers by their own higher productivity.

ii. Keeping cost under check should form an integral part of the wage policy. While the Commission does not think that is a significant factor in distorting the wage structure in India, it does say that DA and other allowances compensating a worker for higher cost of living may cause more inflation.

iii. The main aim of the wage policy should be to bring wages into conformity with the expectations of the working class and in the process, to maximize wage emolument.

iv. Referring to the existence of technological dualism in the Indian economy, the Commission observes wage differentials consequent on the dualism, that is, simultaneous existence of the modern capital-intensive sector and the traditional labour-intensive sector are inevitable and desirable. But this does not necessarily mean that all existing differentials are scientific or based on differences in productivity.

v. The Commission has thus brought out the dilemma of the policy matters in the developing economy of India.

The growth of the economy certainly depends on the rate of investment which in turn depends on the rate of savings. To the extent incomes are consumption oriented rather than savings oriented, rise in wage levels signifies a corresponding diversion of a portion of the total national product from savings and investment to consumption. In certain situations this can retard the process of economic growth and can act as a constraint. On the other hand, in order to maintain the tempo and pace of growth, consumption increases cannot be continuously postponed or kept in abeyance in a period of rising expectations and possible social tensions. In fact, increase in consumption may be necessary to sustain and improve the morale of workers and thereby, the level of production and of economic growth. Wage earners expect to share in the gains of economic development and growth. Commensurate with checks and restraints on consumption required in sustaining the growth process, the standard of living of the workers has to improve. A democratic society with the ideals of social justice will have to reconcile considering of equity and fairness with economic compulsions.

All these seem to induce one to draw the gloomy conclusion that the growth rate in such a society would necessarily be slow and such a society will neither have the political will nor have the social discipline as would enable it to take hard decisions. This is exactly the situation in India.

## The Chakraborty Committee on Wage Policy (1973)

The recommendations of the committee were never accepted by the Government.

The Committee mainly dealt with the employees in the organized private sector, numbering at the time of investigation, about 7 million persons. But the Committee found this sector to be economically very important. This is the modern sector to which the whole nation has contributed.

The main recommendations of the Committee are

1. Wage determination cannot be left to market forces. Free collective bargaining may lead to very high wages reflecting relative strength of unions and excessive profits made by industries rather than real differences in skills and conditions of work. Such bargaining also leads to wasteful work-stoppages. State intervention in wage fixation is essential. But wages in the modern sector need to be deflated so that the gains of this sector can be shared by the community also.

ii. The minimum wage cannot be less than the poverty line.

iii. Wage disparities should be reduced and inter-occupational, inter-industrial and inter-regional wage differentials should be rationalized in a phased manner. Unjustified wage differentials between the organized and unorganized sectors should also be progressively eliminated.

iv. A national wage structure should be evolved by working out a graded structure on the basis of skill differentials and wages should be fixed for each grade. In this national structure the total wages received by all employees will consist of (i) a minimum wage; (ii) skill differential, depending on the grade in which the skill has been included; (iii) compensation for exceptional hazards or other exceptional disadvantages of a job; (iv) growth dividend (a new idea – the concept is that the worker should be paid each year a dividend linked to the increase in average per capita consumption in the previous year. But no reduction in wages should occur if no such increase or any decrease has taken place. This dividend should be merged with the wage at the end of every 10 years); (v) DA (100 per cent compensation for those at the minimum wage level then a tapering DA, (not allowed to those drawing more than Rs. 1,000 as basic pay) and (vi) share in profits (as in bonus payments).

v. Just as the Committee deprecated the earnings of excessive profits so it deprecated excessive salary incomes which, in its view, breed discontent among workers. In its view, salaries should be correlated with the wages of highly skilled labour.

Also the salaries in the private sector should gradually fall in line with those in the public sector.

*Wage Policy in India under Planning:*

It is not necessary for our purpose to examine, at length, what sort of a wage policy, if any, existed before the commencement of formal planning in 1951. This does not mean that there was no wage policy at all before 1951. The Payment of Wages Act, 1936, protected workers against unfair deductions from wages. This was an important measure contributing immeasurably to the welfare of labour in view of the widespread prevalence of serious abuses in the matter of payment of wages in those days. The Indian Trade Disputes Act, 1929, provided a machinery for dealing with disputes relating to wages. This was further strengthened by the provisions for the compulsory adjudication of industrial disputes introduced during the World War II under the Defence of India Rules. Provincial enactments too provided for settlement of wage disputes.

The five-year programme for the amelioration of labour conditions drawn up by the Government of India in 1947 contained several important elements of a desirable wage policy such as the statutory prescription of minimum wages in sweated industries, the promotion of 'fair wage' agreements, the securing of a 'living wage' (i.e., minimum wage) to plantation workers, etc. The Industrial Truce Resolution (1946), the Industrial Policy Resolution (1948), the Report of the Committee on Fair Wages (1949), and the Report of the First Central Pay Commission (1946-47) contained various principles in relation to wages.

## Wage Policy in the Five-Year Plans:

Since wage policy is one of several policies contributing to planned development, it should find the most authoritative expression in the Five Year plans, where each policy is presumed to be set in relation to all others so that maximum coordination for the purpose of national development might be achieved.

Of the eleven Five Year plans that have so far been completed, the First Plan which, more than any of the others, tried to evolve, though not implement sound principles in regard to wages. The First Plan based its approach to labour problems "on considerations which are related on the one hand, to the requirements of the well-being of the working class and on the other to its vital contribution to the economic stability and progress of the country". The Plan clarified that the rate of progress in workers' welfare had to be determined "not only by the needs of the workers but also by the limitations of the country's resources". The attitude of unions towards question of wages had, therefore, to be adjusted to the requirements of economic development in keeping with considerations of social justice.

The Plan then referred to the inflationary pressures that had arisen in the economy as a result of the conditions prevailing during the war and in the post-war period. These pressures had led to greatly increased profits and to substantial increases in wages. Even so, the rise in prices had come in the way of greater improvement in the economic condition of workers and slowed down renovation and modernisation of plants. If the inflationary pressure was to be checked, steps would have to be taken to divert to saving some of the present expenditure on consumption and to increases production. Both profits and wages would have to be subjected to some control by the Government.

"On the side of wages, any upward movement, at this juncture, will further jeopardize the economic stability of the country if it is reflected in costs of production and consequently raises the price of the product. For workers too, such gains will prove illusory because in all likelihood they will soon be cancelled by a rise in the general price level, and in the long run the volume of employment may be adversely affected".

Because of the adverse effect of inflation on the real content of wage increases, the plan laid emphasis on rising productivity as the basis of progress. ". . . . in an undeveloped economy, (if labour) cannot build for itself and the community a better life except on the foundations of a higher level of productivity to which it has itself made a substantial contribution . . . . The whole economic health of the country depends upon rapidly increasing the productivity of labour".

Though the Plan discouraged, in general wage increases unrelated to productivity, it nevertheless permitted wage increases (1) to remove anomalies or where the existing rate were abnormally low and (2) to restore the pre-war level of real wages as a first step towards the living wage through increased productivity.

The Plan recognized that though certain broad principles which could help in the regulation of wages had emerged as a result of the labours of various commissions and committees and had been embodied in existing or proposed legislation "they still do not form an adequate practical basis for a uniform policy in determining wage rates and effecting wage adjustments".

In view of this conclusion, the Plan suggested that the tripartite machinery visualized in the section on industrial relations should evolve in as precise terms as practicable the 'norms' and standards which should guide wage boards or tribunals in settling questions relating to wages, having regard to the claims of the various groups of workers, inter se, of the other participants in industry and of the community as a whole.

The Plan then indulged in some broad, perhaps vague-generalizations, incapable of being translated into precise implementation: (a) all wage adjustments should conform to the broad principles of social policy and disparities of income have to be reduced to the utmost. The worker must obtain his due share in to the national income; (b) the claims of labour should be dealt with liberally in proportion to the distance which the wages of different categories of workers have to cover before attaining the living wage standard; (c) the process of standardisation of wages should be accelerated. There should be a progressive narrowing down of disparities in the rates of remuneration of different classes of workers in the same unit of workers engaged in similar occupations in different units of the same industry, of comparable occupations in different industries and in wages in the same industry in different centres; (d) a scientific assessment of the relative workload in different occupations and industries should be taken up as also pilot studies on payment by results and (e) 50 per cent of the dearness allowance of Government servants drawing a basic pay up to Rs. 750 per month would be amalgamated with pay, and this recommendation should be extended to workers in the private sector.

It may be noted that though the Plan diagnosed the requirements of the economy correctly and gave the correct lead in regard to claims for higher wages, it did not deal with many matters crucial to a consideration of the level or structure of wages. For instance, there was no discussion of the level of industrial wages in relation to subsistence incomes in agriculture, of the merits of a high wage or law wage policy in industry, of the 'room' for increase in consumption and hence in wages, of the problem of high wages island, of the widening or narrowing of skill differentials in recent years, and so on.

The Second Five-Year Plan excused itself of the responsibility for the drawing up of a detailed wage policy by observing: "Much of what has been said in regard to labour policy in the First Five Year Plan holds good as a basis for the future". Its preoccupation was principally with the newly discovered panacea of the "Socialist Pattern of Society"- a slogan which immediately raised the expectations of labour to new and soaring heights. The Plan observed that though what had been said in the First Plan still held good, in the light of the socialist pattern of society which provided the setting for the Second Plan, "suitable alterations in labour policy require to be made". One such alteration was the creation of industrial democracy as a prerequisite to the establishment of a socialist society. Another was the need to evolve a wage policy which aimed at a structure with rising real wages. Though the Plan did not spell out how this was to be done, it observed: "Improvement in wages can result mainly from increased productivity". It added: "Another step in this direction is the introduction of payment by results". If the object of the plan was to raise real wages by raising productivity, this could have been stated more explicitly. On the other hand, to compound the confusion, the Plan referred to two more aspects which required to be examined further. "The first concerns the laying down of principles to bring wages into conformity with the expectations of the working class in the future pattern of society". This laid too much emphasis on the workers' rights without qualifying them with corresponding responsibilities.

The Second Plan did little to carry wage policy planning any further than the First, while it undoubtedly whetted the appetite of the working classes for a greater share in the national product.

The Third Five-Year Plan provided no greater clarity than the second in regard to the development of wage policy. It said: "Labour policy in India have been evolving in response to the specific needs of the situation in relation to industry and the working class and has to suit the requirements of a planned economy". It did not say whether the process of evolution of policy had been satisfactory or whether any positive direction could, with advantage, be imparted to it. The Plan, however, emphasized that the measures adopted "must serve adequately the immediate and that economic progress had to be rapid.

Reference to the working of the Minimum Wages Act, the functioning of wage boards, the need to re-examine the nutritional requirements of a working class family and the setting up of a commission to examine the problem of bonus followed through with little precise guidance in regard to the level or structure of wages.

The Third Plan too paid lip service to the cause of productivity. "For the workers no real advance in their standard of living is possible without a steady increase in productivity, because any increase in wages generally, beyond certain narrow limits, would otherwise be nullified by a rise in prices". But the way to rising productivity indicated in the Plan was too good to be true. Says The Plan: "The term (rationalization) has often been wrongly associated with increase in workloads and added strain on workers in order to swell the volume of private gains. Large gains in productivity and an appreciable reduction in unit costs can be secured in many cases without causing any detriment to the health of the workers and without incurring any large outlays". The way to achieving these desirable goals was clear to the planners: "Greater responsibility in this respect rests on the management which should provide the most efficient equipment, correct conditions and methods of work, adequate training and suitable psychological and material incentives, for the workers". The only missing link here was how the management could achieve the feat of providing the most efficient equipment, correct conditions, and methods of work, adequate training, and suitable material incentives "without incurring any large outlays". One should have thought that each one of these items would call for additional outlays.

The Fourth Five Year Plan, 1969-74, made virtually no mention of wage problems or wage policy. The earlier Draft Outline of 1966 had referred to the fact that labour policy had till then given protection to those engaged in organized industries and stated that in the coming years labour policy and programmes had to be broadened steadily to provide for agricultural labour as well as various groups of unorganized workers.

The Draft Outline stated that price stability was basic to wage policy – a recognition that came none too soon. It suggested although there were obvious difficulties, it was essential for the success of planned development that, in integrated incomes, policy should be evolved for the guidance of both the public and private sectors.

The Draft of the Fifth Five-Year Plan hardly makes any mention of wage policy. It says, however, as follows: "But to the extent such improvement (in the share of wages in total value added) takes place at the expense of capital formation, distribution of incomes will tend to worsen through prevention of additional employment that may have been otherwise created. Improvement of wage share in the organized sector in an economy with a substantial amount of unemployment, open or disguised, is an unambiguous improvement only if the rate of growth of output is kept up at a high enough rate . . . . increases in wages should be closely correlated with increase in productivity". (Vol. I paras 2.83 and 2.84).

From this brief mention of the contents of the various Five-Year Plans in regard to wage policy it is clear that though various elements of such a policy received attention at different times, there was no conscious effort at evolving a cogent and consistent wage policy suited to the requirements of a developing economy.

## Compensation and Reward Management

**To sum up**

Compensation policy in the Indian context is influenced by a number of forces, economic and social. Without controlling non-wage incomes and unaccountable incomes which have a suffocating impact on the economy, formulation of a wage policy would be difficult. The Government has to exercise reasonable control over different forces and take into account not only the interests of the labourers, but also those of the consumers and the entire community generation of employment and need based minimum wage are the two important considerations that should form the basis of such a policy. Every organization must form its own wage policy keeping in mind the interests of the management, the employees, the consumers and the community in general. The wage policy to be more effective, should be examined, evaluated and reviewed periodically to meet the changing needs of the organization. Moreover, a wage policy must be geared to achieving the best prices, the best wages and the best prices. Prices, wages and profits must be thought of together. Only when we have achieved the least balance among them can the economy function in the best possible manner.

**Test Questions**

1. What do you mean by Wage Policy? What are its objectives?
2. Discuss the view of the National Commission (1969) on Labour on Wage Policy.
3. Discuss the Wage Policy in India during the Plan period.
4. No government can avoid having a wage policy. It is a vigorous instrument for achieving social objective. Explain how wage policy achieve social goals.
5. Wage policy in a developing economy will not be the same as in a developed country. What should be the objectives of wage policy in a developing country like India?

# Wage Legislation: The Payment of Wages Act, 1936

## Minimum Wages Act, 1948, Payment of Bonus Act, 1965, Payment of Gratuity Act, 1972, Equal Remuneration Act, 1976

### I. The Payment of Wages Act, 1936

The object of the Act is to regulate the payment of wages to certain classes of persons employed in industry; to pay wages in particular form and at regular intervals and to prevent unauthorized deductions from the wages.

The Act is applicable to persons employed in any factory, railway and to such other establishments to which the State Government may by notification, extend the provisions of the Act, after giving three months' notice to that effect. The term 'establishment' means tramway service, motor transport service engaged in carrying passengers or goods or both, air transport service, dock, wharf or jetty, inland vessel mechanically propelled, mine, quarry, oilfield, plantation, workshop, construction, development and maintenance of buildings, roads, bridges, canals etc.

Employees whose average wages are less than Rs. 1600 in a month are covered under this Act.

The term 'wages' means all remuneration (whether by way of salary, allowance or otherwise) expressed in terms of money or capable of being so expressed which would, if the terms of employment, express or implied were fulfilled, be payable to a person employed in respect of his employment or of work done in such employment.

It includes:
  i. Any remuneration payable under any award or settlement between the parties or order of a court.

ii. Any remuneration to which the person employed is entitled in respect of overtime work or holidays or any leave period.
iii. Any additional remuneration payable under the terms of employment whether called a bonus or by any other name.
iv. Any sum which by reason of the termination of employment of the person employed is payable under any law, contract, or instrument which provides for the payment of such sum whether with or without deductions but does not provide for the time within which the payment is to be made.
v. Any sum to which the person employed is entitled under any scheme framed under any law for the time being in force.

However it does not include:

i. Any bonus (whether under a scheme of profit-sharing or otherwise) which does not form part of the remuneration payable under the terms of employment or which is not payable under any award or settlement between the parties or order of a court.
ii. Value of any house accommodation or of the supply of light water, medical attendance or other amenity or of any service excluded from the computation of wages by a general or special order of the State Government.
iii. Any contribution paid by the employer to any pension or provident fund and the interest which have accrued thereon.
iv. Any travelling concession.
v. Any sum paid to the employed person to defray special expenses entailed on him by the nature of his employment or
vi. Any gratuity payable on the termination of employment.

*Responsibility for payment of wages:* The responsibility for the payment of wages is that of the employer or his representative. In the absence of employer, a person who employs the labourers and with whom they enter into a contract of employment will be regarded as an employer. Application for recovery of wages under the provisions of the Act may be filed against the manager of the factory. But if the manager has resigned or is dead or is removed, it becomes the responsibility of the employer for payment of wages. The responsibility for making such payment on behalf of the employer remains that of the manager as long as one is in office. If there is no manager of the factory, the occupier would be deemed to be the manager.

*Fixation of wage-periods:* No wage period shall exceed one month. The main purpose of this provision is to ensure that inordinate delay is not caused in the payment of wages and a longtime does not elapse before wages are paid for a period for which an employee has worked. Wages may be payable daily, weekly, fortnightly and monthly. But the payment thereof must not extend over a period longer than one month.

Where less than 1000 persons are employed, wages shall be paid before the expiry of the 7th day and in other cases before the expiry of the 10th day, after the last day of the wage period.

In case the employer terminates the services of an employee, the employee is entitled to receive the wage earned by him before the expiry of the 2nd working day from the day on which his employment is terminated.

All wages shall be paid in current coin or currency notes or in both. The employer may, after obtaining the written authorization of the employed persons, pay the wages either by cheque or by crediting the wages into the bank account.

*Deductions which may be made from wages:* Wages are to be paid to an employed person without deductions of any kind except those authorized by the Act. Withholding of increment or promotion (including the stoppage of increment at an efficiency bar); reduction to a lower post or time scale or to a lower stage in a time scale and suspension are not to be deemed to be deductions from wages.

Deductions from wages of an employed person shall be made only in accordance with the provisions of the Act and may be of the following kinds only:
a. Fines;
b. Deductions for absence from duty;
c. Deductions for damage to or loss of goods entrusted to the employed person or for loss of money for which he is required to account where such damage or loss is directly attributable to his neglect or default;
d. Deductions for house accommodation supplied by the employer or by the Government or any or any housing board set up under any law for the time being in force or any other authority engaged in the business of subsidizing house accommodation which may be specified in this behalf by the appropriate Government by notification in the official Gazette;
e. Deductions for such amenities and services supplied by the employer as the appropriate Government many authorize;

f. Deductions for recovery of advances of whatever nature and the interest due in respect thereof or for adjustment of over payment of wages;

g. Deductions for recovery of loans made from any fund constituted for the welfare of labour in accordance with the rules, approved by the appropriate Government and the interest due in respect thereof.

h. Deductions for recovery of loans granted for house building or other purposes approved by the appropriate Government, and the interest due in respect thereof;

i. Deductions of income tax payable by the employed persons;

j. Deductions required to be made by order of a court or other authority competent to make such order;

k. Deductions for subscriptions to, and for repayment of advances from any provident fund to which the Provident Funds Act, 1952 applies or any recognized provident fund as defined or any recognized provident fund as defined in Section 2 of the Income Tax Act, 1961 or any provident fund approved in this behalf by the appropriate Government during the continuance of such approval;

l. Deduction for payments to co-operative societies approved by appropriate government or to a scheme of insurance maintained by the Indian Post Office;

m. Deductions for payment of any premium on his life insurance policy to LIC of India established under the LIC Act, 1956, or for the purchase of securities of the Government of India or for any State Government or for being deposited in any Post Office Savings Bank in furtherance of any savings scheme of any such Government;

n. Deductions made for the payment of his contribution to any fund constituted by the employer or a trade union registered under the Trade Unions Act, 1926, for the welfare of the employed persons or the members of their families or both and approved by the appropriate Government during the continuance of such approval;

o. Deductions made for payments of fees payable by him for the membership of any trade Union registered under the Trade Unions Act 1926;

p. Deductions for payment of insurance premium on Fidelity Guarantee Bonds;

q. Deductions for recovery of losses sustained by a railway administration on account of acceptance by the employed person of counterfoil or base coins or forged currency notes.

r.  Deductions for recovery of losses sustained by a railway administration on account of the failure of the employed person to invoice, to bill, to collect or to account for the appropriate changes due to that administration, whether in respect of fares, freight, demurrage, wharfage and carnage or in respect of sale of good in catering establishment or in respect sale of commodities in grain shops or otherwise;

s.  Deductions for recovery of losses sustained by a railway administration on account of any rebates or refunds incorrectly granted by the employed person where such loss is directly attributable to his neglect or default;

t.  Deductions for contribution to the Prime Minister's National Relief Fund or to such other Fund as the Central Government may specify and

u.  Deductions for contributions to any insurance scheme framed by the Central Government for the benefit of its employees.

3. The total amount of deductions which may be made in any wage period from the wages of any employed person shall not exceed
   i.  In case where such deductions are made for payments to cooperative-societies, 75 per cent of such wages and
   ii. In any other case 50 per cent of such wages.

*Fines:*
1. No fine shall be imposed on any employed person save in respect of such acts and omissions on his part as the employer with the previous approval of appropriate Government.
2. No fine shall be imposed on any employed person until he has given an opportunity of showing cause against the fine.
3. The total amount of fine which may be imposed in any wage period on any employed person shall not exceed an amount equal to 3 per cent of the wages payable to him in respect of that wage period.
4. No fine shall be imposed on any employed person who is under the age of 15 years.
5. Every fine shall be deemed to have been imposed on the day of act or omission in respect of which it was imposed.

*Deductions for absence from duty:* The act authorizes deductions for actual absence from duty. However, if 10 or more employed persons acting in concert absent themselves without due notice and without due cause, such deductions may be made for a maximum period of 8 days.

Deductions from wages for damages or loss caused to the employer by the neglect or default of the employed person are laid down under the Act. Such deductions can be made only after giving the person concerned an opportunity of showing cause against the deduction.

The Act provides for deductions for different services rendered by the employer, recovery of advances and loans, payments to co-operative societies and insurance schemes.

The employer is required to maintain necessary records and registers and display an abstract of the Act at a conspicuous place.

## II. The Minimum Wages Act, 1948

In India, the Royal Commission on Labour appointed in 1929, laid stress on the need for fixing minimum wages for workers employed in certain industries. The Labour Investigation Committee also commented upon the low rates of wages prevailing in some of the industries and recommended immediate steps to remedy them. The question of statutory fixation of minimum rates of wages was discussed in different sessions of the Indian Labour Conferences. In 1945, it approved in principle the enactment of minimum wages legislation. Accordingly the Minimum Wages Act was passed in 1948.

The justification for statutory fixation of minimum wages is obvious. Such provisions which exist in more advanced countries are even more necessary in India, where workers' organizations are yet poorly developed and the workers' bargaining power is consequently poor.

The Act aims to extend the concept of social justice to the workmen employed in certain scheduled employments by statutorily providing for employed in certain scheduled employments minimum rates of wages. It is a piece of social legislation which provides protection to workers in employments in which they are vulnerable to exploitation on accounting of the lack of organization and bargaining power and where sweated labour is most prevalent.

*Main Provisions of the Act:* The Act is not applicable to all employments or industries. A schedule appended to the Act gives a list of employment covered by the Act. It covers an establishment regardless of the number of workers actually employed.

Some of the employments listed in the schedule are (i) employment in any woolen carpet making or shawl weaving establishments; (ii) employment in any rice mill, flour mill or dal mil; (iii) employment in any tobacco (including in bidi making); (iv) employment in any plantation, that is to say, any estate which is maintained for the purpose of growing cinchona, rubber, tea or coffee; (v) employment in any oil mill; (vi) employment under any local authority; (vii) employment on the construction or maintenance of roads or in building operations; (viii) employment in stone breaking or stone crushing; (ix) employment in any lac manufactory; (x) employment in any mica works and (xi) employment in tanneries and leather manufactory.

Part II of the Schedule covers employment in agriculture, that is to say any form of farming, including the cultivation and tillage of the soil, diary farming, the production, cultivation, growing and harvesting of any agricultural or horticultural commodity, the raising of livestock, bees or poultry and any practice performed by a farmer or on a farm as incidental to or in conjunction with farm operations.

The appropriate Government can add to the schedule any other employment in respect of which it is of the opinion that minimum rates of wages should be fixed.

The Act contains a number of definitions. Wages means all remuneration capable of being expressed in terms of money which would, if the terms, of the contract of employment were fulfilled, be payable to a person employed in respect of his employment or of work done in such employment and includes house rent allowance but does not include (i) the value of (a) any house accommodation, supply of light, water, medical attendance or (b) any other amenity or any service excluded by general or special order of the appropriate Government; (ii) any contribution paid by the employer to any pension fund or provident fund or under any scheme of social insurance; (iii) any travelling allowance or value of any travelling concession; (iv) any sum paid to the person employed to defray special expenses entailed on him by the nature of his employment or (v) any gratuity payable on discharge.

Where in respect of an employment the appropriate Government has fixed and notified minimum rates of wages, the employer is bound to pay every employee engaged in that employment at rates not less than whatever is notified. The appropriate Government can review wages at such intervals as they may think fit but not exceeding five years and revise them, if necessary.

The minimum rates of wages may be fixed:
(i) For different scheduled employments;
(ii) Different classes of work in the same scheduled employment;
(iii) Adults, adolescents, children and apprentices and
(iv) Different localities.

The rates of wages may be (i) a time rate, (ii) a piece rate, (iii) a guaranteed time rate and (iv) an overtime rate.

*Procedure for Fixing and Revising Minimum Wages:* In fixing or revising the minimum rates of wages, the appropriate Government shall either

(a) Set up as many committees and sub-committees as it considers necessary to hold enquiries and advise it in respect of such fixation or revision, as the case may be, or

(b) by notification in the official Gazette, publish its proposal for the information, of persons likely to be affected thereby and specify a date on which the proposals will be taken into consideration.

After considering the advice of the Committees, the appropriate Government shall, by notification in the official gazette, fix or revise the minimum rates of wages in respect of each schedule of employment. Unless otherwise provided, it shall come into force on the expiry of three months from the date of its issue.

The Act also empowers the state Government to constitute advisory boards to co-ordinate the work of different committees and subcommittees and advise the Government on the fixation of minimum wages. Similarly, the Central Government is empowered to constitute a central advisory board to advise the central and state Governments and to co-ordinate the work of the advisory boards.

*Wages in kind:* Minimum wages payable under this Act shall be paid in cash. Where it has been the custom to pay wages wholly or partly in kind, the appropriate Government may, by notification in the official gazette, authorize the payment of minimum wages either wholly or partly in kind. It may direct the supply of essential commodities at concessional rates by notifying in the official gazette. Authorized deductions are allowed under the Act. The appropriate Government may fix the number of hours of work, rest day, payment of overtime in respect of scheduled employments.

The Act lays down the penalties for violation of provisions of the Act. If any employer (a) pays to any employees less than the minimum rates of wages fixed for that employee's class of work or (b) contravenes any rule or order made by the appropriate Government under section 13 regarding hours of work, he would be punished with imprisonment up to six months or with fine up to Rs. 500 or with both.

The Central Government is the appropriate authority for enforcing the Act in relation to any scheduled employment carried on by or under the authority of the central Government railway administration, a mine, oil field, a major port, or any corporation established by a

Central Act. The Chief Labour Commissioner (Central) is in charge of implementation of Act in the Central sphere.

## III. Payment of Bonus Act, 1965

The Payment of Bonus Act provides for the payment of bonus to persons employed in certain establishments on the basis of profits or on the basis of production or productivity and for matters connected therewith.

The term 'bonus' is not defined under the Payment of Bonus Act 1965, nor there exist any definition of Bonus under any enactment.

In India, bonus was originally regarded as a gratuitous payment by an employer to his employees. However, in modern times, bonus is clearly regarded as a deferred wage payable to employees which may be claimed by them as of right under the terms of employment. In the conditions under which modern industries function, bonus has now come to be recognized as a right of employees which they can claim from their employers under certain circumstances. The gratuity or bonus is not an act of charity but is regarded as a right of the workers to share in the profits of the company.

The claim for bonus is based on two main considerations, namely (a) that there is a gap between the present wage and the living wage which bonus is intended to shorten (b) that there is an available surplus or profits of the year out of which bonus may be paid.

The Bonus Act came into force from 25 October, 1965. The object of the Act is to maintain peace and harmony between labour and capital by allowing the employees to share the prosperity of the establishment reflected by the profits earned by the contributions made by capital, management and labour.

*Salient Feature of the Act:* The Act applies to all factories and establishment employing 20 or more persons on any day during an accounting year. Establishments also include departments, undertakings and branches.

The Act does not apply to the following establishments: (i) newly setup establishment or units or branches of existing establishments for six years from the date of its starting production unless such establishments make profit; (ii) institutions; (iii) RBI; (iv) Deposit Insurance Corporation; (v) Industrial Development Bank of India; (vi) Agricultural Refinance Corporations; (vii) Unit Trust of India; (viii) IFC and LIC; (ix) Seamen; (x) Stevedore Labour; (xi) Universities and other educational institutions; (xii) Hospitals, Chambers of Commerce and social welfare institutions; (xiii) Inland and water transport and (xiv) Employees employed through contractors on building operations.

Definition of employee means any person other than an apprentice employed on a salary or wage not exceeding Rs. 3500 per month in any industry to do any skilled or unskilled, manual, supervisor, managerial, administrative, technical or clerical work for hire or reward.

The term 'salary' or 'wage' includes basic pay and dearness allowance but does not include any other allowance. It also excludes the value of any house accommodation or of supply of light, water, medical attendance or other amenity or of any service or of any concessional supply of food grains or other articles, any travelling concession, any bonus, any contribution paid by the employer to any pension fund or provident fund, any retrenchment compensation or any gratuity or other retirement benefit payable to the employee.

Determination of gross profit is the first step towards calculating the amount of bonus. The gross profit in the case of a banking company be calculated in the manner specified in the First Schedule and in any other case as specified in the Second Schedule. From gross profit certain prior charges are to be deducted like remuneration to partners or proprietors, a return of 8.5 per cent on equity capital and 6 per cent in reserves, depreciation under the Income Tax Act, development rebate or investment allowance, direct taxes, dividends paid or payable, to arrive at available surplus. But bonus is to be paid out of the allocable surplus. In the case of a company the allocable surplus is 67 per cent of the available surplus and in other cases it is 60 per cent.

Every employee shall be entitled to be paid by his employer, in an accounting year, bonus, provided he has worked in the establishment for not less than 30 working days in that year.

An employee will be disqualified from receiving bonus if he is dismissed from service for (a) fraud; (b) riotous or violent behaviour while on the premises of the establishment or (c) theft, misappropriation or sabotage of any property of the establishment.

The Act imposes a statutory obligation on the employer to pay bonus at the minimum rate of 8.33 per cent of the salary earned by an employee or Rs. 100 whichever is higher in respect of an accounting year. It is to be paid irrespective of profit and loss or whether there is allocable surplus or not in an accounting year. The maximum is fixed at 20 per cent. Where the salary or wage of an employee exceeds Rs. 2500 per month, the bonus payable to such employee shall be calculated as if his salary or wage was Rs. 2500.

Newly setup establishments get exemption from payment of bonus for a period of six years following the accounting year in which the goods produced or manufactured are sold, for the first time and in the alternative, up to the year when the new establishment results in profits, whichever is earlier.

Under the Act, adjustment can be made towards payment of customary or puja bonus against bonus payable under this Act.

If an employee is found guilty of misconduct causing financial loss to the employer, then the employer can deduct the amount of loss, from the amount of bonus payable to the employee for the year in which he was found guilty of misconduct.

The bonus is to be paid within a period of 8 months from the close of the accounting year.

A dispute about bonus payable under the Act will have to be raised by the employees concerned in accordance with the provisions of the Industrial Disputes Act, 1947, or any corresponding State Law as is applicable to them.

The Act provides for the appointment of inspectors and for maintenance of registers and records.

It is open to an employer to pay bonus linked with production or productivity instead of bonus on the basis of profits if there is an agreement to that effect between him and his employees but subject to the provisions of the Act in respect of payment of minimum and maximum bonus. Employees can enter into an agreement with their employer for granting them bonus under a formula different from that under the Act, i.e., bonus linked with production or productivity; but subject to the provisions of the Act in respect of payment of minimum and maximum bonus.

## IV. Payment of Gratuity Act, 1972

The Payment of Gratuity Act, 1972, is to provide for a scheme for the payment of gratuity to employees engaged in factories, mines, oilfields, plantations, ports, railway companies, shops or other establishments and for matters connected therewith or incidental thereto.

The Act shall apply to:
(a) every factory, mine, oilfield, plantation, port and railway company;
(b) Every shop or establishment in which 10 or more persons are employed or were employed on any day of preceding 12 months;
(c) Such other establishments or class of establishments in which 10 or more employees are employed or were employed on any day of the preceding 12 months as the Central Government may, by notification, specify in this behalf.

'Employee' under this Act means any person other than an apprentice employed on wages in any establishment, factory, mine, oilfield, plantation, port, railway company or shop, to do any skilled, semi-skilled or unskilled manual, supervisory, technical or clerical work, whether the terms of such employment are express or implied, and whether or not such person is employed in a managerial or administrative capacity but does not include any such person who holds a post under the Central Government or a State Government and is governed by any other Act or by an rules providing for payment of gratuity.

'Employer' under the Act means, in relation to any establishment, factory, mine, oilfield, plantation, port, railway company or shop.

(i) Belonging to or under the control of the Central Government or a State Government a person or authority appointed by the appropriate Government for the supervision and control of employees or where no person or authority has been appointed, the head of the Ministry or the Department concerned.

(ii) Belonging to or under the control of any local authority, the person appointed by such authority for the supervision and control of employees or where no person has been so appointed, the chief executive office of the local authority.

(iii) In any other case, the person who or the authority which, has the ultimate control over the affairs of the establishment, factory, mine, oilfield, plantation, port, railway company or shop and where the said affairs are entrusted to any other person, whether called a manager, managing director or by any other name, such person.

*Payment of Gratuity:* (i) Gratuity shall be payable to an employee on the termination of his employment after he has rendered continuous service for not less than five years.

(a) on his superannuation or

(b) on his retirement or resignation or

(c) on his death or disablement because of accident or disease.

Provided further that in the case of death of the employee, gratuity payable to him shall be paid to his nominee or if no nomination has been made, to his heirs and where such nominees or heirs is a minor, the share of such minor shall be deposited with the controlling authority who shall invest the same for the benefit of such minor in such bank or other financial institution, as may be prescribed, until such minor attains majority.

(2) For every completed year of service or part thereof in excess of six months, the employer shall pay gratuity to an employee at the rate of 15 days wages based on the rate of wages last drawn by the employee concerned.

Provided that in the case of piece-rated employee, daily wages shall be computed on the average of the total wages received by him for a period of 3 months immediately preceding the termination of his employment and for this purpose, the wages paid for any overtime work shall not be taken into account.

(3) The amount of gratuity payable to an employee shall not exceed 3 lac 50 thousand rupees.

(4) Nothing in this section shall affect the right of an employee to receive better terms of gratuity under any award or agreement or contract with the employer.

(5) (a) The gratuity of an employee, whose services have been terminated for any act, wilful omission or negligence causing any change or loss to, or destruction of property belonging to the employer, shall be forfeited to the extent of the damage or loss so caused.

(b) the gratuity payable to an employee may be wholly or partially forfeited.

(i) if the services of such employee have been terminated for his riotous or disorderly conduct or any other act of violence on his part or

(ii) if the services of such employee have been terminated for any act which constitutes an offence involving moral turpitude, provided that such offence is committed by him in the course of his employment.

*Power to Exempt:* The appropriate Government may exempt any establishment, factory, mine, oilfield, plantation, port, railway company or shop to which this Act applies from the operation of the provisions of this Act if the employees in such establishment, factory, mine, oilfield, plantation, port, railway company or shop are in receipt of gratuity or pensionary benefits not less favourable than the benefits conferred under this Act.

*Nomination:* Each employee who has completed one year of service shall make nomination for payment of gratuity. Any employee may in his nomination, distribute the amount of gratuity amongst more than one nominee.

The employer shall arrange to pay the amount of gratuity within 30 days from the date it becomes payable to the person to whom the gratuity is payable.

If the amount of gratuity payable is not paid by the employer within the specified period, the employer shall pay, from the date on which the gratuity becomes payable to the date on which it is paid, simple interest at such rate not exceeding the rate notified by the Central Government from time to time for repayment of long term deposits, as that Government may specify.

*Recovery of Gratuity*: If the amount of gratuity payable under this Act is not paid by the employer within the prescribed time, to the person entitled thereto, the controlling authority shall issue a certificate for that amount to the Collector who shall recover the same, together with the compound interest thereon at such rate as the Central Government may specify, from the date of expiry of the prescribed time, as arrears of land revenue and pay the same to the person entitled thereto.

The appropriate Government may by notification, make rules for the purpose of carrying on the provision of this Act.

### Equal Remuneration Act, 1976

To give effect to Article 39 of the Indian Constitution, the Equal Remuneration Act was passed on 11 February 1976. The object of the Act is to provide for the payment of equal remuneration to men and women workers and for the prevention of discrimination, on the ground of sex, against women in the matter of employment and for matters connected therewith or incidental thereto.

Main Provisions of the Act: The term 'remuneration' means the basic wage or salary and any additional emoluments whatsoever payable, either in cash or in kind to a person employed in respect of employment or work done in such employment, if the terms of the contract of employment were fulfilled.

"Same work or work of a similar nature" means work in respect of which the skill effort and responsibility required are the same, when performed under similar working conditions, by a man or a woman and the differences, if any, between the skill, effort and responsibility, required of a man and those required of a woman are not of practical importance in relation to the terms and conditions of employment.

It is the duty of the employer to pay equal remuneration to men and women workers for the same work or work of a similar nature.

No employer shall, while making recruitment for the same work or work of a similar nature, make any discrimination against women except where the employment of women in such work is prohibited or restricted or restricted by or under any law for the time being in force.

Advisory Committee: For the purpose of providing increasing employment opportunities to women, the appropriate Government may constitute one or more advisory committees.

The appropriate Government may appoint authorities for hearing and deciding claims and complaints. The authority appointed for this purpose shall have all the powers of a civil court under the Code of Civil Procedure 1908. It is the duty of employers to maintain prescribed registers and other documents in relation to the workers employed by him. The Act provides for penalties for violation of the provisions of the Act.

The Equal Remuneration Act has been brought into force by the Central Government in certain employments such as local authorities, hospitals, nursing homes and dispensaries, banks, insurance companies and other financial institutions, educational, teaching, training and research institutions, mines, Employees' Provident Fund organization, Coal Mines Provident Fund Organization and the Employee's State Insurance Corporation, Food Corporation of India, Central Warehousing Corporations, Textile and Textile Products, Electrical and Electronic machinery, Factories located in plantations, chemicals and chemical products, land and water transport, food products, beverages, tobacco and tobacco products, electricity, gas and water, wholesale and retail trade, restaurants and hotels, agriculture and activities allied to agriculture, transport, storage, warehousing and communications, construction and allied activities, air transport industry, real estate business, and legal services, community, social and personal services.

## Test Questions

1. Discuss briefly the Minimum Wages Act, 1948.
2. Discuss briefly the Payment of Bonus Act, 1965.
3. Explain the Payment of Gratuity Act, 1972.
4. Discuss the Equal Remuneration Act of 1976.
5. Discuss the objectives of the Payment of Wages Act, 1936.
6. Can Minimum Wages be paid in kind?
7. Describe the salient features of the Payment of Bonus Act, 1965.
8. Discuss the salient features of the Payment of Gratuity Act, of 1972.
9. What is the object of the Equal Remuneration Act, 1976? What are the main provisions of the Act?

# University Questions
# Years 2010

## Employment & Compensation Administration

Group-A

**(Multiple Choice Type Questions)**

1. Choose the correct alternatives for any ten of the following:
   (i) Which of the following employees drawing salaries or wages are entitled to get bonus as per the Payment of Bonus Act, 1965?
      (a) Less than Rs. 2500 per annum
      (b) Above Rs. 6000 per annum
      (c) Up to Rs. 3500 per annum
      (d) None of these
   (ii) Gratuity is payable to employee who resigns after completing.
      (a) One year of service
      (b) Three years of service
      (c) Seven years of service
      (d) None of these
   (iii) Under the Contract Labour (Regulation & Abolition) Act, who is responsible for paying the wages to labour?
      (a) The welfare officer
      (b) The contractor
      (c) The contractor in the presence of employer representative
      (d) None of them
   (iv) Equal Remuneration Act, 1976 came to with the object to provide equal remuneration to
      (a) Men
      (b) Women
      (c) Men & women
      (d) None of them

(v) Wage administration deals with
   (a) Payment of dearness allowance on time
   (b) Techniques and procedures for maintaining and designing salary structure and exercising wage control
   (c) Payment of incentives to motivate employees
   (d) None of these

(vi) The Halsey system provides for
   (a) Division of the standard time into a number of points at the rate of one minute per point
   (b) Bonus paid for any time saved
   (c) Fixation of a standard time for the completion of a task
   (d) None of these

(vii) That efficiency depends on plant-wide cooperation is the underlying concept of
   (a) Rowan plan
   (b) Scanlon plan
   (c) Rucker plan
   (d) None of these

(viii) Under the 'Job classification' method
   (a) Certain classes or grades of jobs are defined on the basis of difference in duties, skills, working conditions and other job-related factors
   (b) Jobs are compared with one another and arranged and ranked in the order of their importance
   (c) The relative worth of key jobs are established
   (d) None of these

(ix) Outsourcing refers to
   (a) Outstanding job
   (b) Provide permanent employment to the job seekers
   (c) Contracting with another company or person to do a particular function
   (d) None of these

(x) Employee leasing
   (a) Is similar to the process of hiring temporary workers
   (b) Is not similar to the process of hiring temporary workers
   (c) The process of employing workers
   (d) None of these

(xi) Structural unemployment refers to
   (a) A form of unemployment resulting from a mismatch between the sufficiently skilled workers seeking employment and demand in the labour market.
   (b) The structural change of unemployment
   (c) The disguised unemployment only
   (d) None of those

(xi) The main objective of National Employment in the country is to
   (a) Create full employment in the country
   (b) Provide a framework towards the goal of achieving remunerative and decent employment for all women and men in the labour force
   (c) Provide guaranteed job to every citizen
   (d) All of these

## Group-B

### (Short Answer Type Questions)

Answer any three of the following

1. Write a note on factors that are considered for calculation of consumer price index.
2. What is outsourcing? What are its advantages?
3. Why do we pay dearness allowance? How does DA cost the company?
4. Differentiate between gross pay, net pay and cost to company.
5. What is incentive? What are the advantages of payment of incentive?

## Group-C

### (Long Answer Type Questions)

Answer any three of the following

6. Explain productivity. How does productivity differ from production? What are the principles and others factors, if any, to be borne in mind for effective implementation of an incentive scheme? Discuss one method each of individual and group incentives schemes.

7. (a) Mr. Pritam Banerjee joined a manufacturing scenario on 1st June, 2007 on a basic salary of INR 2500 per month plus DA @ 30 per cent of basic plus HRA @ 12 per cent of basic + DA plus tiff in allowance @ INR 30 per day worked. On 1st January, 2008 he was promoted when his basic salary was enhanced to INR 3500 per month. The company declared bonus for the accounting year 2008-09, 20 per cent. Is Mr. Banerjee entitled to get bonus? If yes, then by how much?

   (b) What is the main objective of Minimum Wage Act, 1948?

   (c) Incentives have a major contribution in keeping the workforce motivated within organizations.' Discuss.

8. Radiant Industries Ltd. is engaged in the business of manufacturing edible oils, soaps etc. It has engaged contract labours through a contract for feeding of hoppers (which is an essential part of the production) and also for supervision work in the godown. The contract labour was not given any benefit of E.S.I. Act. The contract labours demand the permanency of contract labours engaged for feeding of hoppers (being a job perennial in nature) and E.S.I. benefit for all contract labours. The management of Radiant Industries Ltd., being the principal employer, expresses that it would inform about this matter after discussion with the contractor.

   (a) Are the above labours covered under Contract Labour (Regulations and Abolitions) Act, 1970?

   (b) Can the contract labour engaged for feeding of hoppers (being an essential part of the production) be made permanent under law? Can the engagement of contract labour be prohibited in this case? Explain.

   (c) Explain the obligations of the contractor and company relating to rendering benefits of E.S.I. to the contract labour.

9. Define statutory and non-statutory benefits provided in Indian industries. State the guidelines to make employee benefit programmes more effective. What do you mean by "Take Home Pay"?

10. Write short notes on any three of the following:
    (a) Fair wage and capacity to pay
    (b) Productivity bargaining
    (c) Wage differentiation
    (d) Retirement benefits
    (e) Types of fringe benefits

# Employment & Compensation Administration 2011

## Group –A

*(Multiple Choice Type Questions)*

1. Choose the correct alternatives for any ten of the following:

    (i) A written statement of the main duties and responsibilities which a particular job entails is called
    
    (a) Job analysis
    (b) Job specification
    (c) Job description
    (d) Job evaluation

    (ii) Management is bound for labour welfare
    
    (a) Within the factory only
    (b) Outside the factory only
    (c) Both (a) and (b)
    (d) None of these

    (iii) The maximum labour-oriented industry in India is
    
    (a) Cement industry
    (b) Iron and steel industry
    (c) Jute industry
    (d) Cotton industry

    (iv) Piece worker come under .................... class.
    
    (a) Semi skilled
    (b) Skilled
    (c) Manager
    (d) Leader

    (v) A firm uses information technology to break down functional barriers and create a work system based on business processes, products or outputs rather than on functions or inputs in

(a) Restructuring
(b) Benchmarking
(c) Reengineering
(d) Enchmarking

(vi) ............... using financial compensation as a strategic tool is often prevented by ............... control of pay systems.
(a) Line managers, staff
(b) Supervisors, employees'
(c) Staff, line managers'
(d) Employees, top-management's

(vii) More than ............... per cent of American companies have profit-sharing plans.
(a) 80
(b) 30
(c) 95
(d) 60
(e) 50

(viii) Which of the following is not a form of incentive compensation?
(a) Hourly wage
(b) Profit sharing
(c) Gain sharing
(d) All of these are forms of incentive

(ix) An organization provides employees benefits in the form of conveyance facilities, housing facilities and education facilities for children. What kind of benefits is the organization providing the employees?
(a) Incentives
(b) Bonus
(c) Fringe benefits
(d) Security benefits

(x) The special type of stock option plan that protects the holder against any depreciation is known as
(a) Restricted stock plan
(b) Phantom stock plan
(c) Stock option scheme
(d) Stock purchase plan

(xi) Equal Remuneration Act, 1976 came into effect with the object to provide equal remuneration to
  (a) Men
  (b) Women
  (c) Both (a) and (b)
  (d) None of them

(xii) Which amongst the following is not an example of fringe benefit?
  (a) Medical benefits
  (b) Overtime allowance
  (c) House rent allowance
  (d) Educational allowance

## Group-B

### (Short Answer Type Questions)

Answer any three of the following

2. Discuss the types of bonuses common in executive compensation.
3. Distinguish between Minimum, Fair and Living wage.
4. What are the components of retirement benefits?
5. Explain the concept of single linkage and double linkage system of dearness allowance, using hypothetical data.
6. Design a draft pay slip of a Marketing Executive working in a FMCG company with all the pay components, statutory deductions and containing other relevant information.

## Group – C

### (Long Answer Type Questions)

Answer any three of the following

7. (a) What do you mean by incentives? Classify various incentive schemes used by various organizations.

   (b) A company pays a worker for a given job as per the following data:

   Basic Hourly Rate                              Rs. 6
   Increase in the rate                           25 per cent
   Standard hourly output level for the job 800 units

8. Write short notes on any three of the following.
   (a) Scanlon Plan
   (b) Performance Based Pay
   (c) Gratuity
   (d) ESOP
   (e) Fringe benefits
9. Case study

   Even before its recent merger with BP, Amoco was already a major MNC with operations in dozens of countries. One of the most challenging issues that Amoco's HR executives have long had to confront has been juggling the legal, cultural and social factors dictating and reinforcing the needs for different benefit programs in their organization. For example, in the US, Amoco offers insurance, vacation and sick leaves, alternate work schedules, children centres, employees assistance programs and referral services. In Egypt, however, Amoco offers some other benefits. Among these, the more prominent is one-time Haj pilgrimage allowance and two annual subsidized trips to Egyptian resorts. In Netherlands, the emphasis is on flexibility. In Norway, fathers of newborns get five days of paid leave. Amoco employees in Norway get perhaps the most unusual benefit of all. Because the country has an especially high marginal tax rate. Employees are often looking for benefits that their company can provide tax-free.

**Questions for Discussion**
   (a) Comment on the employee benefit scheme offered by MNCs like Amoco.
   (b) What factors are taken into consideration for designing a compensation package for employees working in MNCs like Amoco?

10. What are the two main methods of calculation of dearness allowance in large industry? A Management Trainee joined a company on 1st January, 2006 in the scale Rs. 15,000-1,000-20,000 with a starting dearness pay of 40 per cent and 50 per cent neutralization thereafter, adjustable half yearly. She had been given another option of taking dearness allowance at Rs. 75 per point of 2001 CPI above 120, 140, 160 and 175 respectively on each January of 2006, 2007, 2008 and 2009. Would she regret her decision in January, 2009?

11. What do you mean by Human Resource Outsourcing? Discuss in detail the various steps followed in HR outsourcing process.

# Employment & Compensation Administration 2010

### Group –A

**(Multiple Choice-Questions)**

1. Chose the correct alternatives for any ten of the following:

    (i) Which of the following employees drawing salaries or wages are entitled to get bonus as per the Payment of Bonus Act, 1965?
    
    (a) Less than Rs. 2500 per annum
    
    (b) Above Rs. 6000 per annum
    
    (c) Up to Rs. 3500 per annum
    
    (d) None of these

    (ii) Gratuity is payable to employee who resigns after completing
    
    (a) One year of service
    
    (b) Three years of service
    
    (c) Seven years of service
    
    (d) None of these

    (iii) Under the Contract Labour (Regulation & Abolition) Act, who is responsible for paying the wages to latour?
    
    (a) The welfare officer
    
    (b) The contractor
    
    (c) The contractor in the presence of amours? Representative
    
    (d) None of them

    (iv) Equal Remuneration Act, 1976 came to with the object to provide equal remuneration to
    
    (a) Men
    
    (b) Women
    
    (c) Men & women
    
    (d) None of them

(v) Wage administration deals with
   (a) Payment of dearness allowance on time
   (b) Techniques and procedures for maintaining and designing salary structure and exercising wage control
   (c) Payment of incentives to motivate employees
   (d) None of these

(vi) The Halsey system provides for
   (a) Division of the standard time into a number of points at the rate of one minute per point
   (b) Bonus paid for any time saved
   (c) Fixation of a standard time for the completion of a task
   (d) None of these

   (b) Can the contract labour engaged for feeding of hoppers (being an essential part of the production) be made permanent under law? Can the engagement of contract labour be prohibited in this case? Explain.
   (c) Explain the obligations of the contractor and company relating to rendering benefits of E.S.I to the contract labour.

10. Define statutory and non-statutory benefits provided in Indian industries. State the guidelines to make employee benefit programmes more effective. What do you mean by "Take Home Pay"?

11. Write short notes on any three of the following:
   (a) Fair wage and capacity to pay
   (b) Productivity bargaining
   (c) Wage differentiation
   (d) Retirement benefits
   (e) Types of fringe benefits